The Complete Idiot's Reference Card

The Hierarchy of Poker Hands

Royal Flush
A, K, Q, J, and 10 all of the same suit.

Straight Flush
Five cards in any *sequence*, all of the same suit. (e.g., 9, 8, 7, 6, 5 of diamonds.)

Four of a Kind
Four cards of the same rank, one in each suit. Plus, an additional card that doesn't matter.

Full House
Three cards of one rank plus another two cards of another rank.

Flush
Any five cards of the same suit, in any order.

Straight
Any five cards in sequence.

Three of a Kind
Three cards of the same rank, plus two additional cards.

Two Pair
Two cards of one rank and two cards of another rank, plus an additional card.

One Pair
Two cards of the same rank and three additional cards.

No Pair
All five cards of different ranks and not all of one suit.

Here's How the 36 Craps Combinations Stack Up

Number Rolled	How Many Ways to Roll the Numbers?	True Odds	Winning Combinations
Two	1	135 to 1	
Three	2	17 to 1	
Four	3	11 to 1	
Five	4	8 to 1	
Six	5	6.2 to 1	
Seven	6	5 to 1	
Eight	5	6.2 to 1	
Nine	4	8 to 1	
Ten	3	11 to 1	
Eleven	2	17 to 1	
Twelve	1	35 to 1	

Blackjack Strategy Tips
(From the best-selling The Unofficial Guide® to Las Vegas by Bob Sehlinger)

BASIC STRATEGY *

The Dealer is Showing:	2	3	4	5	6	7	8	9	10	Ace
Your Total is: 4–11	H	H	H	H	H	H	H	H	H	H
12	H	H	S	S	S	H	H	H	H	H
13	S	S	S	S	S	H	H	H	H	H
14	S	S	S	S	S	H	H	H	H	H
15	S	S	S	S	S	H	H	H	H	H
16	S	S	S	S	S	H	H	H	H	H

S=Stand   H=Hit   O=Optional

SOFT HAND STRATEGY *

The Dealer is Showing:	2	3	4	5	6	7	8	9	10	Ace
You Have: Ace, 9	S	S	S	S	S	S	S	S	S	S, H
Ace, 8	S	S	S	S	S	S	S	S	S	S
Ace, 7	S	D	D	D	D	S	S	H	H	S
Ace, 6	H	D	D	D	D	S	H	H	H	H
Ace, 5	H	H	D	D	D	H	H	H	H	H
Ace, 4	H	H	D	D	D	H	H	H	H	H
Ace, 3	H	H	H	D	D	H	H	H	H	H
Ace, 2	H	H	H	D	D	H	H	H	H	H

S=Stand   H=Hit   D=Double Down

SPLITTING STRATEGY

The Dealer is Showing:	2	3	4	5	6	7	8	9	10	Ace
You Have: 2, 2	H	H	SP	SP	SP	SP	H	H	H	H
3, 3	H	H	SP	SP	SP	SP	H	H	H	H
4, 4	H	H	H	H	H	H	H	H	H	H
5, 5	D	D	D	D	D	D	D	D	H	H
6, 6	H	SP	SP	SP	SP	H	H	H	H	H
7, 7	SP	SP	SP	SP	SP	SP	H	H	H	H
8, 8	SP	SP	SP	SP	SP	SP	SP	SP	SP	SP
9, 9	SP	SP	SP	SP	SP	S	SP	SP	S	S
10, 10	S	S	S	S	S	S	S	S	S	S
Ace, Ace	SP	SP	SP	SP	SP	SP	SP	SP	SP	SP

S=Stand   H=Hit   SP=Split D=Double Down

DOUBLING DOWN

The Dealer is Showing:	2	3	4	5	6	7	8	9	10	Ace
Your Total is: 11	D	D	D	D	D	D	D	D	D	H
10	D	D	D	D	D	D	D	D	H	H
9	H	D	D	D	D	H	H	H	H	H

H=Hit   D=Double Down

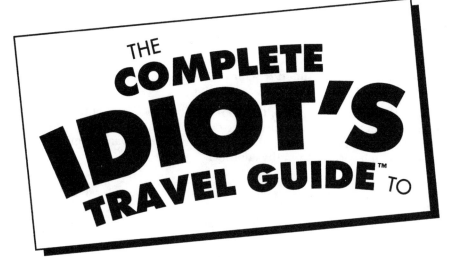

Las Vegas

by Rick Garman

Macmillan Travel   Alpha Books
Divisions of Macmillan Reference USA
A Simon & Schuster Macmillan Company
1633 Broadway, New York NY 10019-6785

ISBN 0-02-862299-5
ISSN 1096-7605

Editors: Bob O'Sullivan and Lisa Renaud
Thanks to Neil Schlecht, Suzanne Jannetta, and Margot Weiss
Production Editor: Mark Enochs
Design by designLab
Digital Cartography by Peter Bogaty & Ortelius Design
Illustrations by Kevin Spear
Page Layout: Laura A. Knox
Proofreaders: Kim Cofer, Mary Hunt

Special Sales

Bulk purchases (10+ copies) of Frommer's and selected Macmillan travel guides are available to corporations, organizations, mail-order catalogs, institutions, and charities at special discounts, and can be customized to suit individual needs. For more information write to: Special Sales, Macmillan General Reference, 1633 Broadway, New York, NY 10019-6785.

Manufactured in the United States of America

Contents

Appendixes

Maps

About the Author

Rick Garman began his writing career after graduating from The American Academy of Dramatic Arts in Pasadena, California. He turned to writing because no one would hire him as an actor and, to be frank, he didn't try all that hard.

His first play, *17 Days*, was produced in 1993 at the Colony Studio Theatre in Los Angeles to critical acclaim and multiple awards. It has since been performed around the country. Rick has gone on to write several more plays, and one of them, *Mountains*, received its world premiere in 1997, also at the Colony. That production has been nominated for several major theater awards. Other writing credits include articles for the *LA Reader* and *New York Newsday*, plus film reviews for *Magill's Cinema*.

The Complete Idiot's Travel Guide to Las Vegas is Rick's second book about the city; he co-wrote *Frommer's Las Vegas 98* with Mary Herczog.

An Invitation to the Reader

In researching this book, we discovered many wonderful places—hotels, restaurants, shops, and more. We're sure you'll find others. Please tell us about them, so we can share the information with your fellow travelers in upcoming editions. If you were disappointed with a recommendation, we'd love to know that, too. Please write to:

The Complete Idiot's Travel Guide to Las Vegas
Macmillan Travel
1633 Broadway
New York, NY 10019-6785

An Additional Note

Please be advised that travel information is subject to change at any time—and this is especially true of prices. We therefore suggest that you write or call ahead for confirmation when making your travel plans. The authors, editors, and publisher cannot be held responsible for the experiences of readers while traveling. Your safety is important to us, however, so we encourage you to stay alert and be aware of your surroundings. Keep a close eye on cameras, purses, and wallets, all favorite targets of thieves and pickpockets.

The following abbreviations are used for credit cards:

AE	American Express	EURO	Eurocard
CB	Carte Blanche	JCB	Japan Credit Bank
DC	Diners Club	MC	MasterCard
DISC	Discover	V	Visa
ER	enRoute		

Introduction

Even though you'll see the skyline of New York, the columns of ancient Rome, the pyramids of Giza, and the streets of New Orleans, Las Vegas is a city like no other. It is equal parts lavish and tacky, endlessly entertaining and completely exhausting, awe-inspiring and overwhelming.

Come to think of it, perhaps overwhelming is an understatement, considering that there are more hotel rooms in Las Vegas than in any other city in the country. No wonder the very thought of coming here has overwhelmed even seasoned travelers.

Las Vegas can make anybody feel like a complete idiot; I often do, and I've been going to Vegas regularly for over a decade. That's where this book comes in. It's written in a simple, straightforward manner that will let even the most inexperienced of you feel like an old pro.

Unlike those monstrous guides for which you need a dozen fingers to keep track of the information on a single topic, my book is easy to use. Stick with me, and I'll eliminate the element of chance (even here in Las Vegas) and turn all of you into winners.

Part 1, "Be Prepared: What You Need to Do Before You Go," answers all those nagging questions you've been asking yourself, such as when to go, how to get there, and how much it's all going to cost. It also gives you addresses, phone numbers, and web sites where you can get more information. It'll get you started and help you take care of all the details you have to handle before you hop on the plane.

Part 2, "Finding the Hotel That's Right for You," addresses one of the biggest decisions you have to make: which hotel to choose. This section picks the best, whatever your taste or budget, and gives you honest, concise reviews, plus handy indexes and maps.

Part 3, "Learning Las Vegas," tells you how to get around Las Vegas, both from the airport to your hotel and in town, so you don't waste any time or money.

Don't read **Part 4, "The Best Restaurants in Las Vegas,"** on an empty stomach, because it's all about the city's restaurants. You'll find detailed reviews—complete with open hours, prices, and more—plus handy indexes and maps. I'll also recommend the best buffets and cheap meal deals in town.

Part 5, "Ready, Set, Go! What to See & Do in Las Vegas," is where I get down to the fun stuff. I'll tell you about the attractions and entertainment, from the Liberace Museum to a side trip to Hoover Dam, to getting married at a drive-through window! I've also included a guide to the best and most bizarre shopping in Vegas, and tips on how to stay active. And, oh yeah, in case you didn't know, you can gamble in Las Vegas, so I've included everything you need to know to play the most popular games and find the best casinos.

Part 6, "On the Town: Nightlife & Entertainment," will tell you everything you need to know about life after dark, from big, splashy production shows, such as Siegfried and Roy, to some of the hottest dance clubs in town.

Extras

This book has several special features you won't find in other guidebooks, which will help you make better use of the information provided and do it faster.

As mentioned earlier, **indexes** cross-reference the information in ways that let you see at a glance what your options are in a particular subcategory— moderately priced restaurants, hotels on the South Strip, and so on.

I've also sectioned off little tidbits of useful information in **sidebars,** which come in five types:

Extra! Extra!

Special tips for readers with special needs.

Bet You Didn't Know

These boxes offer you interesting facts or trivia about the city.

Tourist Traps

These boxes steer you away from rip-offs, activities that aren't worth it, shady dealings, and other pitfalls.

Time-Savers

Here, you'll find ways to avoid lines and hassles, and streamline the business of traveling.

Dollars & Sense

Here, you'll find tips on saving money and cutting corners to make your trip both enjoyable and affordable.

Sometimes the best way to fix something in your mind is to write it down, and with that in mind, I've provided **worksheets** to help you focus your thinking and make your decisions. (Underlining or highlighting as you read along isn't a bad idea, either.) These worksheets will help you feel more in control of your vacation and comfortable with your plans.

Kids A **kid-friendly icon** is used throughout the book to identify activities, attractions, hotels, and restaurants that are especially suited to people traveling with children.

Appendixes at the back of the book give you a handy itinerary planner, Vegas facts you'll need to know, and important numbers and Internet addresses covering every aspect of your trip, from reservations to emergencies.

The last thing I want to mention before you dive in is that Las Vegas is a city built on the concept of fun. Any town that has fake volcanoes, mock pirate battles, and scaled replicas of virtually every major landmark in the world should not be taken too seriously by prospective visitors or travel writers. I certainly had my share of fun writing this book. I hope you'll have as much fun reading it as you will on your Las Vegas vacation.

Okay, now let's roll the dice.

Acknowledgments

It would have been virtually impossible for me to write this book without the help of the following people: Mary Herczog, for advising me on this project and getting me involved in travel writing in the first place. Bob O'Sullivan, for giving me the opportunity to do this. Doug Stallings, for bringing my name up in that meeting. Vern and Pauline Garman, for their research assistance and for giving birth. Fred Ferrier, Mark Rehn, and Jeff Jones for providing research assistance, rides to the airport, and/or cocktails. And the following people in Las Vegas who made my visits more pleasant and/or provided me with invaluable assistance: Robyn Ouchida-Campbell, Cheryl Ladd-Campbell, John Hessling, Mark Hughes, Gene Cataldo, Tim Chanaud, Barbara Mulasky, and Margaret Kurtz.

Part 1

Be Prepared: What You Need to Do Before You Go

I suppose there are free spirits among us who can hop on a plane at the last minute and fly blind. But I'm not one of them. I like to work out the details beforehand so all that's left for me to do is relax and have a great time. I want to help you do that, too.

So, where to start? This first section of the book will guide you painlessly through the basics of planning a trip—from where to find the most useful information on Las Vegas to practical advice on what to pack. Think ahead, you won't have to worry later.

THINGS YOU MAY WANT
TO TAKE
1) UNDERWEAR
2) AIRLINE TICKETS
3) WALLET

Chapter 1

How to Get Started

> **In This Chapter**
>
> ➤ Using general information sources
>
> ➤ Deciding when to go
>
> ➤ Advice for people with special needs

You'd expect a city like Las Vegas—one that makes its living on tourist dollars—to be the subject of a billion books and brochures. Well, you'd be right.

There are tons of valuable resources for information about where to stay, when to go, how to get there, and what to do. This chapter will let you in on the best of these resources, whatever your needs.

How to Be a Las Vegas Know-It-All

You've probably heard the phrase *knowledge is power*—it definitely applies to traveling. It's important to get as much as you can from as many different sources as you can. Just keep in mind that brochures are written to promote places and keep advertisers happy, so take their suggestions with a grain of salt.

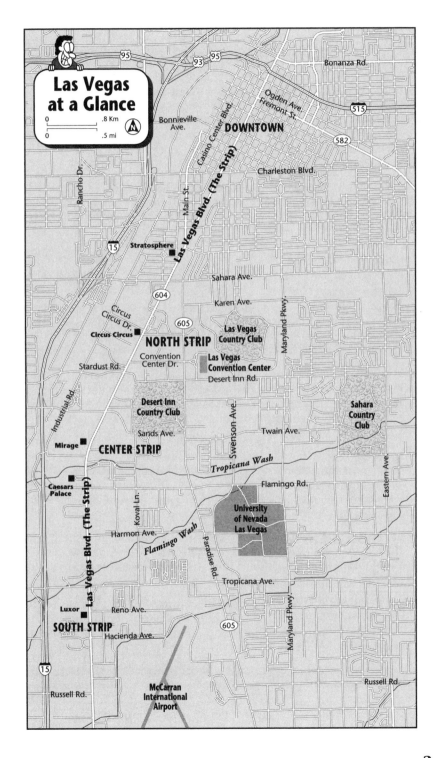

Las Vegas at a Glance

The Official Line

The two most valuable resources for Vegas information are also the two to be most wary of. The first, run by Clark County, is **The Las Vegas Convention and Visitors Authority**, 3150 Paradise Rd., Las Vegas, NV 89109 (☎ 800/332-5333). You'd think with such a title, they'd be all inclusive and unbiased, but that's not always the case. The packet of information they send out is impressive, however, and includes maps, show guides, and an events calendar. They offer prerecorded information on their hotline and a free hotel-locating service. They're open weekdays from 8am to 6pm and weekends from 8am to 5pm.

The other organization doesn't even pretend to be unbiased. It's the **Las Vegas Chamber of Commerce**, 3720 Howard Hughes Pkwy., Las Vegas, NV 89109 (☎ 702/735-1616). They are a member-supported organization, so the stuff you'll receive from them, although valuable, will only recommend businesses that are part of the LVCC. They're open Monday through Friday from 8am to 5pm.

Surfing the Web

There's a veritable avalanche of information available on the web. I did a search on Yahoo! using just the keywords "Las Vegas" and came up with more than 700 links. After checking most of them out, I found the following to be the most informative and user-friendly:

➤ The "Official" Las Vegas Leisure Guide (**www.pcap.com**): This is the best Vegas web site around, with the latest information, terrific resources, and a layout that's easy to follow. With so much hotel, restaurant, and nightlife information, it's no wonder they get more than 2 million hits a month.

➤ Las Vegas Online Entertainment Guide (**www.lvol.com**): The very complete hotel listings in this site include ratings and comments from previous guests, as well as an online reservations system. There's also restaurant information, history, facts, business directories, adult entertainment, and gambling instructions.

➤ *Las Vegas Review-Journal* Website (**www.lvrj.com**): This is the site from the largest Vegas newspaper. In addition to local news and weather, you'll find restaurant listings, show guides, event and concert listings, and tips for getting around town.

➤ Las Vegas Nevada Website (**www.lvnv.com**): This one isn't as complete as the others, but it has some really cool stuff, including lots of pictures, and some live action like the sounds of the Mirage volcano erupting and the roar of a white tiger.

➤ Night on the Town Las Vegas (**www.nightonthetown.com**): This site is loaded with graphics and advertisements, so downloading can take a while, but once you're in, you'll find lots of solid listings, links, contests, and discounts on area restaurants and attractions.

As you surf the web, be warned—a lot of the Vegas sites are horribly obsolete. Also, don't forget that many of the larger hotels have their own web sites complete with pictures, maps, and online reservations systems. It's all promotional, but still, you get to see what each one looks like. You'll find those web addresses in chapter 6, "Hotels A to Z."

Reading Is Fundamental!

No guidebook can tell you *everything* there is to know about any city—especially Las Vegas, which is constantly blowing up hotels, restaurants, and attractions, and building new ones. This book offers you everything you need to plan the perfect trip, but if you want even more detail, *Frommer's Las Vegas* is the best, most thorough Vegas guide around. I also recommend *The Unofficial Guide to Las Vegas*. I can honestly say that I haven't found any guides as complete as these two.

Dollars & Sense

Many Las Vegas web sites (including those for specific hotels) offer discount coupons or deals for restaurants, attractions, and shows. If you're on the Internet, take time to surf around—you might find a great bargain.

When Should I Go?

There are three important points to consider when choosing a date for your departure: climate, crowds, and cost. If you think it doesn't matter how hot it's going to be, how many people are going to be there, or how much money you're going to spend, let me tell you, you're probably fooling yourself.

Climate: "Man, It's Hot!"

Unless you never plan to leave your hotel, you need to consider the climate.

Many people will tell you that since there is little humidity in the desert, the heat is bearable. They're lying. It gets hot as Hades in Las Vegas—often unbelievably, unbearably hot. As you'll see on the chart below, the *average* high temperature in July is 105 degrees, which means that many days it's even hotter than that.

The flip side is that winter months can get chilly, especially at night when the winds tend to pick up.

April, May, September, and October offer the most moderate weather, but you'll still need sunscreen, and many of you will want to wear a hat.

Las Vegas Average Temperatures (in Degrees Fahrenheit)

	Jan	Feb	Mar	Apr	May	June	July	Aug	Sept	Oct	Nov	Dec
Average	44	50	57	66	74	84	91	88	81	67	54	47
Avg. High	55	62	69	79	88	99	105	103	96	82	67	58
Avg. Low	33	39	44	53	60	68	76	74	65	53	41	36

Crowds: "Where Did All These People Come From?!?"

In 1996, almost 30 million people visited Las Vegas, and if you have my kind of luck, most of them will be ahead of you in line at your hotel's reception desk when you arrive.

A few pointers: Summer months are the slowest, weekends are always busier than weekdays, and holidays tend to bring out the masses (even the smaller ones like Valentine's Day—you know, the wedding chapels and all). Also, major conventions and sporting events like major boxing matches and the Super Bowl will almost guarantee a lot of reservations agents saying, "Sorry, sold out!"

So basically, if you don't like crowds, try for a non-holiday weekday during the summer when there is no convention in town. Simple, huh?

Use the reference list below to rule out high-traffic times—or to find something of interest that may make you willing to join the throng.

Dollars & Sense

If you're one of those people who just doesn't mind the heat, try coming to Las Vegas during the summer. It is the slowest time of the year for hotels and casinos, and hotels often offer drastic rate reductions and terrific bargains. If you're into serious gambling, you'll be spending most of your time in an air-conditioned casino, anyway.

Cost: "I Thought This Was Supposed to Be a Cheap Vacation!"

In the past, Vegas offered lots of cheap hotel rooms on the premise that this would lure visitors who would drop lots of money in the casinos. Sadly, that doesn't happen much these days. In fact, most of the newer hotels offer rooms for $100 or more per night.

There are ways to get cheap rooms, but as you should already know, your best chance for good deals is during summer months and non-convention times.

Bet You Didn't Know

Watch out, Mickey! More people choose Las Vegas as their vacation destination than Disneyland, Walt Disney World, and all of America's other theme parks combined. In fact, Las Vegas is the number-one tourist spot in America and the fifth most popular destination in the world. And that's not all—between 4,000 and 6,000 people move to Las Vegas every month, making it the fastest growing city in the U.S.

Convention Dates from Hell (and Other Major Annual Events That Bring Visitors Out of the Woodwork):

This is a short list and is not intended to be complete, so get a more detailed listing of convention and event dates from the **Las Vegas Convention and Visitor's Authority** (☎ **800/332-5333**) and ask for their brochures on these topics.

January

➤ **Consumer Electronics Show**: A major convention with attendance of over 100,000. Usually the second week. 1998 dates: January 8–11; 1999 dates: January 7–10.

➤ **The PBA Players Classic**: A bowling tournament held at The Showboat Hotel, 2800 Fremont St. (☎ **702/385-9123**). 1998 dates: January 10–14.

➤ **The Super Bowl**: Sports fans galore flock to Vegas to wager on this football showdown. Last Sunday in January.

February

➤ **Valentine's Day:** Lots of people love to get married in Vegas. February 14.

➤ **Men's Apparel Guild in California (MAGIC)**: Another big convention that brings in over 70,000 people. Usually the third week. 1998 dates: February 18–21.

April

➤ **The World Series of Poker**: High-stakes gamblers flock to Binion's Horseshoe Casino, 128 East Fremont St. (☎ **702/382-1600**), for this three-week event.

➤ **Gay & Lesbian Pride Celebration**: Festival held every year, usually the last weekend. Call ☎ **702/225-3389.**

May

➤ **Networld/Interop**: Sixty thousand people are expected at this high-tech convention. Usually the first week. 1998 dates: May 4–8.

➤ **Memorial Day**: A big getaway weekend for Vegas, with the crowds to prove it. Last Monday in May.

June

➤ **The PBA Invitational**: Another bowling tournament, also at The Showboat Hotel. 1998 dates: June 7–13.

➤ **Helldorado**: A Western heritage celebration with rodeos, trail rides, and barbecues at the Thomas and Mack Center at the University of Nevada Las Vegas (UNLV). Sponsored by the Elk's Lodge. Call ☎ **702/ 870-1221.** Usually mid-month.

July

➤ **Independence Day**: The fireworks shows are spectacular and so are the numbers of people who come to watch them. July 4th.

Tourist Traps

Hotels usually charge substantially higher room rates during peak holiday or convention times. If you're not careful, you could wind up paying three or four times the regular rate. You have to shop around and be flexible: hotels may be charging $200 for a room one week and $50 for the same room the next.

August

If you don't mind the heat (and I mean serious heat), this is a good time to go. No really huge conventions or major holidays.

September

➤ **Labor Day**: Celebrate work by playing all day in Las Vegas! First Monday.

➤ **Oktoberfest**: Polka, polka, polka from mid–September through the end of October at the Mount Charleston Resort (☎ **800/955-1314**).

October

➤ **PGA Tour Las Vegas Invitational**: A five-day championship golf event. For more details, call ☎ **702/242-3000.**

➤ **Halloween**: Ghosts and ghouls roam the casinos, with both the guests and employees getting in on the action. October 31.

November

➤ **Softbank Comdex**: This computer convention is the biggest of the year, with almost 200,000 people expected. Second or third week. 1998 dates: November 16–19.

➤ **Thanksgiving**: Loads of people take advantage of the four-day weekend to come to town—and yes, the hotel buffets serve turkey. Fourth Thursday.

December

➤ **National Finals Rodeo**: The biggest rodeo event in the country, with 170,000 attendees each year. For more info, call ☎ **702/895-3900.** First two weeks of the month.

➤ **Christmas**: The week leading up to the holiday is one of the slowest times of the year, but the week right after is one of the busiest.

➤ **New Year's Eve**: Over 200,000 visitors jam the city to count down the year, and the Las Vegas Strip is closed off to accommodate nearly twice that number of revelers, rivaling the attendance in Times Square! You've got to book well in advance for this party.

Should I Bring the Kids?

A few years ago, the great minds of Vegas decided to try to go after the family market. Amusement parks, roller coasters, and arcades sprang up, along with hotel childcare centers—all aimed at trying to get mom and dad to bring the kids to Las Vegas instead of Disneyland.

It didn't work.

Almost all the hotels that were designed with the kids in mind (Treasure Island, MGM Grand, Stratosphere, Excalibur) have scaled back their initial offerings and in some cases scrapped them all together. Therefore, there just isn't a lot for kids to do now.

The main lure of Vegas is, of course, gambling, and you have to be 21 to even enter a casino. In other words, little Johnny and Becky can't hang out next to you at the slot machines. So if you intend to spend any significant time gambling, you'll have to find a video arcade or the like in which to park them while you hit the tables. And, quite frankly, it'll probably wind up costing you more to do this than you'll win.

But I HAVE to Bring the Kids!

Okay, okay, with a little bit of creativity and some fairly loose purse strings, you can bring your entire family and everybody will have a good time.

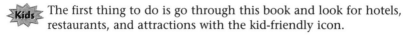 The first thing to do is go through this book and look for hotels, restaurants, and attractions with the kid-friendly icon.

As far as hotels are concerned, you'll only see the icon if there is something special about the property that will keep kids entertained while you gamble away their college funds. Examples might be large video arcades, rides or games, childcare centers, or family pool areas. If you are bringing children, these hotels should be your first choices, no matter how cool others may seem. If they aren't, your kids might have a lousy time—and if *they* have a lousy time, you can bet they'll see to it that you do, too. Also, be sure to check out the appendixes in the guide for a list of important phone numbers for families.

Think Ahead & Then Call Ahead

Nobody knows your children better than you (no matter how often you feel you don't understand them). Think about what you need to get through a typical day in your household. Now, envision yourself trying to meet those requirements without the comforts of home. If your child is young enough to require a car seat, for example, be sure to ask the car rental company if they provide them. Or maybe you'll want to go out for a romantic dinner while the kids stay with a baby-sitter. Many hotels offer baby-sitting services—so be sure to inquire about costs, references, and arrangements before you arrive at the front desk.

Get Them Involved

Read some of the descriptions in the following chapters to your children and let them decide which ones they think sound the most interesting. If they feel like they've had a hand in planning the trip, they may be more invested in having a good time. This will be especially valuable in chapters 12, "The Top Attractions A to Z," and 13, "More Fun Stuff to Do."

Travel Advice for the Senior Set

People over the age of 60 are traveling more than ever before. And why not? Being a senior citizen entitles you to some terrific travel bargains.

If you're not a member of **AARP (American Association of Retired Persons),** 601 E St. NW, Washington, DC 20049 (☎ **202/434-AARP**), do yourself a favor and join. You'll get discounts on car rentals and hotels.

Mature Outlook, P.O. Box 9390, Des Moines, IA 50306-9519 (☎ **800/ 336-6330**; fax 847/286-5024), is a similar organization, offering discounts on car rentals and hotel stays at many Holiday Inns, Howard Johnsons, and Best Westerns. The $20 annual membership fee also gets you $100 in Sears coupons and a bimonthly magazine. Membership is open to all Sears customers 18 and over, but the organization's primary focus is on the 50-and-over market.

In addition, most of the major domestic airlines, including American, United, Continental, U.S. Airways, and TWA, offer discount programs for senior travelers—be sure to ask whenever you book a flight. In most cities, people over the age of 60 get reduced admission at theaters, museums, and other attractions, and they can often get discount fares on public transportation. Carrying identification with proof of age can pay off in all these situations.

The Mature Traveler, a monthly, 12-page newsletter on senior-citizen travel, is a valuable resource. It's available by subscription ($30 a year) from GEM Publishing Group, Box 50400, Reno, NV 89513-0400. GEM also publishes **The Book of Deals**, a collection of more than 1,000 senior discounts on airlines, lodging, tours, and attractions around the country that sells for $9.95. You can order *The Mature Traveler* and *The Book of Deals* by calling ☎ **800/460-6676**. Another helpful publication is **101 Tips for the Mature Traveler,** available from Grand Circle Travel, 347 Congress St., Suite 3A, Boston, MA 02210 (☎ **800/221-2610** or 617/350-7500; fax 617/350-6206).

Grand Circle Travel is also one of the literally hundreds of travel agencies specializing in vacations for seniors. But beware: Many of them are of the tour-bus variety, with free trips thrown in for those who organize groups of 20 or more. Seniors seeking more independent travel should probably consult a regular travel agent. **SAGA International Holidays,** 222 Berkeley St., Boston, MA 02116 (☎ **800/343-0273**), offers inclusive tours for those 50 and older.

Advice for Travelers with Disabilities
A disability shouldn't stop anybody from traveling, particularly in Las Vegas, which has really gone to great lengths to accommodate individuals with special needs. Every major hotel comes equipped with the basics like ramps and elevators, and most have rooms outfitted with the latest technology designed for accessibility. Just be sure to inform your reservations agent of your requirements.

There are more options and resources available to travelers with disabilities than ever before. One great tool is **A World of Options**, a 658-page book of resources for disabled travelers. It costs $45 and is available from **Mobility International USA,** P.O. Box 10767, Eugene, OR, 97440 (☎ **541/343-1284,** voice and TDD, www.miusa.org). For more personal assistance, call the **Travel Information Service** at ☎ **215/456-9603** or 215/456-9602 (for TTY).

Many of the major car-rental companies now offer hand-controlled cars for drivers with disabilities. Avis can provide such a vehicle at any of its locations in the U.S. with 48-hour advance notice; Hertz requires between 24 and

72 hours notice at most of its locations. **Wheelchair Getaways** (☎ **800/ 642-2042**; or fax 606/873-8039; www.blvd.com/wg.htm) rents specialized vans with wheelchair lifts and other features for the disabled in more than 100 cities across the U.S.

Travelers with disabilities may also want to consider joining a tour that caters specifically to them. One of the best operators is **Flying Wheels Travel,** 143 West Bridge (P.O. Box 382), Owatonna, MN 55060 (☎ **800/535-6790**). They offer various escorted tours and private tours in minivans with lifts. Another good company is **FEDCAP Rehabilitation Services**, 211 W. 14th St., New York, NY 10011. Call ☎ **212/727-4200** or fax 212/721-4374 for information about membership and summer tours.

Vision-impaired travelers should contact the **American Foundation for the Blind**, 11 Penn Plaza, Suite 300, New York, NY 10001 (☎ **800/ 232-5463**), for information on traveling with seeing-eye dogs.

Out & About: Advice for Gay & Lesbian Travelers

The hotels and casinos in Las Vegas want your money—it doesn't matter who you're dating. In fact, many of the mega-resorts are now actively advertising in gay and lesbian papers to try to lure some of those disposable-income dollars away from you.

A few of the best gay bars are listed in chapter 16, "Hitting the Bars & Clubs," but for more detailed information, call and ask for a copy of *The Las Vegas Bugle* (☎ **702/369-6260**). This is the local monthly gay and lesbian newspaper, listing all the bars, restaurants, and events in town. Make sure you pick one up when you get to town for the latest information on what's happening.

You can also check out **The Damron Guide**, which is a great nationwide travel guide for the gay community. It's available at most gay and lesbian bookstores, or you can call the Damron Company at ☎ **415/255-0404**. An abbreviated version is available online at **www.damron.com.**

Speaking of web sites, Gay Las Vegas (**www.gaylasvegas.com**) is a terrific resource, with information on bars, gay-friendly restaurants, and even weather forecasts. This is not to be confused with www.gay-las-vegas.com, a similar but (in my humble opinion) inferior web site.

Chapter 2

Money Matters

> **In This Chapter**
>
> ➤ Money: How much and what kind?
>
> ➤ Budgeting your trip
>
> ➤ Pinching pennies

Money matters, all right, especially in Vegas. One thing is certain: This city is well set up for separating you from your bread. There are plenty of places to get it—cash machines galore—and even more places to spend it. In this chapter, we'll take a look at different options for keeping yourself funded while making sure you don't go bankrupt in the process.

Should I Carry Traveler's Checks or the Green Stuff?

Traveler's checks are something of an anachronism from the pre-ATM days. Because they could be replaced if lost or stolen, traveler's checks were a sound alternative to filling your wallet with cash at the beginning of a trip.

These days, traveler's checks are less necessary because most cities have 24-hour ATMs linked to a national network that most likely includes your bank at home.

Still, if you feel you need the security of traveler's checks and don't mind the hassle of showing identification every time you want to cash a check, you can get them at almost any bank. **American Express** offers checks in denominations of $10, $20, $50, $100, $500, and $1,000. You'll pay a service charge ranging from 1 to 4 percent, although AAA members can obtain checks without a fee at most AAA offices. You can also get American Express traveler's checks over the phone by calling ☎ **800/221-7282**; Amex gold and platinum cardholders who call this number are exempt from the 1 percent fee.

Visa also offers traveler's checks, available at Citibank locations across the country and at several other banks. The service charge ranges between 1.5 and 2 percent; checks come in denominations of $20, $50, $100, $500, and $1,000. **MasterCard** also offers traveler's checks. Call ☎ **800/223-9920** for a location near you.

Bet You Didn't Know

There is no state income tax in Nevada. Gambling is the number-one source of income for the state, providing over 43 percent of Nevada's general funding.

ATMs to the Left of Me, ATMs to the Right of Me

The last thing you need to worry about in Las Vegas is not having access to your money—there's an ATM around every corner. After all, if you were out of cash and couldn't use your ATM card at 3am, you wouldn't be able to drop any more quarters in that double-diamond slot machine that you're just *sure* is going to pay off big at any moment. And Las Vegas cares about your being able to access your money in such situations.

Cirrus (☎ **800/424-7787** or 800/ 4CIRRUS) and **Plus** (☎ **800/843-7587**) are the two most popular networks; check the back of your ATM card to see which network your bank belongs to. The 800 numbers will give you specific locations of ATMs where you can withdraw money away from home.

Dollars & Sense

Although you can get in touch with your money through ATMs, you may have to pay a price for the privilege, particularly at non-bank locations. There are cash machines every five feet in Las Vegas, which is convenient, but they may clip you $1 or more for each transaction. Many banks have also begun to impose a fee ranging from 50¢ to $3 every time you use the ATM in a different city. Your own bank may also charge you a fee for using ATMs from other banks. Try to anticipate your cash needs to cut down on the number of trips you'll make to the ATM.

Consider Yourself Warned

If you get that gleam in your eye when you're near a blackjack table and have a hard time exercising self-restraint, you really need to take some extraordinary measures, such as leaving your ATM card at home or in your hotel room and carrying only as much cash as you're willing to lose.

Plastic

Credit cards are invaluable when traveling. They are a safe way to carry money and provide a convenient record of all your travel expenses when you arrive home. You can also get **cash advances** off your credit cards at any bank (although you'll start paying interest on the advance the moment you receive the cash, and you won't receive frequent-flyer miles on an airline credit card). At most banks, you don't even need to go to a teller; you can get a cash advance at the ATM if you know your PIN number. If you've forgotten your PIN number or didn't even know you had one, call the phone number on the back of your credit card and ask the bank to send it to you. It usually takes five to seven business days, although some banks will do it over the phone if you tell them your mother's maiden name or give them some other security clearance.

Tourist Traps

Most casinos will make it easy to get a cash advance from your credit card. Isn't that nice of them? The problem is that they charge outrageous processing fees—usually 7–10% of the amount you are advancing ($200 costs you an additional $16). Don't do it!

Stop, Thief! (What to Do If Your Money Gets Stolen)

Almost every credit-card company has an emergency 800 number you can call if your wallet or purse is stolen. The company may be able to wire you a cash advance immediately, and in many places, it can get you an emergency credit card in a day or two. The issuing bank's 800 number is usually on the back of the credit card. (But that doesn't help you much if the card was stolen, does it? So just call 800-information—that's **800/555-1212**—to find out the number.) **Citicorp Visa's** U.S. emergency number is ☎ **800/645-6556. American Express** cardholders and traveler's check holders should call ☎ **800/221-7282** for all emergencies. **MasterCard** holders should call ☎ **800/307-7309.**

If you opt to carry traveler's checks, be sure to keep a record of their serial numbers and store them in some other place, so that you can handle just such an emergency.

Odds are that if your wallet is gone, you've seen the last of it, and the police aren't likely to recover it for you. However, after you realize that it's gone and you cancel your credit cards, it is still worth a call to inform the police. You may need the police report number for credit card or insurance purposes later.

What Will This Trip Cost?

Budgeting a trip to Vegas is different from planning a trip to Europe or Yosemite. Some things, such as show tickets, cost more than you'd care to imagine; others, like hotel rooms, swing wildly in price. And the amount of money you want to spend on gambling is entirely up to you and your own self-control. But the good news here is that there are loads of bargains to be had, and it's entirely possible to enjoy a really affordable Vegas vacation.

The budget worksheet at the end of this chapter will help you figure out where your money's going to go.

Transportation

Getting here is going to cost you either airfare or gas money. Whether you're flying or driving, refer to chapter 3, "How Will I Get There?", for more details on how to save serious dough. Since Las Vegas is such a major destination, many airlines offer competitive rates and frequent sales.

Chapters 4, "Tying Up the Loose Ends," and 8, "Getting Around," deal with rental cars, taxis, and other modes of transportation. If you're renting a car (which I highly recommend), you can probably get a rate of $25 to $30 per day for a basic economy car. And that's a fair number to budget for transportation even if you don't rent a car, because that's about the same amount you can expect to pay per day for taxis.

A Place to Lay Your Head

In chapter 6, "Hotels A to Z," you'll find listings of hotels in all price ranges. The average price for a hotel room in Las Vegas is around $60 per night based on double occupancy, but you can spend significantly more or less, depending on what you're looking for. Chapter 5, "Pillow Talk: The Lowdown on the Las Vegas Hotel Scene," offers tons of pointers on how to get the best rate.

What Things Cost in Las Vegas

Taxi from airport to the Strip	$8–$12
Taxi from airport to downtown	$16–$20
Minibus from airport to the Strip	$3.50
Minibus from airport to downtown	$4.75
Double room at the Desert Inn ($$$$$)	$175–$185
Double room at the Mirage ($$$$)	$79–$129
Double room at the Luxor ($$$)	$49–$99
Double room at Orleans ($$)	$39–$79
Three-course meal at Gatsby's ($$$$$)	$65–$85
Three-course meal at Chin's ($$$$)	$35–$45
Three-course meal at Hard Rock Cafe ($$$)	$15–$20
Three-course meal at Liberty Cafe ($)	$5–$10
All-you-can-eat buffet dinner at the Luxor	$8.99
All-you-can-eat buffet dinner at The Mirage	$12.95
Cup of coffee	$1.50
Roll of ASA 100 color film, 36 exposures	$4.70
Show ticket for Lance Burton ($$$)	$34.95
Show ticket for Jubilee ($$$$)	$49.50
Show ticket for headliners at Caesars	$45–$75
Show ticket for Siegfried and Roy ($$$$$)	$89.95

Dollars & Sense

Most hotels offer guests discounts on their shows, restaurants, and attractions. Check with the hotel representative when making your reservation to see what kinds of goodies you can get.

Restaurants

This is where your taste really comes into play. If you're a champagne-and-caviar type, then plan on at least $100 per person per day for food. Vegas used to be a culinary wasteland, but the restaurant scene has really taken off, and there are dozens of high-end choices now.

Average Joes with beer-and-popcorn tastes can get by with $25 per day—sometimes less. Vegas is famous for its low-cost, all-you-can-eat buffets, so if you want to save money in this area, you really can. Restaurants are listed (with prices) in chapter 10, "Making Your Restaurant Choice."

Shows & Nightlife

The average show ticket runs around $50 per person, but that price may include drinks, tax, gratuities, or even dinner. Some of the big-name shows, though, such as Siegfried and Roy, can run up to $90 a ticket—enough to shock even New Yorkers used to Broadway ticket prices! See chapter 15, "The Shows A to Z," for more details.

If you plan on hitting any of the big nightclubs on a weekend, expect a substantial cover charge ($10–$20) and very high drink prices. Weekdays can be expensive, too, but to a lesser extent.

Bet You Didn't Know

If you're going to Vegas primarily for the gambling, you're actually in the minority. Only 5 percent of visitors cite games of chance as their main reason for visiting. However, once they get to town, almost 90 percent of tourists spend some time gambling. So even if you don't think you're gonna roll the dice, remember that almost everyone gets sucked into the casinos.

Shopping

Again, personal taste is a big factor here. If you're a shop-a-holic, keep in mind that this is not a cheap town, especially in tourist areas such as the Strip and downtown. Even souvenirs can cost you dearly, so budget accordingly.

Gambling

Be strict with this part of your budget by setting aside as much money as you're prepared to lose. Once that runs out, don't steal from other areas of the budget. Also, don't expect to come home with any of the cash that you put into this column—the sad reality is that most people lose while gambling in Las Vegas.

Dollars & Sense

Here are some handy tips on tipping:

Bartenders	10–15% of total check or about $1 a drink
Bellhops	$1 per bag
Cab drivers	10–15% of the fare
Casino dealers	A few dollars if you have a big win
Domestic staff	At least $1 per day (everybody forgets them, but really, who does more for you on your whole vacation than the person who makes your bed and picks up your dirty towels?)
Checkroom attendants	$1 per garment
Showroom maitre d's	$5–$10, depending on total show ticket price and how good a seat you want
Waiters	15% of the total check or more for exceptional service
Valet parking attendants	$1–$2

What If I'm Worried I Can't Afford It?

If you're now thoroughly frightened that you'll be washing dishes to pay for your meals, relax. Go over the worksheet at the end of this chapter carefully. If the number comes out too high, think about where you can, or are willing to, economize.

There are plenty of ways to cut down on costs. Note the "Dollars & Sense" boxes scattered throughout this book, which offer hints on how to save. Here are just a few strategies right off the bat:

➤ **Go during the off-season.** If you can travel at non-peak times (notably, summer), you'll find hotel prices that are significantly reduced from peak months.

➤ **Travel on off-days of the week.** Airfares vary depending on the day of the week. If you can travel on a Tuesday, Wednesday, or Thursday, you may find cheaper flights to your destination. When you inquire about airfares, ask if you can obtain a cheaper rate by flying on a different day.

➤ **Try a package tour.** You can book airfare, hotel, ground transportation, and even some sightseeing just by making one call to a travel agent or packager, and it may cost a lot less than if you tried to put the trip together yourself. (See "The Pros & Cons of Package Tours" in chapter 3 for specific suggestions of companies to call.)

➤ **Always ask for discount rates.** Membership in AAA, frequent-flyer plans, trade unions, AARP, or other groups may qualify you for discounted rates on car rentals, plane tickets, hotel rooms, and even meals. Ask about everything; you could be pleasantly surprised.

➤ **Ask if your kids can stay in your room with you.** A room with two double beds usually doesn't cost any more than a room with a queen-size bed. And many hotels won't charge you the additional person rate if the additional person is pint-sized and related to you. Even if you have to pay $10 or $15 for a rollaway bed, you'll save hundreds by not taking two rooms.

➤ **Try expensive restaurants at lunch instead of dinner.** Lunch tabs are usually a fraction of what dinner would cost at most top restaurants, and the menu often boasts many of the same specialties.

➤ **Skip the souvenirs.** Your photographs and your memories should be the best mementos of your trip. If you're worried about money, you can do without the T-shirts, key chains, Elvis salt-and-pepper shakers, fuzzy dice for your dashboard, and other trinkets.

Budget Worksheet: You Can Afford This Trip

Expense	Amount
Airfare (× no. of people traveling)	
Car Rental (if applicable)	
Lodging (× no. of nights)	
Breakfast *may be included in your room rate* (× no. of nights)	
Lunch (× no. of nights)	
Dinner (× no. of nights)	
Baby-sitting	
Gambling	
Attractions (admission charges to museums, theme parks, tours, theaters, nightclubs, etc.)	
Transportation (cabs, subway, buses, etc.)	
Souvenirs (t-shirts, postcards, that antique you just gotta have)	
Tips (think 15% of your meal total plus $1 a bag every time a bellhop moves your luggage)	
Don't forget the cost of getting to and from the airport in your home town, plus long-term parking (× no. of nights)	
Grand Total	

How Will I Get There?

With nothing but miles of barren desert surrounding it, Las Vegas is literally in the middle of nowhere. In fact, it's the most isolated major city in the country.

Getting here is easy. You'll either fly or drive, because there is no passenger train service to the city. So let's take a closer look at your options and get this show on the road!

Travel Agent: Friend or Foe?

A good travel agent is like a good mechanic or a good plumber—hard to find, but invaluable after you've zeroed in on the right person. And the best way to find a good travel agent is the same way you find a good plumber or mechanic or doctor: word of mouth.

Any travel agent can help you find a bargain airfare, hotel, or rental car. A good travel agent will stop you from ruining your vacation by trying to save a few dollars. And the best travel agents can tell you how much time you should budget in a destination, find a cheap flight that doesn't require you to change planes in Atlanta or Chicago, get you a better hotel room for about the same price, arrange for a competitively priced rental car, and even give you restaurant recommendations.

Travel agents work on commission. The good news is that *you* don't pay the commission—the airlines, hotels, and tour companies do. The bad news is that unscrupulous travel agents will try to persuade you to book the vacations that get them the most money in commissions instead of a trip that might suit you better.

To make sure that you get the most out of your travel agent, do a little homework. Read about your destination (you've already made a sound decision by buying this book) and pick out what you think you want to see and do. If necessary, get a more comprehensive travel guide like *Frommer's Las Vegas* or *The Unofficial Guide to Las Vegas*. If you have access to the Internet, check prices on the web in advance (see "Happy Landings: Winning the Airfare Wars," later in this chapter, for more information on how to do that). You'll be a well-informed consumer when you meet with your agent, and you won't be talked into anything that's not right for you.

Bring your guidebook and web information to the travel agent and ask him or her to make the arrangements for you. Because they have access to more resources than even the most complete web travel site, travel agents should be able to get you an even better price than you could get by yourself. And they can issue your tickets and vouchers right there. If they can't get you into the hotel of your choice, they can recommend an alternative, and you can look for an objective review in your guidebook right there and then.

Tourist Traps

Make sure you are 100 percent positive about your vacation plans before making your airline reservations. Most airlines will charge a fee for changing your flight schedule, especially if you initially received a bargain fare.

In the past two years, some airlines and resorts have begun limiting or eliminating travel-agent commissions altogether. The immediate result has been that travel agents don't bother booking these services unless the customer specifically requests them (another reason why you need to be well-informed). But some travel-industry analysts predict that if other airlines and accommodations throughout the industry follow suit, travel agents may have to start charging customers for their services. When that day arrives, the best agents should prove even harder to find.

The Pros & Cons of Package Tours

Package tours are not the same thing as escorted tours. They are simply a way of buying your airfare and accommodations at the same time.

And for popular destinations like Las Vegas, package tours are really the smart way to go, because they save you a ton of money. In many cases, a package that includes airfare, hotel, and transportation to and from the airport will cost you less than just the hotel alone if you booked it yourself. That's because packages are sold in bulk to tour operators who resell them to the public. It's kind of like buying your vacation at Sam's Club, except that it's the tour operator who buys the 1,000-count box of garbage bags and resells them 10 at a time at a cost that undercuts what you'd pay at your average neighborhood supermarket.

Packages vary as much as garbage bags, too. Some packages offer a better class of hotels than others. Some offer the same hotels for lower prices. Some offer flights on scheduled airlines, while others book charters. In some packages, your choices of accommodations and travel days may be limited. Some allow you to add on excursions or escorted day trips (also at prices lower than if you booked them yourself).

Each destination usually has one or two packagers that are better than the rest because they buy in even bigger bulk. The time you spend shopping around will be well rewarded.

Pick a Peck of Pickled Packagers

The best place to start looking is the travel section of your local Sunday newspaper. **Liberty Travel** (many locations; check your local directory, since there's not a central 800 number) is one of the biggest packagers in the Northeast and usually boasts a full-page ad in Sunday papers. You won't get much in the way of service, but you will get a good deal.

American Express Vacations (☎ **800/241-1700**) is another option.

Another good resource is the airlines themselves, which often package their flights together with accommodations. When you pick the airline, you can choose one that has frequent service to your home town and the one on which you accumulate frequent-flyer miles. And although disreputable packagers are uncommon, they do exist; but by buying your package through the airline, you can be pretty sure that the company will still be in business when your departure date arrives.

Among the airline packages, your options include **American Airlines FlyAway Vacations** (☎ 800/321-2121), **America West Vacations** (☎ 800/356-6611), **Delta Dream Vacations** (☎ 800/872-7786), **Southwest Airlines Vacations** (☎ 800/423-5683), **United Airlines Vacations** (☎ 800/328-6877), and **U.S. Airways Vacations** (☎ 800/455-0123).

The prices and availability of package tours change constantly, but here are a few examples that were available at press time: **Southwest Airlines Vacations** was offering round-trip airfare from Los Angeles and two nights at the Luxor, with a bunch of other goodies, like ground transportation included, for only $149 per person based on double occupancy. Granted, this was for traveling during the week in an off period, but the airfare and hotel alone would have cost over $200 without the package deal. **Delta Dream Vacations** (☎ **800/872-7786**) had a mid-week package from New York that was only $349 per person (based on double occupancy) that included airfare, two nights' accommodations (at a variety of hotels), one day car rental, and assorted goodies.

The biggest hotels may also offer packages. If you already know where you want to stay, call the resort itself and ask if they can offer land/air packages.

Happy Landings: Winning the Airfare Wars

Airfares are capitalism at its purest. Passengers within the same cabin on an airplane rarely pay the same fare. Instead, they pay what the market will bear.

Business travelers who need the flexibility to purchase their tickets at the last minute, change their itinerary at a moment's notice, or want to get home before the weekend, usually pay the premium rate, known as the *full fare*. Passengers who can book their tickets long in advance; who don't mind staying over Saturday night; or who are willing to travel on a Tuesday, Wednesday, or Thursday pay the least—usually a fraction of the full fare. On most flights, even the shortest hops, the full fare is close to $1,000 or more, but a 7-day or 14-day advance purchase ticket is closer to $200–$300. Obviously, it pays to plan ahead.

The airlines also periodically offer specials in which they lower the prices on their most popular routes. These fares have advance-purchase requirements and date-of-travel restrictions, but you can't beat the price: usually no more than $400 for a cross-country flight. Keep your eyes open for these sales as you are planning your vacation, and then pounce on them. The sales tend to take place in low seasons. You'll almost never see a sale around the peak holiday seasons, when people have to fly regardless of what the fare is.

Dollars & Sense

Consolidators, also known as bucket shops, are a good place to check for the lowest fares. Their prices are much better than the fares you could get yourself and are often even lower than what your travel agent can get you. You see their ads in the small boxes at the bottom of the page in your Sunday Travel section. Some of the most reliable consolidators include **1-800-FLY-4-LESS** or **1-800-FLY-CHEAP**. Another good choice, **Council Travel** (☎ **800/226-8624**), caters especially to young travelers, but their bargain-basement prices are available to people of all ages.

Surfing the Web to Fly the Skies

Another way to find the cheapest fare is to let the Internet to do your searching for you. After all, that's what computers do best—search through millions of pieces of data and return information in rank order. The number of *virtual travel agents* on the Internet has increased exponentially in recent years.

There are too many online sites to mention, but a few of the better-respected ones are **Travelocity (www.travelocity.com)**, **Microsoft Expedia (www.expedia.com)**, and **Yahoo!'s Flifo Global (http://travel.yahoo.com/travel/)**. Each has its own little quirks (Travelocity, for example, requires you to register with them), but they all provide variations of the same service. Just enter the dates you want to fly and the cities you want to visit, and the computer looks for the lowest fares. The Yahoo! site has a feature called *Fare Beater* that will check flights on other airlines or at different times or dates in hopes of finding an even cheaper fare. Expedia's site will email you the best airfare deal once a week if you so choose. Travelocity uses the SABRE computer reservations system that most travel agents use and has a "Last Minute Deals" database that advertises really cheap fares for those who can get away at a moment's notice.

Great last-minute deals are also available directly from the airlines through a free email service called **E-savers**. Each week, the airline sends you a list of discounted flights—usually leaving the upcoming Friday or Saturday and returning the following Monday or Tuesday. You can sign up for all the major airlines at once by logging onto **Epicurious Travel (http://travel.epicurious.com/travel/c_planning/02_airfares/email/signup.html)**, or by visiting each airline's web site:

> **American Airlines:** www.americanair.com
>
> **Continental Airlines**: www.flycontinental.com
>
> **TWA:** www.twa.com
>
> **Northwest Airlines**: www.nwa.com
>
> **US Airways:** www.usairways.com

The Comfort Zone: How to Make Your Flight More Pleasant

The seats in the front row of each airplane cabin, called **bulkhead seats,** usually have the most leg room. They have some drawbacks, however. Because there's no seat in front of you, there's no place to put your carry-on luggage, except in the overhead bin. The front row also may not be the best place to see the in-flight movie. And often, airlines will put passengers with small children in the bulkhead row so the kids can sleep on the floor. This is terrific if you have kids but a nightmare if you have a headache.

Emergency-exit row seats also have extra leg room. They are assigned at the airport, usually on a first-come, first-serve basis. Ask when you check in whether you can be seated in one of these rows. In the unlikely event of an emergency, you'll be expected to open the emergency exit door and help direct traffic.

Ask for a seat toward the front of the plane. The minute the captain turns off the Fasten Seat Belts sign after landing, people jump up out of their seats as though Ken Griffey, Jr. just hit a home run. They then stand in the aisles and wait for 5 to 10 minutes while the ground crew puts the gangway in place. The closer to the front of the plane you are, the less hurry-up-and-waiting you'll have to do. Why do you think they put first class in the front?

Time-Savers

When you buy your ticket, find out if your airline offers electronic ticketing. If so, you simply show a picture ID (passport or driver's license) and present your confirmation number at the counter or gate on the day of your trip. You never actually handle a physical ticket, so you can't possibly lose it, and you'll speed up the whole process, especially if you aren't checking any luggage.

Wear comfortable clothes. The days of getting dressed up in a coat and tie to ride an airplane went out with Nehru jackets and poodle skirts. And dress in layers; the supposedly controlled climate in airplane cabins is anything but predictable. You'll be glad to have a sweater or jacket that you can put on or take off as the temperature on board dictates.

Bring some toiletries aboard on long flights. Airplane cabins are notoriously dry places. Take a travel-size bottle of moisturizer or lotion to refresh your face and hands at the end of the flight. If you're taking an overnight flight (a.k.a. the *red eye*), don't forget to pack a toothbrush to combat that feeling upon waking that you've been sucking on your seat cushion for six hours. If you wear contact lenses, take them out before you get on board and wear glasses instead. Or at least bring eye drops.

Extra! Extra!

If you have special dietary needs, be sure to order a special meal. Most airlines offer vegetarian meals, macrobiotic meals, kosher meals, meals for the lactose intolerant, and several other meals in a large variety of categories. Ask when you make your reservation if the airline can accommodate your dietary restrictions. Some people without any special dietary needs order special meals anyway, because they are made to order, unlike the mass-produced dinners served to the rest of the passengers.

Jet lag is not usually a problem for flights within the U.S., but some people are affected by three-hour time-zone changes. The best advice is to get acclimated to local time as quickly as possible. Stay up as long as you can the first day, and then try to wake up at a normal time the second day. Drink plenty of water both days, as well as on the plane, to avoid dehydration.

And if you're flying with kids, don't forget chewing gum for ear-pressure problems with swallowing, a deck of cards or favorite toys to keep them entertained, extra bottles or pacifiers, diapers, and so on.

For Fear of Flying or Love of Driving

Get out that map; we're going on a road trip!

Las Vegas is located in the southern tip of Nevada right along Interstate 15, the major north-south route from Los Angeles to the Canadian border. I-15 actually runs through the city, past downtown and less than a mile from the Strip, where all the big hotels are.

A good choice if you're coming from Northern or Central California is Highway 99 from Sacramento to Highway 58 in Bakersfield, which will take you to I-15 in Barstow. Portions of that route are still a two-lane, undivided highway, but most of the trip is freeway-style driving. From Southern California, take I-15 all the way.

If you're coming from the upper Midwest, your best bet is probably I-80, which stretches from Pennsylvania all the way to San Francisco. It may not be an extremely scenic drive, but it's the safest and fastest route to the point where it intersects with I-15 in Utah.

Another option is I-70, which runs from Missouri to I-15 in Utah.

The best way from the Northwest is probably I-84 running from Oregon to I-15 in Utah.

The Road Less Traveled

If you're coming from anywhere east of Las Vegas, why not take historic Route 66? It's been replaced by interstates in a few spots, but for the most part, it still winds from Chicago to Los Angeles, offering more than 2,000 miles of Americana all the way. You can get your kicks all the way to Kingman, Arizona, where you can hook up with Highway 93, which will take you past the famous Hoover Dam and then right into Las Vegas.

Does It Look Like Rain?

The mountains and deserts between you and Las Vegas make it imperative that you check the weather forecast before you leave. If your local TV station or newspaper doesn't give you enough information, check out The Weather Channel on cable, call them at ☎ **1-900-WEATHER**, or visit their web site (**www.weather.com**). An impending snowstorm through the Rockies or a heat wave across the desert Southwest may make you reconsider your travel route.

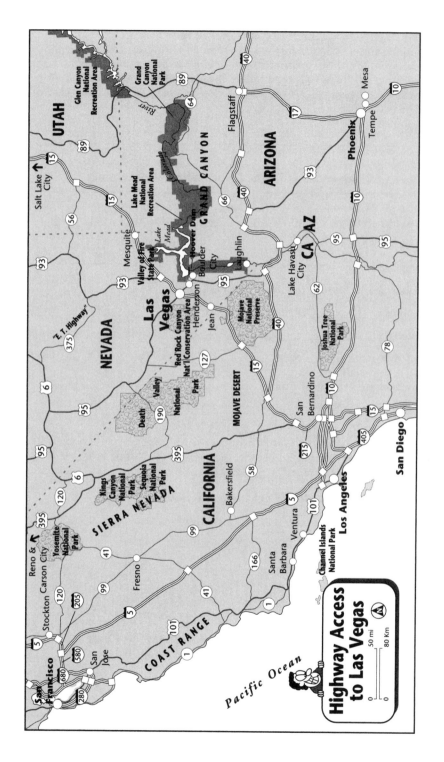

Highway Access to Las Vegas

29

Fare Game: Choosing an Airline

Arranging and booking flights is a complicated business; that's why a whole industry has grown up to handle it for you. If you're searching around for a deal, though, it helps to leave a trail of breadcrumbs through the maze so you can easily find your way to your destination and back. You can use this worksheet to do just that.

1 Schedule & Flight Information Worksheets

Travel Agency: _____ **Phone #:** _____

Agent's Name: _____ **Quoted Fare:** _____

Departure Schedule & Flight Information

Airline: _____ Airport: _____

Flight #: _____ Date: _____ Time: _____am/pm

Arrives in _____ Time: _____ am/pm

Connecting Flight (if any)

Amount of time between flights: _____ hours/mins.

Airline:_____ Flight #:_____ Time: _____am/pm

Arrives in _____ Time: _____ am/pm

Return Trip Schedule & Flight Information

Airline:_____ Airport: _____

Flight #: _____ Date: _____ Time: _____am/pm

Arrives in _____ Time: _____ am/pm

Connecting Flight (if any)

Amount of time between flights: _____ hours/mins.

Airline:_____ Flight #:_____ Time: _____am/pm

Arrives in _____ Time: _____ am/pm

2   Schedule & Flight Information Worksheets

Travel Agency: _____ **Phone #:** _____

Agent's Name: _____ **Quoted Fare:** _____

Departure Schedule & Flight Information

Airline: _____ Airport: _____

Flight #: _____ Date: _____ Time: _____am/pm

Arrives in _____ Time: _____ am/pm

Connecting Flight (if any)

Amount of time between flights: _____ hours/mins.

Airline:_____ Flight #:_____ Time: _____am/pm

Arrives in _____ Time: _____ am/pm

Return Trip Schedule & Flight Information

Airline:_____ Airport: _____

Flight #: _____ Date: _____ Time: _____am/pm

Arrives in _____ Time: _____ am/pm

Connecting Flight (if any)

Amount of time between flights: _____ hours/mins.

Airline:_____ Flight #:_____ Time: _____am/pm

Arrives in _____ Time: _____ am/pm

3   Schedule & Flight Information Worksheets

Travel Agency: _____ **Phone #:** _____

Agent's Name: _____ **Quoted Fare:** _____

Departure Schedule & Flight Information

Airline: _____ Airport: _____

Flight #: _____ Date: _____ Time: _____am/pm

Arrives in _____ Time: _____ am/pm

Connecting Flight (if any)

Amount of time between flights: _____ hours/mins.

Airline:_____ Flight #:_____ Time: _____am/pm

Arrives in _____ Time: _____ am/pm

Return Trip Schedule & Flight Information

Airline:_____ Airport: _____

Flight #: _____ Date: _____ Time: _____am/pm

Arrives in _____ Time: _____ am/pm

Connecting Flight (if any)

Amount of time between flights: _____ hours/mins.

Airline:_____ Flight #:_____ Time: _____am/pm

Arrives in _____ Time: _____ am/pm

4 Schedule & Flight Information Worksheets

Travel Agency: _____ **Phone #:** _____

Agent's Name: _____ **Quoted Fare:** _____

Departure Schedule & Flight Information

Airline: _____ Airport: _____

Flight #: _____ Date: _____ Time: _____am/pm

Arrives in _____ Time: _____ am/pm

Connecting Flight (if any)

Amount of time between flights: _____ hours/mins.

Airline:_____ Flight #:_____ Time: _____am/pm

Arrives in _____ Time: _____ am/pm

Return Trip Schedule & Flight Information

Airline:_____ Airport: _____

Flight #: _____ Date: _____ Time: _____am/pm

Arrives in _____ Time: _____ am/pm

Connecting Flight (if any)

Amount of time between flights: _____ hours/mins.

Airline:_____ Flight #:_____ Time: _____am/pm

Arrives in _____ Time: _____ am/pm

Chapter 4

Tying Up the Loose Ends

In This Chapter

➤ Advice on car rentals and travel insurance

➤ Handling emergencies while on vacation

➤ Making reservations

➤ Packing tips

➤ Taking Care of last-minute details

So you have a flight booked. Now all you need to do is decide where you're going to stay (you'll deal with that question separately in chapters 5, "Pillow Talk: The Lowdown on the Las Vegas Hotel Scene," and 6, "Hotels A to Z"), and what you're going to do once you get there. You also need to make reservations, put the dog in the kennel, pack your bags, and do 50 other last-minute things. Organizing everything coherently and thoroughly ahead of time will save you precious time in Vegas waiting on line, trying to get tickets, calling around town, being miserable, buying the underwear you forgot to bring, and dealing with all the other annoyances that plague the unprepared traveler. In this chapter, you're going to learn how to take care of all the pesky details you need to handle before you leave on your trip, right down to packing comfortable walking shoes. The worksheet at the end of this chapter will help you keep track.

Do I Need to Rent a Car in Las Vegas?

Yes, yes, yes! This is my single best piece of advice to make your trip to Las Vegas more enjoyable. You could do without one, but you'll either wind up missing out on things or spending more money on taxis than you would on a rental car. Don't believe me? Take a taxi from the airport to the Stardust hotel, for example, and you'll wind up paying around $15, including tip. What's that? You want to see the pyramid-shaped Luxor hotel? Okay, but it's a solid 3 miles away and it's over 100 degrees outside. Another $20 round trip. Suppose that later that night, you want to go see the Fremont Street Experience downtown and then finish off the night with a cocktail at the top of the Stratosphere Tower. Rack up another $20 minimum—more if traffic is heavy. Right there, you've spent $55 on taxis, and for that amount, you could be cruising the Strip in your own convertible. With car rentals usually available for as low as $20 a day, the value is obvious.

Add the freedom it gives you and the fact that every hotel in town offers free parking to guests and non-guests, and the obvious answer is "Yes, rent a car!"

However, if you're dead set against renting a car, you can reach your hotel via one of the airport shuttle services. You don't have to arrange any of this in advance; just refer to chapter 7, "Getting Your Bearings," for more details. Once you're settled in, though, your only viable alternative for getting around will be taxis and walking. There is regular city bus service, but in my experience, the routes don't make a lot of sense, the buses are usually over-crowded, and the whole system rarely runs on time.

Be a Smart Shopper

Okay, now that you've made your decision, here's the inside scoop.

Car-rental rates vary even more than airline fares. The price depends on the size of the car, the length of time you keep it, where and when you pick it up and drop it off, where you take it, and a host of other factors.

Asking a few key questions could save you hundreds of dollars. Weekend rates may be lower than weekday rates, for example. Ask if the rate is the same for pickup Friday morning as it is, say, for Thursday night. If you're keeping the car five or more days, a weekly rate may be cheaper than the daily rate. Some companies may assess a drop-off charge if you do not return the car to the same rental location; others, notably National, do not. Ask if the rate is cheaper if you pick up the car at the airport or a location in town. If you see an advertised price in your local newspaper, be sure to ask for that specific rate; otherwise you may be charged the standard (higher) rate. Don't forget to mention membership in AAA, AARP, frequent-flyer programs, and trade unions. These usually entitle you to discounts ranging from 5 to 30 percent. Ask your travel agent to check any and all of these rates.

In addition, one local car-rental agency is offering a special deal to readers of *The Complete Idiot's Guide to Las Vegas*. **Allstate Car Rental** will deduct 20 percent off your rate if you show them this book at the rental counter. Not only is that a great deal; it's a great company to deal with—a genuinely friendly staff and a large, well-maintained fleet of vehicles. You can reach them at **800/634-6186**.

And most car rentals are worth at least 500 miles on your frequent-flyer account!

35

Time-Savers

There are Internet resources that make comparison shopping for rental cars easier. Yahoo!'s partnership with Flifo Global travel agency, for example, allows you to look up rental prices for any size car at more than a dozen rental companies in hundreds of cities. Just enter the size of the car you want, the rental and return dates, and the city where you want to rent, and the server returns a price. It will even make your reservation for you. Point your browser to **http://travel.yahoo.com/travel/** and then choose Reserve Car from the options listed.

On top of the standard rental prices, other optional charges apply to most car rentals. The **Collision Damage Waiver (CDW),** which requires you to pay for damage to the car in a collision, is illegal in some states but is covered by many credit-card companies. Check with your credit-card company before you go so that you can avoid paying this hefty fee (as much as $10/day).

The car-rental companies also offer additional liability insurance (if you harm others in an accident), personal accident insurance (if you harm yourself or your passengers), and personal effects insurance (if your luggage is stolen from your car). If you have insurance on your car at home, you are probably covered for most of these unlikelihoods. If your own insurance doesn't cover you for rentals, or if you don't have auto insurance, you should consider the additional coverages, keeping in mind that the car-rental companies are liable for certain base amounts, depending on the state.

Dollars & Sense

Some rental-car companies also offer refueling packages, in which you pay for an entire tank of gas up front. The price is usually fairly competitive with local gas prices, but you don't get credit for any gas remaining in the tank. If you reject this option, you pay only for the gas you use, but you have to return the car with a full tank or face charges of $3–$4 a gallon for any shortfall. If a stop at a gas station on the way to the airport will make you miss your plane, then by all means take advantage of the fuel-purchase option. Otherwise, skip it.

Car-Rental Comparison Worksheet

Company	Type of Car	Number of Days	Rate
Allstate 800/634-6186			
Avis 800/331-1212			
Budget 800/527-0700			
Dollar 800/800-8000			
Hertz 800/654-3131			
National 800/227-7368			
Thrifty 800/367-2277			
Other			
Other			
Other			

What About Travel Insurance?

There are three kinds of travel insurance: trip-cancellation insurance, medical, and lost luggage. Trip-cancellation insurance is a good idea if you have paid a large portion of your vacation expenses up front—by purchasing a package, for example. It can also protect you if you have to cancel your plans at the last minute because of a health emergency.

But the other two types of insurance don't make sense for most travelers. Your existing health insurance should cover you if you get sick while on vacation (although if you belong to an HMO, you should check to see whether you are fully covered when away from home). And your homeowner's insurance should cover stolen luggage if you experience off-premises theft. Check your existing policies before you buy any additional coverage.

Dollars & Sense

The airlines are responsible for $1,250 on domestic flights if they lose your luggage; if you plan to carry anything more valuable than that, keep it in your carry-on bag.

Some credit cards (American Express and certain gold and platinum Visas and MasterCards, for example) offer automatic flight insurance against death or dismemberment in case of an airplane crash. If you still feel that you need more insurance, though, try one of the companies listed below. But don't pay for more insurance than you need. If you only need trip-cancellation insurance, for example, don't purchase coverage for lost or stolen property. Trip-cancellation insurance costs approximately 6 to 8 percent of the total value of your vacation (and you shouldn't purchase it from the packager who sold you the trip).

Here are some of the reputable issuers of travel insurance:

➤ **Access America**, 6600 W. Broad St., Richmond, VA 23230 (☎ 800/284-8300)

➤ **Mutual of Omaha**, Mutual of Omaha Plaza, Omaha, NE 68175 (☎ 800/228-9792)

➤ **Travel Guard International**, 1145 Clark St., Stevens Point, WI 54481 (☎ 800/826-1300)

➤ **Travel Insured International, Inc.**, P.O. Box 280568, East Hartford, CT 06128 (☎ 800/243-3174)

What If I Get Sick Away from Home?

Avoid it at all costs!

It can be hard to find a doctor you trust when you're away from home. Plus, getting sick will ruin your vacation.

Bring all your medications with you, as well as a prescription for more if you worry that you'll run out. If you have health insurance, be sure to carry your identification card in your wallet. Bring an extra pair of contact lenses in case you lose one. And don't forget over-the-counter medications for common travelers' ailments like upset stomach or diarrhea.

If you suffer from a chronic illness, talk to your doctor before taking your trip. For such conditions as epilepsy, diabetes, or a heart condition, wear a **Medic Alert Identification tag,** which will immediately alert any doctor to your condition and give him or her access to your medical records through Medic Alert's 24-hour hotline. Membership is $35, plus a $15 annual fee. Contact the Medic Alert Foundation, P.O. Box 1009, Turlock, CA 95381-1009 (☎ 800/825-3785).

If you do get sick, ask the concierge at your hotel to recommend a local doctor—even his or her own doctor if necessary. This is probably a better

Extra! Extra!

The most convenient location for medical emergencies is the 24-hour Urgent Care Facility at the Imperial Palace in the heart of the Strip. It's a fully staffed, licensed facility independent of the hotel. You'll find it on the eighth floor, and no appointment is necessary.

recommendation than any national consortium of doctors available through an 800 number can give you. If you can't get a doctor to help you right away, try the emergency room at the local hospital. Many hospital emergency rooms have walk-in clinics for emergency cases that are not life-threatening. You may not get immediate attention, but you won't pay the high price of a genuine emergency-room visit (usually a minimum of $300 just for signing your name, on top of whatever treatment you receive).

Making Reservations & Getting Tickets Ahead of Time

Las Vegas is pretty informal, and the practice of making reservations here is, too. For the most part, it's not really necessary to book your meals and entertainment weeks in advance. Even the best restaurants and the biggest shows need only a few days' notice, and some won't even accept reservations more than a week in advance.

Of course, there are exceptions. Las Vegas is a major concert and sporting venue, and the big-ticket events (Bette Midler or Rolling Stones concerts, boxing matches, and so on) sell out quickly. You may also have a problem if you're going during a peak holiday or convention period.

If you read about a restaurant or a show that you just *have* to experience, place a call and find out if it's possible to make reservations now so that you won't be disappointed later.

Where to Get the Latest on What's Happening

These are the best resources for finding out what's going on in Las Vegas at the time you plan to visit:

➤ This book, of course! In the following chapters, you're going to find descriptions of the best restaurants (see chapters 9, "The Lowdown on the Las Vegas Dining Scene," and 10, "Making Your Restaurant Choice"), shows (see chapter 15, "The Shows A to Z"), and attractions (see chapter 12, "The Top Attractions A to Z") in town, with phone numbers listed for making reservations.

Time-Savers

The **"Official" Las Vegas Leisure Guide Website (www.pcap.com)** is probably the most comprehensive and up-to-date web resource around, with listings of music and comedy concerts, shows, attractions, and restaurants. It's a terrific way to find out if your favorite singer is going to be in town or to find out the latest gossip.

➤ ***What's On Magazine*** is a free weekly publication found everywhere around Las Vegas. It's crammed with all the latest information on shows, attractions, hotels, and restaurants. There are also a lot of coupons and specials in the advertisements, plus a really cool horoscope that tells you which game of chance to play. To get a copy of the magazine before you arrive in Vegas, call ☎ **800/494-2876** or check out their web site (whats-on.com); you won't find the coupons and horoscope online, though.

➤ The ***"Official" Las Vegas Leisure Guide*** at www.pcap.com is probably the most comprehensive and up-to-date web site around with listings of music and comedy concerts, shows, attractions, and restaurants. A terrific resource for finding out if your favorite singer is going to be in town or to find out the latest gossip.

➤ Go to your local newsstand or call for a copy of ***The Las Vegas Review-Journal*** (☎ **702/383-0205**). This is the biggest newspaper in town, and the Friday edition has a full Entertainment section. They'll send you back copies (for a hefty fee), or you can visit their web site at www.lvrj.com. ***The Los Angeles Times*** (☎ **800/LATIMES x75951**) also has a multipage Las Vegas advertising supplement in its Sunday Calendar section that includes upcoming concerts and ongoing shows.

➤ The ***Las Vegas Convention and Visitor's Authority*** (☎ **800/332-5333**) and the ***Las Vegas Chamber of Commerce*** (☎ **702/735-1616**) will send you full packets of information about what to do and where to go.

➤ ***Frommer's Las Vegas*** contains extensive and detailed listings of restaurants, production shows, and sightseeing opportunities. It's updated annually.

➤ Once you've chosen a hotel, ask your reservations agent what's going on during your stay. These agents can fill you in on all the hotel restaurants, give you details and times for any resident shows or upcoming concerts, and may even be able to offer you a discount on reservations. Sure, they'll only tell you about their specific property, but who else knows it better?

Pack It Up!

Start your packing by taking everything you think you'll need and laying it out on the bed. Then get rid of half of it.

I don't say this because the airlines won't let you take it all (they will, with some limits), but because you don't want to get a hernia from lugging half your house around with you. Suitcase straps can be particularly painful to sunburned shoulders.

Some essentials: comfortable walking shoes, a camera, a versatile sweater and/or jacket, a belt, a bathing suit, toiletries and medications (pack these in your carry-on bag so that you'll have them if the airline loses your luggage), and something to sleep in. Unless you're attending a board meeting, a funeral, or one of the city's finest restaurants, you probably won't need a suit or a fancy dress. You'll get much more use out of a pair of jeans or khakis and a comfortable sweater. (See the packing checklist below for other essential packing advice.)

Consider bringing a hat or cap, no matter what the weather forecast. During especially hot and sunny days, a hat will keep you from getting sunburned, and on cold nights, it will retain some of your body's natural warmth. A jacket should be the most you'll need to stay warm, but if you're coming anytime from November to March, consider bringing a slightly heavier coat for evenings.

Sunscreen is a must if you're going to be outside for long, no matter when you're planning to visit. Even during the cooler winter months, the sun can be brutal during the day.

Bet You Didn't Know

As a rule, you're still allowed two pieces of carry-on luggage, both of which must fit in the overhead compartment or under the seat in front of you. But note that some airlines are beginning to limit this to only one carry-on—so ask when you book your flight! And then show your carry-on bag when you first check in to avoid problems at the gate or on board. All airlines are getting more strict about not letting passengers exceed the size limit.

When choosing your suitcase, a bag with wheels makes sense. A fold-over garment bag will help keep dressy clothes wrinkle-free but can be a nuisance if you'll be packing and unpacking a lot. Hard-sided luggage protects breakable items better but weighs more than soft-sided bags.

When packing, start with the biggest, hardest items (usually shoes), and then fit smaller items in and around them. Pack breakable items between several layers of clothes or keep them in your carry-on bag. Put things that could leak, like shampoo, suntan lotion, and so on, in zip-lock bags. Lock your suitcase with a small padlock (available at most luggage stores) if your bag doesn't already have one, and put an identification tag on the outside.

You'll want to consider carrying on board a book, any breakable items you don't want to put in your suitcase, a personal headphone stereo, a snack in case you don't like the airline food, any vital documents you don't want to lose in your luggage (like your return tickets, passport, wallet, and so on), and some empty space for the sweater or jacket you won't want to be wearing while you're waiting for your luggage in an overheated terminal.

Packing Checklist: Don't Forget Your Toothbrush!

☐ Socks

☐ Underwear

☐ Shoes (Try to keep these to two or three; don't forget a good pair of walking shoes.)

☐ Pants and/or skirts

☐ Shirts or blouses

☐ Sweaters and/or jackets (I know it's hot in Vegas, but there's over-zealous air conditioning everywhere.)

☐ A belt

☐ A coat and tie or a dress (only if you plan to go somewhere fancy in the evening)

☐ Shorts

☐ Bathing suit

☐ Workout clothes (if you're planning to use the gym at your hotel)

☐ Toiletries (Don't forget a razor, toothbrush, comb, deodorant, make-up, contact-lens solutions, hair dryer, an extra pair of glasses, and a sewing kit.)

☐ Sunscreen

☐ Camera (Don't forget the film; it can be outrageously expensive if you have to buy it on the Strip.)

☐ Medications (Pack these in a carry-on bag so that you'll have them even if you lose your luggage.)

Part 2

Finding the Hotel That's Right for You

One thing's for sure—you won't have a shortage of choices. Las Vegas is one serious hotel town. It has more hotel rooms than any other city in America, and the numbers just keep climbing. As of this writing, there are just over 100,000 rooms, with another 25,000 expected by the turn of the century!

Overkill, you say? Consider this: Las Vegas has the highest hotel occupancy rate of any major city, running at roughly 90 percent. Another way of looking at it is that 9 times out of 10, there will be somebody sleeping in any given hotel room at any given time. That means you'll want to make your choice and book your room right away, and that's where this book comes in.

With all these choices, you'd be forgiven for breaking out into a cold sweat at the thought of finding a hotel that suits your needs. But never fear, because this chapter does just what its title promises: It finds the best hotel for your needs and your wallet. I've inspected and compared them all, and I'll tell you how to master the ins and outs and get a great deal. It's all here for you, from insider tips on saving money to quick, easy-to-use reviews, followed by a handy work-sheet to help you put all the information together and make a selection.

Happy hunting!

Chapter 5

Pillow Talk: The Lowdown on the Las Vegas Hotel Scene

In This Chapter

➤ Choosing where you want to stay

➤ Finding out what a hotel room will cost you—plus tips on how to save

➤ Deciding what kind of accommodation is right for you

➤ Tips for people who didn't plan ahead

An Egyptian pyramid. A pirate ship. A mini-version of the New York skyline. A medieval castle. An ode to Roman decadence. A circus complete with acrobats and trapeze artists.

Clearly, Toto, we're not in Kansas anymore.

Hotel amenities in this town go way beyond room service and a swimming pool. I'm talking roller coasters, flamingos and toucans, Elvis's gold lamé jacket, talking animatronic camels, wedding chapels, a volcano that erupts every 15 minutes, and slot machines galore. It's not exactly your everyday choice between a Holiday Inn and a Howard Johnson.

But there's no need to be overwhelmed by the crowds, the ever-shifting prices, and the gimmicks. There's a method to the madness; here, you'll learn what you need to know to negotiate your way through the scene like a pro.

Location, Location, Location

There are three main areas in Las Vegas where the major hotels and attractions are grouped: *the Strip*, *downtown*, and *Paradise Road*.

Your mission, should you choose to accept it, is to read the pros and cons of each area and decide which part of town you'll choose as your base of operations.

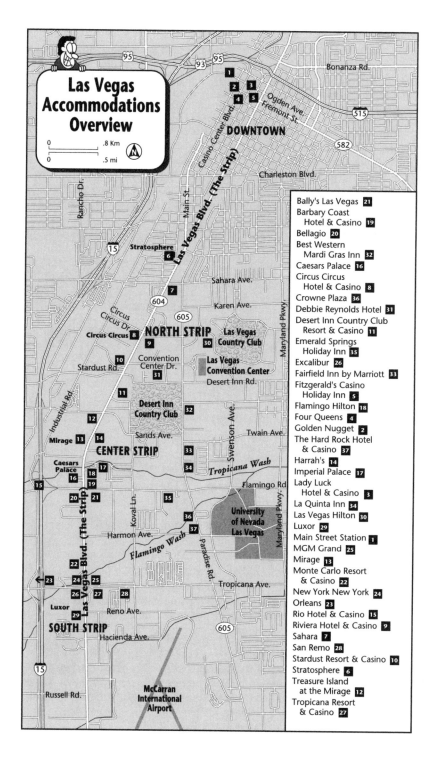

Las Vegas Accommodations Overview

0 .8 Km
0 .5 mi

DOWNTOWN

Bally's Las Vegas **21**
Barbary Coast
  Hotel & Casino **19**
Bellagio **20**
Best Western
  Mardi Gras Inn **32**
Caesars Palace **16**
Circus Circus
  Hotel & Casino **8**
Crowne Plaza **36**
Debbie Reynolds Hotel **31**
Desert Inn Country Club
  Resort & Casino **11**
Emerald Springs
  Holiday Inn **35**
Excalibur **26**
Fairfield Inn by Marriott **33**
Fitzgerald's Casino
  Holiday Inn **5**
Flamingo Hilton **18**
Four Queens **4**
Golden Nugget **2**
The Hard Rock Hotel
  & Casino **37**
Harrah's **14**
Imperial Palace **17**
Lady Luck
  Hotel & Casino **3**
La Quinta Inn **34**
Las Vegas Hilton **30**
Luxor **29**
Main Street Station **1**
MGM Grand **25**
Mirage **13**
Monte Carlo Resort
  & Casino **22**
New York New York **24**
Orleans **23**
Rio Hotel & Casino **15**
Riviera Hotel & Casino **9**
Sahara **7**
San Remo **28**
Stardust Resort & Casino **10**
Stratosphere **6**
Treasure Island
  at the Mirage **12**
Tropicana Resort
  & Casino **27**

The Strip

Officially known as Las Vegas Boulevard South, this four-mile stretch of road is home to the biggest, splashiest, and (in some cases) gaudiest hotels on earth. All the major players you've heard about are here: New York New York, the Luxor (that's the pyramid-shaped one), Caesars Palace, and The Mirage, just to name a few.

No matter what people may tell you, the Strip is very spread out, and walking from one end to the other is only for hardy souls on nice days. For this reason, I've divided the Strip into three sections. The **South Strip** runs roughly from Harmon Avenue south and includes the MGM Grand, New York New York, and the Luxor. The **North Strip** is everything north of Fashion Show Lane up to the Stratosphere Tower; it's here that you'll find Circus Circus, the Sahara, and the Desert Inn, to name a few. The **Center Strip** is basically everything between and includes Caesars Palace, The Mirage, and Treasure Island.

If you're a first-time visitor to Vegas, the Strip is probably where you'll want to stay, but consider the pros and cons.

In a nutshell:

➤ All the mega-resorts are here—many within walking distance of one another (and trust me, you'll want to spend time gawking at these hotels).

➤ A wide variety of choices, from super-luxurious casino resorts to standard motels.

➤ This is why you're coming to Vegas!

But...

➤ This is why *everyone* comes to Vegas, so this is where the crowds are.

➤ Most places are on the expensive side, and the few cheap hotels are cheap in every sense of the word.

➤ With so much to do on the Strip, it's easy to miss out on the rest of the city.

Downtown

This is where Las Vegas was born. The first hotels and casinos popped up here decades before the Strip was anything more than cactus and tumbleweeds. Downtown is informally known as *Glitter Gulch* (narrower streets make the neon seem brighter here).

The bulk of the action is concentrated on and around Fremont Street between Main and 9th (about a five-minute drive from the north end of the Strip). A recent revitalization, led by the Fremont Street Experience (see chapter 12, "The Top Attractions A to Z"), has transformed downtown from a seedy, unsafe row of low-rent hotels and strip joints to a more pleasant, friendly row of medium-rent hotels and strip joints.

Tourist Traps

The Strip is one of the most popular destinations in the country, so it's not surprising that tourist traps abound here. Be aware that anything you buy on the Strip—a meal, film, a souvenir, or a tube of toothpaste—will cost more than anywhere else in town. Be careful to pack enough film and an adequate supply of all your toiletries so that you don't run out and fall victim to the outrageous price tags in hotel stores, and try to resist buying those kitschy souvenirs until you're in another part of town.

In a nutshell:

➤ Downtown is less crowded and overwhelming than the Strip.

➤ You can get better bargains on hotels and entertainment.

➤ Everything is within walking distance.

But...

➤ There are fewer hotels and places to play than you'll have on the Strip.

➤ It's somewhat isolated from all the really famous, big-ticket venues in town.

➤ Downtown is still seedy in spots and, on the whole, it doesn't cater to families.

Dollars & Sense

Staying downtown will usually save you money on your hotel bill—*and* just about everything else. Everything you need, including dozens of casinos, is within walking distance, so you won't need to take cabs. And, as a general rule, meals, shows, and attractions are cheaper.

Paradise Road

This section of town, just east of the Strip, is the main choice for convention-goers, since it's near the Las Vegas Convention Center. The street runs parallel to Las Vegas Boulevard, about a mile away, and most hotels and casinos are located between Harmon and Sahara Avenues. (Keep in mind when you read the hotel reviews that a "Paradise Road" designation does not necessarily mean the hotel is right *on* Paradise Road, but it will be in the vicinity.)

There aren't as many big, flashy hotels here—which may be a blessing or a curse, depending on your outlook.

In a nutshell, Paradise Road offers:

➤ More non-casino hotels as a quiet alternative to the busy Strip and downtown.

➤ A close proximity to all the action without being right in the middle of it.

➤ Often the best deals for budget-conscious travelers.

But...

➤ It has fewer hotel, entertainment, and recreation choices than either the Strip or downtown.

➤ None of the fun stuff is within walking distance.

➤ If there's a convention in town, forget it!

The Price Is Right

Here's where I get down and dirty about the price tag on all these flashy hotels. If money is no object, feel free to skip over this next part of the book. But there aren't too many people I know who don't care about the bottom line when they get their bill.

Other than airfare, your hotel bill will be your single biggest vacation expense, so I'll tell you what to expect and help you avoid sticker shock. I'll help you avoid blowing your life savings on a hotel room (so you can go blow it at the roulette wheel if you want).

Bet You Didn't Know

Bigger apparently equals better in Las Vegas. The sheer size of the new hotels scheduled to open in the next couple of years is mind-blowing. Look for a new Planet Hollywood Hotel (with 3,200 rooms) and a 3,000-room Paris Casino Hotel, complete with a 540-foot replica of the Eiffel Tower. And yes, the largest hotel in the world is coming! The Venetian will boast more than 6,000 (yes, you read that right) rooms, plus actual canals and gondoliers. The price tag? A cool $2 billion.

What's a Rack Rate?

The *rack rate* is the maximum rate that a hotel charges for a room. It's the rate you'd get if you walked in off the street and asked for a room for the night. You sometimes see the rate printed on the fire/emergency exit diagrams posted on the back of your door.

Hotels are happy to charge you the rack rate, but you don't have to pay it! Hardly anyone does. Perhaps the best way to avoid paying the rack rate is surprisingly simple: Just ask for a cheaper or discounted rate. You may be pleasantly surprised. Hotels make a lot of extra profit from people who don't bother to ask a simple question.

In all but the smallest accommodations, the rate you pay for a room depends on many factors, not the least of which is how you make your reservation. A travel agent may be able to negotiate a better price with certain hotels than you could get by yourself. (That's because the hotel gives the agent a discount in exchange for steering his or her business toward that hotel.)

Dollars & Sense

If you're traveling with your family or a group of friends who are willing to share a room, you can save big bucks. Be sure to ask the reservations agent at each hotel about its policy on occupancy. Most room rates are based on double occupancy, and charges for extra guests vary wildly. Some hotels will let small children stay for free in their parents' room but charge anybody else up to $30 a night extra. However, some hotels will allow up to four people to a room at no extra charge.

Reserving a room through the hotel's 800-number may also result in a lower rate than if you call the hotel directly. On the other hand, the central reservations number may not know about discount rates at specific locations. (Local franchises may offer a special group rate for a wedding or a family reunion, for example, but they may neglect to tell the central booking line.) Your best bet is to call both the local number and the 800 number to see which one gives you a better deal.

Room rates also change with the season and as occupancy rates rise and fall. If a hotel is close to full, it is less likely to extend discount rates; if it's close to empty, it may be willing to negotiate. Resorts are most crowded on weekends and usually offer discounted rates for midweek stays. The reverse is true for business and convention hotels. See chapter 1, "How to Get Started," for a list of dates for the biggest Vegas conventions; these will be expensive times to go, so try to avoid them if you can.

Room prices are subject to change without notice, so even the rates quoted in this book may be different than the actual rate you get when you call. Rates can and do swing *wildly* in Las Vegas, so comparison shopping and being flexible with your dates is the best advice. The same hotel that charges $150 this week may offer you a rate of $95 the next.

Be sure to mention your membership in AAA, AARP, frequent-flyer programs, and any other corporate rewards program when you make your reservation. You never know when it might be worth a few dollars off your room rate.

It never hurts to ask!

The Price Categories

Here's where you get your first taste of the categories I use throughout this book. They're easy to scan, because I've marked each review with an icon to indicate relative expense—from $ to $$$$$.

Unfortunately, the days of the super-cheap room at a famous, big-name hotel are over. I remember staying at the Dunes Hotel (before it was blown up in 1993, of course) for $19!—and that was a deluxe tower room facing the Strip. Now you just can't find a room for less than $30 that's clean and in a safe neighborhood.

The good news, though, is that in general, I'm not talking about New York–style prices here. There are tons of bargains to be had, and a Las Vegas vacation is a pretty good value.

Price Categories

$$$$$	Very Expensive	$100 and up per night
$$$$	Expensive	$80–$99 per night
$$$	Moderate	$60–$79 per night
$$	Inexpensive	$40–$59 per night
$	Unbelievably Cheap	$40 or less per night

All these categories are based on what you can expect to pay on average for a standard room based on single or double occupancy.

How to Find Those Blue-Light Specials

Here's a few hints on how to find the best hotel bargains:

➤ **Be Flexible.** Choose a few different times for your trip and then call to find out which dates offer the best deals.

Here's living proof: I recently booked a trip for my parents, who were willing to travel either the first or second weekend in November. One hotel quoted me a rate of $189 a night for the first set of dates but only $69 a night for the second—a savings of $120 per night! Another place offered the same rooms for $85 one week and $28 the next—that second rate is better than what you'd pay at the local Motel 6, and this was at a major Las Vegas hotel.

➤ **Go When Nobody Else Is Going.** As you would expect, you'll find the best bargains during off-peak times. Hotel rooms are cheaper during the week (Sunday through Thursday) than they are on the weekend, and the slower summer months often offer better deals than you'll find during the winter. Avoid holidays and big convention dates (see chapter 1 for a list of the biggies, when the crowds really drive up hotel prices). Again, flexibility is the key here. Unless your boss is dictating your vacation schedule, try to think in year-round terms.

➤ **Call Around—twice.** Every hotel listed in this book has a toll-free phone number. Seeing as how it won't cost you anything, call around and see who is offering the best prices. When you're finished, wait a day and call again. You'll often get different prices—maybe higher, but maybe an even better deal.

➤ **Don't Limit Yourself.** The hotels in Las Vegas *are* the tourist attractions, so you don't have to actually stay in the biggest and brightest to experience most of what it has to offer. Unless you've got your heart set on a spa or you plan to do a lot of relaxing at a fabulous pool at your own hotel, it doesn't matter where you sleep, right? Consider checking into a cheaper, more out-of-the-way hotel, drop your luggage off, and then go explore!

➤ **Try a package tour.** Package tours (discussed in detail in chapter 3, "How Will I Get There?") combine airfare and accommodations in one purchase. Because package-tour companies buy in bulk, they can pass major savings along to you. Just be sure that you understand their restrictions and can live with the terms.

Taxes & Service Charges

Of course, the tax people get their share. As of this writing, Las Vegas has a hotel tax of 9 percent. That can really add up, *so don't forget to figure this into your budget.*

Most room rates cover whatever is inside your room and that's it. Any additional services you might need will probably cost you. Even something innocuous like requesting an iron may add a couple of dollars to your bill (it happened to me—don't laugh). Ask what everything costs before you commit.

Tourist Traps

Most hotels have surcharges for telephone calls; you might be charged as much as $1 every time you make an outside call. This even applies to local calls and calls charged to a credit card or home phone. During a business trip, I once racked up more in telephone surcharges than the cost of my hotel room. The hotel's policy should be clearly posted in your room, but if it's not, be sure to ask before you reach out and touch someone.

What Kind of Place Is Right for You?

So you've chosen a location, and you know from the size of your bank balance what kind of price range you can afford. But, as I've told you already, Vegas is not your typical hotel town. There are still a few more things to consider.

Casino Versus Non-Casino Hotels

This is a big decision. If you're itching to roll the dice, it's pretty clear cut, but some of you might want to gamble a bit but don't consider it a high priority. In that case, here's what you need to know.

Casino hotels usually offer round-the-clock entertainment, dining, and fun, while in most non-casino hotels, you get a room, a pool (maybe), and a parking space. On the other hand, casino hotels are often loud, crowded, enormous places that actively discourage relaxing (it hinders your gambling), while non-casino hotels offer quiet getaways from the hustle and bustle. You'll have to decide for yourself whether you'd rather be in the center of the action or whether you'd like to desert the action for a little peace and quiet at the end of the day.

Dollars & Sense

There's a popular misconception that non–casino hotels offer cheaper rooms. But that's not necessarily true. You may find a good deal occasionally, but most non-casino hotels have to make up for a lack of gaming revenue by charging higher room rates.

David Versus Goliath

There really is no such thing as a small hotel in Las Vegas. So your options are not big versus small—they're big versus gargantuan. (For the sake of this argument, I'll call it small versus big, though.)

In this corner, we have the small hotels, which often give more personalized service. Here you won't need to leave a trail of bread crumbs to find your room, and you won't get stuck for an eternity in a line at the front desk. However, the smaller hotels usually offer less in the way of amenities like pools, health clubs, and restaurants.

In the opposing corner, we have the big hotels. They have spared no expense in keeping you entertained and pampered, and they're full of action. However, these hotels give you a map when you check in. (I'm not joking.) Consider a 15-minute walk from your room to the pool—in your bathing suit—through a crowded casino. 'Nuff said.

Each review you'll find in the following chapter discusses the relative size of each hotel. This has to do with more than just the number of rooms—it's about the sprawl, how far you have to walk from the elevator to the front door, and how easily you can negotiate the place. It's a tradeoff between convenience and personal service and having every conceivable amenity and amusement available right at your hotel.

Theme Versus Non-Theme Hotels
Basically, this question boils down to whether you'd rather spend a day at the beach or a day at Disneyland.

Theme hotels have most of the pluses and minuses of the "Happiest Place on Earth," including big fun, big crowds, and general sensory overload. Non-theme hotels are usually for those who want to get away from these things and therefore have fewer roller coasters. Your call.

Family-Friendly Versus Adult Hotels
By *adult hotels*, I don't mean vibrating beds and mirrors on the ceiling.

Some places aim for the grown-up market by deliberately leaving out the things that appeal to children, like video arcades and water rides.

Kids If you have kids, look for the kid-friendly icon when you read the hotel reviews in chapter 6, "Hotels A to Z." These icons highlight the places that cater to families.

For Free Spirits Having Second Thoughts
Okay, so you're standing in the bookstore in the Las Vegas airport having just arrived in town on a last-minute whim. Now you've realized that you don't have hotel reservations, and the prospect of sleeping at the bus station is beginning to loom over you. What do you do?

Find a Pay Phone
All the hotels in this book have local numbers listed in addition to the toll-free numbers (which usually don't work in Las Vegas). This will sound obvious at first, but stick with me... start by calling a few and seeing if they have any vacancies. If they do, you can relax and take your time in selecting a hotel that fits your needs and budget. If you get nothing but "Sorry, sold out," read on.

Bet You Didn't Know

Gangster Bugsy Siegel helped put Vegas on the map in the 1940s when he and fellow mobsters Lucky Luciano and Meyer Lansky opened the Flamingo Hotel— "a real class joint." They lined up Jimmy Durante to open their showroom, and the hotel was so luxurious for its time that even the janitors wore tuxedos. Life's a gamble when you're in the Mob, so Bugsy's own lavish suite came complete with escape routes and tunnels.

You could go through the phone book and call numbers at random, but you're risking getting stuck in a bad neighborhood or an overpriced dump. Instead, try a hotel reservations service that can find a place for you to sleep and book the room for you for free: **The Las Vegas Convention and Visitors Authority** (☎ 702/892-0711) is open weekdays from 8am to 6pm and weekends from 8am to 5pm; **Las Vegas Reservations Systems** (☎ 702/369-1919) is open 24 hours a day; **Reservations Plus** (☎ 702/795-3999)** is also available around the clock.

Tourist Traps

You'll notice that I've listed a couple of reservations agencies in this section for travelers who arrived without reservations and aren't having any luck finding a vacancy. But I don't recommend these agencies for anybody else, because these services are usually tied, in some way or another, to specific businesses. This means that they will often try to steer you toward a place where they collect a commission instead of helping you find another option that may suit you better.

...And If All Else Fails

Still no luck, huh? Serves you right for not reading this book sooner!

Okay, you have one more chance, but it's going to require some work. Go get a rental car (you can't do what I have in mind on foot or by taxi) and start driving. There are lots of little hotels near the airport, so you can begin there, and then head to the Strip—that's where most of the rooms are located. Even if you got a "sold out" on the phone, try the front desk anyway, in case there's been a last-minute cancellation.

Your next hunting ground should be Paradise Road and the streets crossing it, like Flamingo, Convention Center, and Harmon. There are lots of nice, smaller hotels here that might not be included in this book or the reservations systems.

Finally, go downtown, but be careful—some areas are not very safe.

Also, don't forget that many of the hotels are owned by the same companies (like Luxor, Excalibur, and Circus Circus). Throw yourself on the mercy of the front-desk clerk and ask if any "sister" hotels may have vacancies.

Getting the Best Room

Somebody has to get the best room in the house—it might as well be you.

Always ask for a corner room. They're usually larger, quieter, and have more windows and light than standard rooms, and they don't always cost more.

When you make your reservation, ask if the hotel is renovating; if it is, request a room away from the renovation work.

Many hotels now offer non-smoking rooms; by all means, ask for one if smoke bothers you.

Inquire, too, about the location of the restaurants, bars, and discos in the hotel—these could all be a source of irritating noise.

I've talked a lot in this chapter about landing great deals. But keep a caveat in mind: Be careful when shopping for a bargain that you aren't getting stuck in an older section of the hotel that isn't as nice as the rest. Ask for details on amenities and conditions from your hotel reservation agent and tell him or her that you are writing it down. If it doesn't match when you get there, cause a stink!

If you aren't happy with your room when you arrive, talk to the front-desk clerk before you settle in. If they have another room, they should be happy to accommodate you, within reason.

A Word About Smoking

All Las Vegas hotels have at least some no-smoking rooms; most have entire floors set aside for those without the habit. As far as the rest of the hotel is concerned, however, it's pretty much open season—smoking is allowed just about everywhere. If you're a non-smoker, it's important that you request a smoke-free room when you reserve it, or you may live to regret it.

There are some casinos that have small no-smoking sections of slot-machines or no-smoking gaming tables, but it really doesn't mean much, since they aren't separate from the rest of the casino. If you're especially sensitive to cigarette/pipe/cigar smoke, don't plan on spending a lot of time in the casino area.

All hotel restaurants have no-smoking areas, but most bars and nightclubs don't.

Chapter 6

Hotels A to Z

In This Chapter

➤ Quick indexes of hotels by location and price

➤ Reviews of all the best hotels in the city

➤ A worksheet to help you make your choice

OK, let's get down to business: It's time to choose your place to snooze. I've started this chapter with some handy lists that break down my favorite hotels by neighborhood and price, then reviewed them all, giving you all the information you need to make your decision.

If I included every single hotel in town, the pages of this book would fill a room. My goal here is to save you the time and energy of having to slog through endless descriptions of hotels that, ultimately, I wouldn't recommend. This guide is selective so you don't have to waste any time—I'm sending you straight to my favorites. I've only put in the best that Las Vegas has to offer, but I've tried to give you a broad range of choices in size, cost, location, family friendliness, amenities, and the like.

The reviews are arranged alphabetically, so they're easy to refer back to, and the each hotel's location appears right below its name.

As far as price goes, I've noted rack rates in the listings and also preceded each with dollar signs to make quick reference easier. The more dollar signs under the name, the more you pay. But don't forget that the prices listed here are the "official" rack rates; they're rarely what you're going to wind up paying. If one of these hotels strikes your fancy but appears to be out of your price range, call anyway. It may be having a special promotion or a slow week that could get you in for a lower rate than normal. Rates swing wildly in Vegas all the time; they just might swing in your favor.

All the hotels listed have free parking for guests (usually self and valet), so I won't waste your time by rehashing that point in every listing.

The Price Categories

Each hotel listing has a handy dollar-sign rating so that you can see at a glance how expensive each place is. Here's how it breaks down:

$$$$$	Very Expensive	$100 and up per night
$$$$	Expensive	$80–$99 per night
$$$	Moderate	$60–$79 per night
$$	Inexpensive	$40–$59 per night
$	Unbelievably Cheap	$40 or less per night

These categories are based on what you can expect to pay on average for a standard room based on single or double occupancy. They do not necessarily correspond with the rack rates that are printed with the listing, simply because those rates are often higher than what you would normally pay. Trust me: I know where you might be able to get a good deal.

Excalibur **5**		New York New York **3**	
MGM Grand Hotel/Casino **4**		Orleans **2**	
Luxor Las Vegas **8**		San Remo **7**	
Monte Carlo Resort & Casino **1**		Tropicana Resort & Casino **6**	

There's also a kid-friendly icon marking those hotels that are especially good for families.

Keep an eye out, too, for sections called "Extra! Extra!", where I direct you to the best choice if you have a special consideration in mind—the best for romance, the best for serious pampering, and so on.

Hint: As you read through the reviews, you'll want to keep track of the ones that appeal to you. I've included a chart at the end of this chapter where you can rank your preferences, but to make matters easier on yourself now, just put a little check mark next to the ones you like. Remember how your teachers used to tell you not to write in your books? Now's the time to rebel. Scrawl away.

Quick Picks: Las Vegas Hotels at a Glance
Hotel Index by Location

South Strip

Excalibur $$

Luxor $$

MGM Grand Hotel/Casino $$$$

Monte Carlo Resort & Casino $$$$

New York New York $$$$

Orleans $

San Remo $

Tropicana Resort & Casino $$$$

Center Strip

Bally's Las Vegas $$$$$

Barbary Coast Hotel & Casino $$

Bellagio $$$$$

Caesars Palace $$$$$

Flamingo Hilton $$$$

Harrah's Las Vegas $$$$

Imperial Palace $

The Mirage $$$$$

Rio Hotel & Casino $$$$

Treasure Island $$$$

North Strip

Circus Circus $

Desert Inn Country Club Resort & Casino $$$$$

Riviera Hotel & Casino $$$

Sahara Hotel & Casino $$$

Stardust Resort & Casino $$

Stratosphere Las Vegas $$$

Downtown

Fitzgerald's Casino Holiday Inn $$

Four Queens $$$

Golden Nugget $$$

Lady Luck Casino Hotel $$

Main Street Station $$

Paradise Road

Best Western Mardi Gras Inn $$

Crowne Plaza Holiday Inn $$$$$

Debbie Reynolds Hotel & Casino $$$

Emerald Springs Holiday Inn $$$

Fairfield Inn by Marriott $$$

The Hard Rock Hotel & Casino $$$$

Las Vegas Hilton $$$$$

La Quinta Inn $$$

Hotel Index by Price

$$$$$

Bally's Las Vegas (Center Strip)

Bellagio (Center Strip)

Caesars Palace (Center Strip)

Crowne Plaza Holiday Inn (Paradise Road)

Desert Inn Country Club Resort & Casino (North Strip)

Las Vegas Hilton (Paradise Road)

The Mirage (Center Strip)

$$$$

Flamingo Hilton (Center Strip)

The Hard Rock Hotel & Casino (Paradise Road)

Harrah's Las Vegas (Center Strip)

MGM Grand Hotel/Casino (South Strip)

Monte Carlo Resort & Casino (South Strip)

New York New York (South Strip)

Rio Hotel & Casino (Center Strip)

Treasure Island (Center Strip)

Tropicana Resort & Casino (South Strip)

$$$

Debbie Reynolds Hotel & Casino (Paradise Road)

Emerald Springs Holiday Inn (Paradise Road)

Fairfield Inn by Marriott (Paradise Road)

Four Queens (Downtown)

Golden Nugget (Downtown)

La Quinta Inn (Paradise Road)

Riviera Hotel & Casino (North Strip)

Sahara Hotel & Casino (North Strip)

Stratosphere Las Vegas (North Strip)

$$

Barbary Coast Hotel & Casino (Center Strip)

Best Western Mardi Gras Inn (Paradise Road)

Excalibur (South Strip)

Fitzgerald's Casino Holiday Inn (Downtown)

Lady Luck Casino Hotel (Downtown)

Luxor (South Strip)

Main Street Station (Downtown)

Stardust Resort & Casino (North Strip)

$

Circus Circus (North Strip)

Imperial Palace (Center Strip)

Orleans (South Strip)

San Remo (South Strip)

Las Vegas Hotels A to Z

Bally's Las Vegas
$$$$$. Center Strip.

No, it's not cheap, but you really get your money's worth at Bally's. They're aiming for the upscale crowd by providing resort-level service and plush surroundings. You'll enter from the Strip via moving sidewalks that pass through muted neon-light pillars, waterfalls, and lush landscaping. Bright and cheerful marble, wood, and crystal are the rule throughout. The oversized rooms contain a sofa—a rarity in Las Vegas. The hotel is not huge in comparison to other Vegas hotels, but it does have more than 2,500 rooms; a light and airy casino; a noteworthy spa and fitness center; tennis and basketball courts; one of the loveliest swimming pools in town (Olympic size, no less); and a whole range of restaurants.

3645 Las Vegas Blvd. S. (at Flamingo Rd.) ☎ ***800/634-3434*** *or 702/739-4111, fax 702/739-3848, Internet www.ballyslv.com.* **Rack rates:** *$99–$175 double. AE, CB, DC, JCB, MC, V.*

Dollars & Sense

If you're looking to save a few bucks on transportation, there is a free monorail that runs from Bally's to the MGM Grand about a mile away. If nothing else, it'll save wear and tear on your feet.

Barbary Coast Hotel & Casino
$$. Center Strip.

Here's an inexpensive option right in the heart of all the Strip action. Since it's (relatively) small, with only 200 rooms, you forego niceties like a pool, health club, and showrooms (although there are two restaurants, two bars, and a casino). But the upside is a friendly, attentive staff and opulent, faux-Victorian–style rooms with touches like gas-style lamps and canopied beds—they could have been tacky, but they're actually kind of charming.

3595 Las Vegas Blvd. S. (at Flamingo Rd.) ☎ ***800/634-6755*** *or 702/365-7506, fax 702/737-6304.* **Rack rates:** *$39–$100 double. AE, CB, DC, DISC, JCB, MC, V.*

Bellagio
$$$$$. Center Strip.

Scheduled to debut a few months after this book hits the stands in 1998, this $1.3 billion resort will be mammoth. It's supposed to resemble an Italian village, complete with classical gardens, pools, and a 12-acre lake (where they plan on doing water ballet extravaganzas). They're after a crowd with well-padded wallets, so it won't be cheap, but if it's as nice as the artists' renderings I've seen, it may very well be worth every penny.

3600 Las Vegas Blvd. S. (at Flamingo Rd.) ☎ ***888/987-6667*** *(note: this is the sales office number; a reservations number is scheduled to open in April '98.), Internet www.bellagiolasvegas.com.* **Rack rates:** *Not available at press time (but expect it to be comparable to the other hotels in the $$$$$ range).*

Best Western Mardi Gras Inn

$$. Paradise Road.

This is like a typical Best Western motor inn you'd find anywhere in the U.S. in terms of quality and cleanliness, but this one has larger-than-normal rooms, manicured lawns, and a small casino in the lobby. Single king rooms have small sitting areas with convertible sofas, and all units have kitchenettes, so it feels like your home away from home. A large pool area, two sun decks, and a gazebo-covered picnic area are bonuses.

Time-Savers

First-timers to Las Vegas should take a serious look at properties in the Center Strip area. It's centrally located (hence the name) to just about everything and will save you a lot of time and energy over the other choices.

3500 Paradise Rd. (between Sands Ave. and Desert Inn Rd.) ☎ **800/634-6501** *or 702/731-2020, fax 702/731-2020.* **Rack rates:** *$49–$125 double. AE, CB, DC, DISC, JCB, MC, V.*

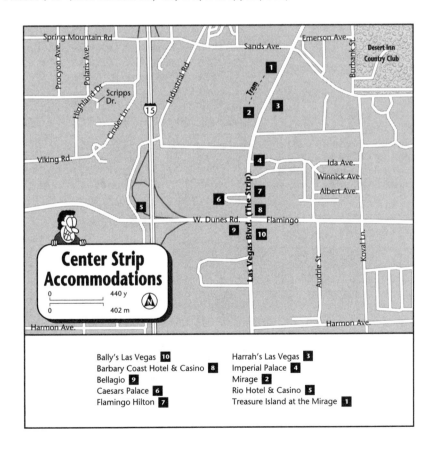

Bally's Las Vegas **10**
Barbary Coast Hotel & Casino **8**
Bellagio **9**
Caesars Palace **6**
Flamingo Hilton **7**
Harrah's Las Vegas **3**
Imperial Palace **4**
Mirage **2**
Rio Hotel & Casino **5**
Treasure Island at the Mirage **1**

Caesars Palace
$$$$$. Center Strip.

This is the ultimate sprawling Vegas hotel, where high class meets high kitsch. A major $300-million remodeling is making Caesars brighter and more truly elegant, but have no fear: The campy Roman theme lives on, with marble columns, talking statues, and toga-wearing employees. True glamour has replaced most of the tacky sort (kind of sad for those of us who love all things kitschy), but this is still pure Vegas at its best. The newer rooms are beautiful and huge—some with his and hers baths. And even the older rooms have character—some with sunken tubs in the sleeping areas.

You name it, Caesars has it. A moving sidewalk carries you to a ritzy shopping arcade, and the hotel is known for having some of the best restaurants in town. Other facilities include a stunning swimming pool with a classical Roman theme, three casinos, and a cutting-edge video arcade. A fabulous new health spa is in the works, set to open in 1998.

3570 Las Vegas Blvd. S. (just north of Flamingo Rd.) ☎ **800/634-6661** *or 702/731-7110, fax 702/731-6636, Internet www.caesars.com.* **Rack rates:** *$109–$500 double. AE, CD, DC, DISC, MC, V.*

Extra! Extra!

If you're traveling with children, I recommend **Circus Circus** ($/North Strip/☎ **800/444-CIRC**), with its big-top fun, carnival games, and indoor amusement park. **Treasure Island** ($$$$/Center Strip/☎ **800/944-7444**) offers a cool pirate theme and a large arcade. The **MGM Grand** ($$$$/South Strip/☎ **800/929-1111**) also has a huge arcade, plus its own theme park.

 ### Circus Circus
$. North Strip.

If you're bringing the kiddies, make a beeline for this massive hotel (with more than 3,700 rooms). It's basically Barnum & Bailey run amok, complete with chaotic carnival and arcade games on the midway. Don't miss the circus acts (trapeze, high wire, jugglers, and so on) that run most of the day, visible from the midway and much of the casino. There are plenty of amusements to keep the tots happy: an aerial tramway, the Grand Slam Canyon indoor theme park, two swimming pools, and even a branch of the Golden Arches. It's almost always a great deal for travelers on a budget—but try to avoid the Manor rooms, which are in glorified motel buildings that have seen better days.

2880 Las Vegas Blvd. S. (between Sahara Ave. and Convention Center Dr.)
☎ *800/444-CIRC or 702/734-0410, fax 702/734-2268, Internet www.circuscircus-lasvegas.com.* **Rack rates:** *$39–$99 double. AE, CB, DC, DISC, MC, V.*

Crowne Plaza Holiday Inn
$$$$$. Paradise Road.

Crowne Plaza is the upscale division of Holiday Inn, and it caters mostly to business folk with this all-suite hotel. A six-story atrium lobby done in marble and muted tones greets guests. Rooms are large, with unique layouts offering separate sleeping quarters, wet bars, and mini-fridges, plus nice touches such as bathrobes. Also worth noting is the pool area, where Calypso bands play during the summer, and a small gym.

4255 Paradise Rd. (just north of Harmon Ave.) ☎ *800/2-CROWNE or 702/369-4400, fax 702/369-3770.* **Rack rates:** *$149–$189 double.*

Extra! Extra!

If you want to avoid other people's kids, try a downtown hotel instead of staying on the Strip. Downtown, I recommend the **Golden Nugget** ($$$/ ☎ **800/634–3454**) and **Fitzgerald's Casino Holiday Inn** ($$/☎ **800/ 274–LUCK**). On the North Strip, I'd head for the exclusive **Desert Inn Country Club Resort & Casino** ($$$$$/☎ **800/634–6906**). Its price tag will probably buy you some peace and quiet.

Debbie Reynolds Hotel & Casino
$$$. Paradise Road.

Another small hotel (and very small casino), this place primarily draws older Debbie Reynolds fans and some convention goers. Although there's Hollywood memorabilia throughout the public areas, the rooms themselves are pretty unremarkable, except that they have balconies (almost unheard of in Vegas). Mini-suites offer minibars and sleeper sofas. I like this place but only recommend it if you're a real fan of Ms. Reynolds—and even then, be aware that she's not exactly roaming the halls or greeting the guests at the front door. There's a large swimming pool and a 24-hour coffee shop/lounge where Debbie and some of her showbiz friends occasionally perform.

305 Convention Center Dr. (between the Strip and Paradise Rd.) ☎ *800/633-1777 or 702/734-0711, fax 702/734-7548.* **Rack rates:** *$75–$99 double. AE, CB, DC, DISC, MC, V.*

Desert Inn Country Club Resort & Casino
$$$$$. North Strip.

It's mighty pricey, but this is the place for you if you want graciousness rather than glitz and if you're dying to be pampered in a luxurious resort atmosphere. Smaller than most Strip hotels (700 rooms), the Desert Inn oozes elegance with a turn-of-the-century Palm Beach theme that extends from the casino to the spacious and comfortable but surprisingly unspectacular rooms (great bathrooms, though). Active types should take special note of the exceptional golf course and tennis facilities; gamblers will head for the small but very chic casino. There's also a wonderful gym and a spa for massages, facials, and the like, plus a pool and six restaurants. The Desert Inn draws a lot of business travelers since it's near the convention center.

3145 Las Vegas Blvd. S. (at Desert Inn Rd.) ☎ *800/634-6906 or 702/733-4444, fax 702/733-4676.* **Rack rates:** *$175–$185 double. AE, CB, DC, DISC, JCB, MC, V.*

Extra! Extra!

If you have a disability, I recommend the **Monte Carlo** ($$$$/South Strip/☎ **800/311-8999**). It's close to other major hotels, the lobby/casino is all one level (no ramps to negotiate), and you don't have to go through the casino to get to the elevators, as in most of the other major hotels. Other possibilities include **Harrah's Las Vegas** ($$$$/Center Strip/☎ **800/HARRAHS**), which offers similar features but has a few more ramps and levels, and **The Mirage** ($$$$$/Center Strip/☎ **800/627-6667**), which has a one-level lobby/casino and is centrally located, although it's a real trek from the lobby to the elevators.

Emerald Springs Holiday Inn
$$$. Paradise Road.

A cut above your typical Holiday Inn, this exceptionally clean and well-tended place offers a low-key, non-casino alternative to the overwhelming Strip—although it's only three (big) blocks away when you want to go out on the town. The emphasis is on providing friendly, family-style service. Standard rooms are large, with sofas, desks, and wet bars with a fridge. Larger suites with kitchenettes are available but cost more.

325 E. Flamingo Rd. (between Koval Lane and Paradise Rd.) ☎ *800/732-7889 or 702/732-9100, fax 702/731-9784.* **Rack rates:** *$79–$99 studio double. AE, CB, DC, DISC, MC, V.*

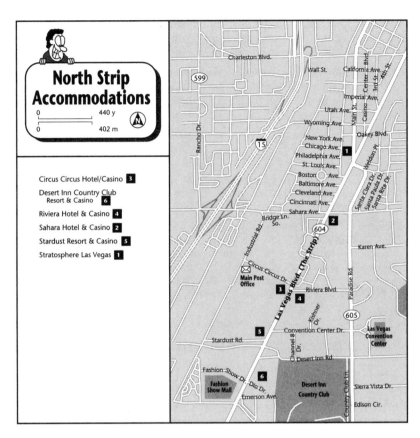

North Strip
Accommodations

0   440 y
0   402 m

Circus Circus Hotel/Casino **3**
Desert Inn Country Club
    Resort & Casino **6**
Riviera Hotel & Casino **4**
Sahara Hotel & Casino **2**
Stardust Resort & Casino **5**
Stratosphere Las Vegas **1**

 ### Excalibur
$$. South Strip.

A gigantic, medieval castle, complete with moat and drawbridge—yep, it's typical over-the-top Las Vegas style. But it's a good and reasonably priced choice for families, since kids will probably be enchanted with the attractive swimming pools (complete with waterfalls and water slides) and will love the sheer enormity and spectacle of it all. (Adults often quickly tire of the place for the same reasons.) The castle motif in the casino and rooms strike me as claustrophobic, despite the vast size of the place (more than 4,000 rooms, 7 restaurants, a casino, and medieval-theme video and shopping arcades).

3850 Las Vegas Blvd. S. (at Tropicana Ave.) ☎ **800/937-7777** *or 702/597-7777, fax 702/597-7040, Internet www.excalibur-casino.com.* **Rack rates:** *$75–$119 for up to four people. AE, CB, DC, DISC, MC, V.*

Fairfield Inn by Marriott
$$$. Paradise Road.

If you're going to Vegas but don't want the neon, frenetic Vegas experience, this is a good choice. It's within walking distance to several major restaurants but not much else. Friendly, personal service is the main draw to this small, non-casino hotel. There's a continental breakfast, a living room–style lobby, and a "guest of the day" who gets a basket of goodies. Rooms are basic motel-style, but they're clean and comfortable, and they offer sleeper sofas.

3850 Paradise Rd. (between Twain Ave. and Flamingo Rd.) ☎ *800/228-2800 or 702/791-0899, fax 702/791-2705, Internet www.marriott.com.* **Rack rates:** *$61–$150 for up to five people. AE, CB, DC, DISC, MC, V.*

Extra! Extra!

If you're an active type, I recommend the **Las Vegas Hilton** ($$$$$/Paradise Road/☎ **800/732-7117**), which is adjacent to a major golf course and has its own tennis courts, jogging track, putting green, and a huge gym. The **Desert Inn Country Club Resort & Casino** ($$$$$/North Strip/☎ **800/634-6906**) has excellent golf and tennis facilities. And **Bally's Las Vegas** ($$$$$/Center Strip/☎ **800/634-3434**) also offers a health club, plus tennis and basketball courts.

Fitzgerald's Casino Holiday Inn
$$. Downtown.

A solid, middle-of-the-road choice for affordable downtown accommodations with a fun and understated luck o' the Irish theme throughout (don't miss the Blarney Stone!). Rooms are pretty standard but comfortable (slightly larger Jacuzzi units are available for a few bucks more), but the tall tower offers great views of the mountains or the Strip. As with most downtown hotels, there is no pool or recreational facilities, but there is a casino and a few restaurants and bars. Of special note is the outdoor balcony off the casino from which you can watch the Fremont Street Experience.

301 E. Fremont St. (at 3rd St.) ☎ *800/274-LUCK or 702/388-2400, fax 702/ 388-2181.* **Rack rates:** *$40–$85 double. AE, CB, DC, DISC, MC, V.*

Extra! Extra!

If you want to lounge by the pool, lots of Vegas hotels could make you happy. My top picks are **The Mirage** ($$$$$/Center Strip/☎ **800/627-6667**) and the **Flamingo Hilton** ($$$$/Center Strip/☎ **800/732-2111**), both of which offer your choice of pools, surrounded by lush landscaping and waterfalls. The Flamingo even has swans, ducks, penguins, and yes... flamingos. **Caesars Palace** ($$$$$/Center Strip/☎ **800/634-6661**) has a stunning new pool area, done in a Greco-Roman theme with three large pools (one with a covered colonnade in the center), cabanas, beverage bars, and garden areas.

Flamingo Hilton
$$$$. Center Strip.

Infamous gangster Bugsy Siegel opened this hotel/casino in 1946 on what would eventually become the Strip. More than 50 years and a $130 million renovation later, it still lives up to its reputation as a class act, sporting a vaguely art deco/tropical theme. The standard rooms and casino are nice but nothing to write home about. The gorgeous, lush pool and spa area, on the other hand, with its dense foliage and live birds, is worth at least a postcard. There's also a casino, excellent tennis facilities, a wedding chapel, and more bars and restaurants than you could shake a stick at.

3555 Las Vegas Blvd. S. (just north of Flamingo Rd.) ☎ *800/732-2111 or 702/ 733-3111, fax 702/733-3353, Internet www.hilton.com.* **Rack rates:** *$69–$269 double. AE, CB, DC, DISC, JCB, MC, V.*

Four Queens
$$$. Downtown.

This is one of the last remnants of the 1960s Rat-pack glory days of old Las Vegas. It's rather dated (and a bit worn in spots), especially when compared to the new mega-resorts on the Strip, but the elegance still lingers, and the price is right. The clientele is older, and these folks are definitely here to gamble, not to sightsee. You'll get clean, comfortable, quiet rooms and a handful of restaurants on site but alas, no pool.

202 Fremont St. (at Casino Center Blvd.) ☎ *800/634-6045 or 702/385-4011, fax 702/387-5160, Internetwww.savenet.com/702/4queens.htm.* **Rack rates:** *$59–$179 double. AE, CB, DC, DISC, MC, V.*

Golden Nugget
$$$. Downtown.

Indisputably the nicest downtown hotel, the Golden Nugget has miles of white marble and gleaming brass fixtures evoking a French Riviera feel. Larger-than-average rooms are comfortable and elegant, with marble entryways, armoires, and plush chairs. There's also a beautiful health club and spa, a large pool (rare for downtown), and several different restaurants, including a California Pizza Kitchen. Despite its grandeur, the Nugget can be a surprisingly good deal; I once booked a mid-week room there for $39 a night!

129 E. Fremont St. (at Casino Center Blvd.) ☎ *800/634-3454 or 702/385-7111, fax 702/386-8362.* **Rack rates:** *$49–$299 double. AE, CB, DC, DISC, MC, V.*

The Hard Rock Hotel & Casino
$$$$. Paradise Road.

Rock 'n' roll memorabilia adorn every square inch of this place, which tries to draw a younger crowd than the typical Vegas hotel. The spacious rooms have some distinctive touches, like leather headboards, bigger-than-average TVs, and French windows that open up for fresh air. Everything's loud, loud, loud and crowded, too (especially the wildly and playfully decorated casino), but it's definitely an upbeat and happening scene. There's a stunning pool area, plus a health club and three restaurants.

4455 Paradise Rd. (at Harmon Ave.) ☎ *800/473-ROCK or 702/693-5000, fax 702/ 693-5010, Internet www.hardrock.com.* **Rack rates:** *$75–$300 double. AE, CB, DC, DISC, MC, V.*

Accommodations Downtown

Fitzgerald's Casino Holiday Inn **5**

Four Queens **4**

Golden Nugget **2**

Lady Luck Casino Hotel **3**

Main Street Station **1**

Fremont Street Experience

Bet You Didn't Know

Music buffs will want to check out the memorabilia in the **The Hard Rock Hotel & Casino.** Some of it's a little lame, but there's some cool stuff, too, such as a smashed guitar from Pete Townsend, James Brown's "King of Soul" cape and crown, menus signed by Elvis and Jimi Hendrix, and Greg Allman's favorite biker jacket. The hotel's music theme is everywhere, from the casino, with its grand piano-shaped craps tables and guitar necks as slot-machine handles to the quotation over the front entrance from Stevie Ray Vaughn: "If the house is a rocking, don't bother knocking, come on in."

Harrah's Las Vegas
$$$$. Center Strip.

Harrah's is one of the friendliest places in town; the location, price, and overall theme make it one of my top choices. A great renovation has made the hotel classy (think marble and a grand piano in the lobby) but still light and fun (okay, so the piano is painted bright colors). I love the carnival atmosphere, which is not overwhelming, and the rooms, which are large and comfortably furnished. The casino is downright festive, and there's also a beautiful pool, several restaurants, a shopping and entertainment plaza, and an already outstanding gym that's been renovated to become even better.

3475 Las Vegas Blvd. S. (between Spring Mountain and Flamingo Rds.) ☎ *800/* **HARRAHS** *or 702/369-5000, fax 702/369-5008, Internet www.harrahs.lv.com.* **Rack rates:** *$75–$289 double. AE, CB, DC, DISC, MC, V.*

Extra! Extra!

If you don't want to stay in a casino hotel, forget about staying on the Strip or downtown; head for Paradise Road and its vicinity. My top picks would be the **Fairfield Inn by Marriott** ($$$/☎ **800/228-2800**), **La Quinta Inn** ($$$/☎ **800/531-5900**), and the **Emerald Springs Holiday Inn** ($$$/☎ **800/732-7889**). La Quinta and Fairfield Inn have incredibly friendly, family-oriented service; Emerald Springs has big rooms and great low-cost rates, plus an equally welcoming staff.

Imperial Palace
$. Center Strip.

Have I got a deal for you! Okay, it's an older hotel that's showing some wear, but if you can get past that, it's hard to find a better value in cost, facilities, and location. It's in the heart of the Center Strip, within walking distance of many major hotel/casinos, and offers large, inexpensive rooms. Add in a large casino (with a separate no-smoking area), a tropical pool, an adequate health club, and entertainment options like the auto collection (see chapter 13, "More Fun Stuff to Do"), and you have a solid choice worth considering.

3535 Las Vegas Blvd. S. (between Spring Mountain and Flamingo Rds.). ☎ *800/* **634/6441** *or 702/731-3311, Internet www.imperial-palace.com.* **Rack rates:** *$29–$99 double. AE, CB, DC, DISC, MC, V.*

Kids **La Quinta Inn**
$$$. Paradise Road.

Everything is clean and quiet here, making La Quinta a perfect choice for those who want to avoid the Vegas mayhem. At this writing, renovations are underway to upgrade the already comfortable decor and facilities here. Rooms range from standard hotel rooms to two-bedroom suites that feel like apartments; some have kitchens and all have whirlpool tubs. There are lots of great restaurants within walking distance. Also of note is the heated pool and friendly staff, plus the free 24-hour shuttle to and from the airport and several casinos on the Strip.

3970 Paradise Rd. (between Twain Ave. and Flamingo Rd.) ☎ ***800/531-5900*** *or 702/796-9000, fax 702/796-3537.* **Rack rates:** *$65–$99 double. AE, CB, DC, DISC, MC, V.*

Extra! Extra!

If you're going for serious gambling, I recommend **The Mirage** ($$$$$/Center Strip/☎ **800/627-6667**), which has an airy, tropical-theme casino offering all the games you'd want in a relaxing atmosphere. **New York New York** ($$$$/South Strip/☎ **800/693-6763**) is sheer spectacle—there's nothing quite like playing blackjack in the middle of Central Park.

Lady Luck Casino Hotel
$$. Downtown.

Eighty percent of this hotel's clientele is repeat business, so they've got to be doing something right. I attribute it mainly to the friendly atmosphere and bargain rates. There's not as much glitz and glamour as in the newer hotels, but it is brighter and more attractive than many other downtown options. The rooms, although standard, are large and airy, with a Southwestern motif; there's even a pool and sundeck—one of the few downtown.

206 N. 3rd St. (at Ogden Ave.) ☎ ***800/523-9582*** *or 702/477-3000, fax 702/ 382-2346, Internet www.lady-luck.com.* **Rack rates:** *$40–$105 double. AE, CB, DC, DISC, JCB, MC, V.*

Las Vegas Hilton

$$$$$. Paradise Road.

Adjacent to the Las Vegas Convention Center, this flagship of the Hilton chain caters mostly to business travelers. Large, comfortable rooms are top-of-the-line, with marble desks and bathrooms plus minibars upon request. The 1998 opening of Star Trek: The Experience and the Spacequest Casino (see chapters 13 and 14, "Charge It! A Shopper's Guide to Las Vegas") may change the upscale atmosphere, but ultimately this is still an elegant and expensive place to stay. There's an incredible selection of restaurants—including Benihana Village, with its outrageous decor. In addition, the Hilton offers both a plush main casino and the high-tech Spacequest casino, a beautiful recreation deck with a swimming pool and tennis courts, and a terrific health club/spa where you'll really feel pampered.

3000 Paradise Rd. (at Riviera Blvd.) ☎ *800/732-7117 or 702/732-5111, fax 702/732-5584, Internet www.lv-hilton.com.* **Rack rates:** *$99–$349 double. AE, CB, DC, DISC, ER, MC, V.*

Extra! Extra!

For top-notch service, I give the nod to **The Mirage** ($$$$$/Center Strip/ ☎ 800/627-6667), **Treasure Island** ($$$$/Center Strip/☎ 800/944-7444), or the **Golden Nugget** ($$$/Downtown/☎ 800/634-3454). These three hotels are owned by the same company, and obviously the management teaches the staff that the customer comes first.

Luxor

$$. South Strip.

You've probably seen pictures of this behemoth: It's the 30-story pyramid with the Sphinx in front and an Egyptian motif throughout. After a $300 million renovation, it's not so much of a tacky theme park anymore, and it's pretty impressive. It has become one of my favorite hotels. The rooms in the new towers are stunning—I've never seen anything like their Egyptian/art-deco decor. The pyramid rooms have cool sloped walls, making them larger than average. There are five big pools, a shopping arcade, a large and airy casino, numerous places to drink and dine, and an attractions level with games and rides (see chapter 14). Friendly staff and affordable rates, too!

3900 Las Vegas Blvd. S. (just south of Tropicana Ave.) ☎ *800/288-1000 or 702/262-4000, fax 702/262-4452, Internet www.luxor.com.* **Rack rates:** *$49–$299 double. AE, CB, DC, DISC, MC, V.*

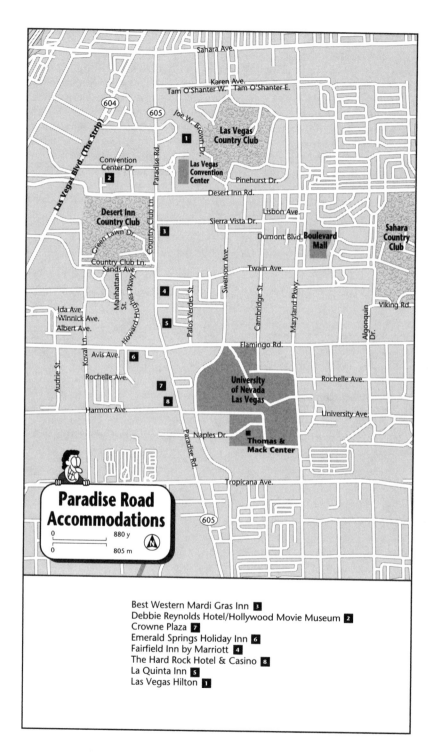

Best Western Mardi Gras Inn **3**
Debbie Reynolds Hotel/Hollywood Movie Museum **2**
Crowne Plaza **7**
Emerald Springs Holiday Inn **6**
Fairfield Inn by Marriott **4**
The Hard Rock Hotel & Casino **8**
La Quinta Inn **5**
Las Vegas Hilton **1**

Main Street Station
$$. Downtown.
This newly renovated hotel (two short blocks from Fremont Street) evokes turn-of-the-century San Francisco with charming decor. It's one of the nicest downtown choices and a really great bargain to boot. There are gas lanterns, stained-glass windows, and lazy ceiling fans in the casino, plus plantation shutters and comfy furniture in the rooms, which are of pretty average size. The only drawbacks are potential freeway noise and no pool or health club.

200 N. Main St. (between Fremont and I-95) ☎ ***800/465-0711*** *or 702/387-1896, fax 702/388-2660.* **Rack rates:** *$45–$65 double. AE, CB, DC, DISC, MC, V.*

 ## MGM Grand Hotel/Casino
$$$$. South Strip.
If you think bigger is better, read on. The MGM is the largest hotel in the world (until it's soon eclipsed by another soon-to-be-completed Vegas whopper), and, of course, it boasts the largest casino in the world. It can be overwhelming, so consider yourself warned. The original Wizard of Oz theme, with its vile overuse of emerald green, is mostly gone (as are some of the family-friendly aspects of the hotel). Now the theme is of classic MGM movies, and the rooms, which are perfectly comfortable, have four main motifs: Hollywood (movie stars), Oz (Wizard of), Casablanca (think Morocco), and Old South (à la Scarlett O'Hara). The MGM Grand has the best lineup of restaurants of any hotel in town: the Wolfgang Puck Cafe, Emeril Legasse's New Orleans Fish House, Gatsby's, an outpost of Hollywood's Brown Derby, and a newly added Rain Forest Cafe, to name just a few. And there's every facility and diversion imaginable—a full-fledged theme park, a spa, a swimming pool and sundeck, a carnival midway, bars and lounges, and a really outstanding kids activity center.

3799 Las Vegas Blvd. S. (at Tropicana Ave.) ☎ ***800/929-1111*** *or 702/891-7777, fax 702/891-1030, Internet www.mgmgrand.com.* **Rack rates:** *$69–$129 double. AE, DC, DISC, MC, V.*

Extra! Extra!
If you want a room with a view, check into **New York New York** ($$$$/South Strip/☎ **800/693-6763**), which has the tallest hotel-room towers in town (over 40 stories), so nothing impedes your view. At **Treasure Island** ($$$$/Center Strip/☎ **800/944-7444**), you can get a room overlooking a swashbuckling pirate battle staged periodically. The **Las Vegas Hilton** ($$$$$/Paradise Road/☎ **800/732-7117**) is a half-mile east of the Strip; its top-floor west-facing rooms offer views of the entire thing in all its neon glory.

The Mirage
$$$$$. Center Strip.

Simply put, this is one of the best hotels in town. From its lovely tropical-theme casino to the tasteful marble and wood decor of the rooms, it's worth the high price tag. The friendly staff provides excellent service. It's all much more understated than the typical Vegas hotel extravaganza (yes, I say that despite the indoor rain forest and the 200,000-gallon aquarium in the lobby), although it's an immense place to negotiate. The Mirage has (arguably) the loveliest pool and the best health club/spa in town, plus tons of restaurants and bars. Be sure to ask for a room overlooking the volcano, which stands on the tropically landscaped hotel grounds and erupts every 15 minutes! Siegfried and Roy's white tigers are housed here, and The Mirage is also home to the Dolphin Habitat (see chapter 12, "The Top Attractions A to Z"). A free tram runs between The Mirage and Treasure Island all day and most of the night, being closed only from 4am–6am.

3400 Las Vegas Blvd. S. (between Flamingo Rd. and Sands Ave.) ☎ *800/627-6667 or 702/791-7111, fax 702/791-7446, Internet www.themirage.com.* **Rack rates:** *$99–$299 double. AE, CB, DC, DISC, MC, V.*

Monte Carlo Resort & Casino
$$$$. South Strip.

This immense hotel reproduces the opulence of its namesake with colonnades, arches, and fountains—it's definitely an upscale resort atmosphere. Spacious rooms have a warm European feel (created by marble and fine furnishings). There's the usual array of restaurants and bars, plus a showroom and casino, but more noteworthy is the hotel's 20,000-acre pool area, with lush landscaping, wave pool, surf pond, waterfalls, and a "river" for tubing. (Kids will like that part but will probably be bored by the rest.) Grownups will go for the fabulous spa, with all the equipment and treatments you could want.

3770 Las Vegas Blvd. S. (between Flamingo Rd. and Tropicana Ave.). ☎ *800/311-8999 or 702/730-7777, fax 702/730-7250, Internet www.monte-carlo.com.* **Rack rates:** *$69–$269 double. AE, CB, DC, DISC, MC, V.*

New York New York
$$$. South Strip.

You have to see it to believe it—New York New York is pure, mind-blowing, Las Vegas fun. It's almost impossible to do this place justice in just a few sentences, but here goes. The exterior is an actual reproduction of the New York skyline, with one-third–scale replicas of the Empire State Building, the Chrysler Building, the Statue of Liberty, and the Brooklyn Bridge. Inside, you'll stroll through versions of Greenwich Village, Times Square, and Central Park. Oh, and just for flavor, a roller coaster runs through the whole thing. The rooms are smallish (just like New York!) but have lovely art-deco decor. The spa and pool aren't as great here as at other hotels; it's overcrowded; and there's definitely a sensory overload factor, especially in the casino. But it's a hoot. You've got to at least stop by to see it.

3790 Las Vegas Blvd. S. (at Tropicana Ave.) ☎ ***800/693-6763*** *or 702/740-6969, fax 702/740-6920, Internet www.nynyhotelcasino.com.* **Rack rates:** *$89 and up double. AE, CB, DC, DISC, MC, V.*

Extra! Extra!

If you want a romantic escape, you can get a lavish room or honeymoon suite at just about any hotel. So I'll focus here on the ones with cool tubs for... well, you know. I recommend **Caesars Palace** ($$$$$/Center Strip/☎ **800/ 634-6661**), where older rooms have Greco/Roman Jacuzzi tubs in the sleeping areas. The Jacuzzi suites at the **Luxor** ($$/South Strip/☎ **800/288-1000**) have the tubs placed under the sloping glass of the pyramid, offering an under-the-stars kind of experience. The **Imperial Palace** ($/Center Strip/☎ **800/ 634-6441**) has something called Luv-Tub rooms, which feature enormous whirlpool baths surrounded by mirrors.

Orleans
$. South Strip.

This is one terrific value. As the name implies, this is the Las Vegas interpretation of New Orleans, complete with French Quarter decor and Cajun influences everywhere. It's actually located about a mile west of the Strip. I'm recommending this place primarily for the rooms: They are the biggest in town, with comfortable Victorian parlor–style furnishings. This is a medium-size hotel (for Vegas), with the usual array of bars and restaurants (including a New Orleans–theme nightclub), plus two medium-size swimming pools, a wedding chapel, and a 70-lane bowling alley.

4500 W. Tropicana Ave. (west of I-95) ☎ ***800/ORLEANS*** *or 702/365-7111, fax 702/365-7505, Internet www.orleanscasino.com.* **Rack rates:** *$39–$79 standard double. AE, DC, DISC, MC, V.*

Rio Hotel & Casino
$$$$. Center Strip.

This place is not too high on my list, but lots of people love this hotel for its carnival ambiance, tropical theme, and oversized rooms (they're big, all right, featuring sectional sofas and small refrigerators, but they're not quite the "suites" the hotel touts). Downsides include location (it's a solid 20-minute walk from the Strip) and a sometimes unfriendly staff. I also find the hectic, party-all-the-time atmosphere a little overwhelming and claustrophobic (it's not a good choice for families with kids). There's a newer addition to the hotel—a 41-story tower and a "European" village of shops and restaurants. A live-action show with a carnival theme, called "Masquerade in the Sky," runs periodically throughout the day. The Rio has a mind-boggling array of restaurants and bars (including a wine bar where you can indulge in tastings), plus three swimming pools (one sandy and palm-fringed, the other two pretty but quite small), a rather dark casino, Jacuzzis, and a fitness center.

3700 W. Flamingo Rd. (just east of I-15) ☎ *800/752-9746 or 702/252-7777, fax 702/253-6090, Internet www.playrio.com.* **Rack rates:** *$95–$149 double. AE, CB, DC, MC, V.*

Extra! Extra!

If you want something big and splashy, you've certainly chosen the right destination! There are lots of options that will suit you, but I'd narrow it down to **New York New York** ($$$$/South Strip/☎ **800/693-6763**), which is so over-the-top it's awe-inducing, or the **Luxor** ($$/South Strip/☎ **800/288-1000**), which is an equally impressive giant glass pyramid with all the attendant Egyptian detail. Oh, and the **MGM Grand** ($$$$/South Strip/☎ **800/929-1111**) is simply the biggest hotel *in the world!*

Riviera Hotel & Casino
$$$. North Strip.

Now in its fifth decade, this Vegas institution often gets overshadowed by the bigger and more boisterous competition. To be honest, the place seems to be in search of a personality. Elegant trappings seem to collide with the topless revues that are heavily featured (the Riviera is definitely not a good choice for families). However, the rooms are quite nice, and there are tons of facilities, restaurants, and shows to keep you entertained—including a vast, vast casino; an Olympic-size pool and sundeck; a large video arcade; a well-equipped health club; two tennis courts; and a wedding chapel.

2901 Las Vegas Blvd. S. (at Riviera Blvd.) ☎ *800/634-6753 or 702/734-5110, fax 702/794-9451.* **Rack rates:** *$59–$99 double. AE, CB, DC, MC, V.*

Sahara Hotel & Casino
$$$. North Strip.

This Vegas institution, a major player since 1952, recently got a real facelift. It sports the prerequisite chandeliers and marble, but there's an Arabian Nights theme, so they've thrown in onion domes and mosaic tile, evoking Morocco (sort of). The rooms are on the smallish side (and whoever picked out the eye-straining striped bedspreads should be shot), but they can be cheap. The Northern Strip location puts it out of the way, which is a pro or con, depending on your point of view. There's a very attractive, Olympic-size pool with Moroccan tiles and a sun deck, plus a large casino and several restaurants and bars (including the Casbah Lounge, which offers really good, live entertainment). Not a good choice for families with kids.

2535 Las Vegas Blvd. S. (at E. Sahara Ave.) ☎ ***800/634-6666*** *or 702/737-2111, fax 702/791-2027.* **Rack rates:** *$35–$85 double. AE, CB, DC, DISC, MC, V.*

Extra! Extra!

If you want something small and intimate, I recommend **Main Street Station** ($$/Downtown/☎ **800/465-0711**), whose 400 rooms are as comfortable and beautiful as the rest of this small gem. **Barbary Coast** ($$/Center Strip/☎ **800/634-6755**) has only 200 rooms and a small casino and is only steps away from the sensory overload of the nearby splashy mega-hotels if you get bored. **La Quinta Inn** ($$$/Paradise Road/☎ **800/531-5900**) is smaller than both of these (with about 180 rooms) and offers multiple room layouts to choose from (up to two-bedroom suites) and very friendly service. You won't get lost or overwhelmed in any of these places.

San Remo
$. South Strip.

This is a great alternative if you want to be near the Vegas madness but not right in the middle of it. It's a small hotel located just off the Strip with nice rooms done in vaguely French provincial decor. Many of the tower rooms include balconies and sleeper sofas. There is a small casino, several moderately priced restaurants, and two lounges featuring entertainment daily.

115 E. Tropicana Ave. (just east of the Strip) ☎ ***800/522-7366*** *or 702/736-1120.* **Rack rates:** *$69–$299 double. AE, CB, D, DISC, JCB, MC, V.*

Stardust Resort & Casino
$$. North Strip.

This is an old-timer among Vegas hotels. It seems to be in search of a personality, but I don't mind that fact here as much as at the Riviera. Everything is bright and cheery, including the rooms, which are entirely forgettable but certainly nice enough. Try to avoid the Garden rooms, which offer terrific prices but not-so-terrific accommodations. The casino here is large, crowded, and lively. In addition to the usual array of shops and restaurants, there are also two large, attractive pools and a few whirlpools. Guests have access to a fabulous, 24-hour health club that's located behind the hotel. Check out the nifty water-ballet fountains in the front.

3000 Las Vegas Blvd. S. (at Convention Center Dr.) ☎ ***800/634-6757** or 702/732-6111, fax 702/732-6257, Internetwww.vegas.com/hotels/stardust.* **Rack rates:** *$26–$200 double. AE, CB, DC, DISC, JCB, MC, V.*

Extra! Extra!

If you want to be pampered, head straight for the Desert Inn ($$$$$/North Strip/☎ **800/634-6906**), with its wonderful spa; it's the pinnacle of the resort-style vacation in Las Vegas (although it has a price to match). **Caesars Palace** ($$$$$/Center Strip/☎ **800/634-6661**) offers tremendous luxury, from the plush rooms to the gorgeous pool/spa and everything between. **The Mirage** ($$$$$/Center Strip/☎ **800/627-6667**) also has a stunning pool and health club/spa, plus an attentive staff.

Stratosphere Las Vegas
$$$. North Strip.

A 106-story observation tower makes this the tallest building west of the Mississippi. Aside from really stunning views, the tower has the world's highest roller coaster, a thrilling free-fall ride, and a wedding chapel complete the aforementioned views. Cool! But the rest of the hotel has drawbacks: It's quite a trek to anything else on the Strip; the rooms aren't in the tower itself (so don't expect tremendous views from your own windows); and, as of this writing, the entire place is in bankruptcy, although it's still open and operating. I'm including it because the incredibly nice staff and the tower views make it a good backup choice if my first preferences are full. Other extras include a casino, a huge pool, and a big shopping arcade with a World's Fair theme.

2000 Las Vegas Blvd. S. (between St. Louis St. and Baltimore Ave.) ☎ **800/99-TOWER** *or 702/380-7777, fax 702/383-5334, Internet www.grandcasinos.com.* **Rack rates:** *$39–$129 double. AE, CB, DC, DISC, JCB, MC, V.*

 Treasure Island
$$$$. Center Strip.

Remember Disneyland's Pirates of the Caribbean? Replace the boats with slot machines, and you get a pretty good idea of what this place is like, although it's a little more upscale than you're probably imagining. From the huge pirate-village exterior to the nautical-theme rooms, this is a fun alternative that remains kid-friendly (a blessing or a curse, depending on your outlook). Rooms are comfortable; try to get one overlooking the pirate-battle stunt-show stage in front of the hotel every 90 minutes. The intense theme and the sheer number of kids can be distracting in the casino. There's a gigantic video arcade and carnival midway, a very good spa and health club, and a surprisingly run-of-the-mill pool area.

3300 Las Vegas Blvd. S. (at Spring Mountain Rd.) ☎ **800/944-7444** *or 702/894-7111, fax 702/894-7446, Internetwww.treasureislandlasvegas.com.* **Rack rates:** *$69 and up double. AE, DC, DISC, JCB, MC, V.*

Tropicana Resort & Casino
$$$$. South Strip.

Picture a tropical Caribbean theme, complete with waterfalls; exotic flowers; towering palms; and real, live flamingos, macaws, and toucans everywhere you look. It's really appealing. Tower rooms are the nicest, with either a French provincial or tropical theme. Pedestrian walkways link the hotel with the Luxor, the MGM Grand, and Excalibur. Other bonuses include an attractive casino, a well-equipped health club, a range of restaurants (all with smashing decor), and three pools (one Olympic-size) located with a few whirlpools in a beautifully landscaped garden with waterfalls and lagoons. One of the pools even has a swim-up blackjack table so that you can gamble and work on your tan at the same time.

3801 Las Vegas Blvd. S. (at Tropicana Ave.) ☎ **800/634-4000** *or 702/739-2222, fax 702/739-2469, Internet http://tropicana.lv.com (note the lack of www).* **Rack rates:** *$69–$169 double. AE, CB, DC, DISC, MC, V.*

So what you want to do is jot down the names and vital statistics of those places in the chart below, get everything lined up and orderly, and then scan the line to see how they stack up against each other. As you rank them in your mind, rank them in the column on the right too; that way you can have your preferences all ready when making reservations, and if there's no room at the inn for choice number 1, you can just move on to number 2.

Hotel Preferences Worksheet

Hotel	Location	Price per night

Advantages	Disadvantages	Your Ranking (1–10)

Part 3

Learning Las Vegas

In most major cities, finding a specific neighborhood or landmark requires maps, directions, and frustration. But Las Vegas is a little different. It's going to be a snap.

Finding the Strip is the least of your problems—you couldn't miss it if you tried. Just look for a bunch of big buildings and lights bordered by a giant black pyramid at one end and a 106-story tower at the other. You can see it as your plane lands, from the airport, and from about 20 miles of freeway in every direction.

Vegas as a whole is very spread out, but the parts of town where you'll be spending most of your time are not. Learning Las Vegas really isn't hard, so take a break from all decision making and spend a moment getting acquainted with the airport, the roads, and the neighborhoods. You'll be negotiating this town like a pro in no time.

Chapter 7

Getting Your Bearings

> **In This Chapter**
>
> ➤ An airport like no other
>
> ➤ Your car made it across the desert, now what?
>
> ➤ Helping hands

No matter how you get here, you'll probably be dazzled at first. I've been going to Las Vegas regularly for over a decade, sometimes every weekend on business, and yet each time I see the city and all that neon, my jaw drops. It's a mind-blowing sight, so take it in and enjoy it. As for getting through the airport, here are some useful insider tips.

Your Plane Just Landed. Now What?

McCarran International Airport is located at the southern end of the city, at 5757 Wayne Newton Boulevard. In some big cities, you have to drive for what seems like hours to get to your hotel from the airport, but McCarran is only about a mile from the Strip.

The location is super-convenient, and so is the airport itself. Sure, it's busy (it's the eighth busiest airport in the world, with over 30 million people passing through annually, to be precise), but it's simple to navigate. Big, modern, and well planned, it has three concourses and more than 60 gates, with an additional 70 planned by the year 2010. The A and B concourses are connected by walkways to the main terminal; these concourses are for both international and domestic flights. The C concourse, for domestic flights only, is separate from the main terminal and is serviced by a monorail system. Everything is well marked with overhead signs pointing the way.

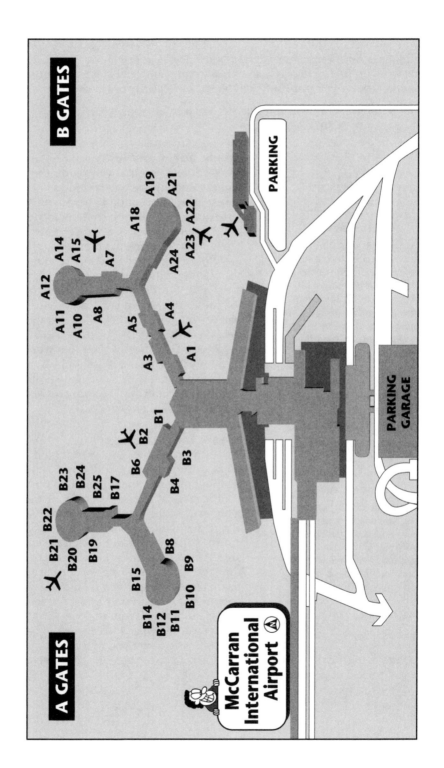

B GATES

A12
A14
A15
A7
A11
A10
A8
A18
A19
A21
A23 A22
A24
A5
A4
A3
A1
B1
B2
B6
B3
B23
B24
B25
B17
B22
B21
B20
B19
B4
B8
B15
B14
B12
B11
B10 B9

A GATES

PARKING

PARKING GARAGE

McCarran International Airport Ⓐ

85

So you couldn't eat the airline food, and now you're starving? Each satellite terminal has restaurants, food stands, and stores near just about every gate. You'll wind up paying more for food here than you would at a place outside the airport, but if you just can't wait, you'll have plenty to choose from.

For more information, you can call McCarran International Airport Information at ☎ **702/261-5743**.

Time-Savers

If your flight arrives in the C terminal at a high gate number, say 22 and above, don't bother with the monorail. Just past gate 27, there is a moving sidewalk to the main terminal that is much faster and less crowded than the trains.

Time-Savers

As you exit the luggage claim area, you will be asked to show your claim tickets to verify that you're taking the right bag. Make sure to have your ticket handy so that you don't have to fumble through your carry-on luggage or purse.

Ready, Set, Gamble!

As you'll see as soon as you get off the plane, gambling is *everywhere* in Las Vegas. Even in the airport. Yup, there are more than 1,000 slot machines and video-poker games right here at McCarran. These banks of machines (known as *carousels*) are in all the satellite terminals, the main terminal, and the baggage-claim area. Hint: Most people will advise avoiding these "one-armed bandits" like the plague—supposedly, they offer lower winnings (known as *paybacks*) than hotel machines. They may be right, but who could resist such a quintessential Las Vegas experience as shaking hands with a one-armed bandit while waiting for your luggage? Speaking of which...

Where Is My Luggage?

Provided the airline hasn't lost it (and don't worry—people joke about it, but it seldom happens), you'll be able to find your luggage at a central point near the main exit. Again, there are signs everywhere, but if all else fails, follow the crowd. Once you get to the baggage-claim area, there are eight carousels to choose from, each with an electronic message board announcing which flight's bags are coming out. It can take a while for your luggage to make it from the plane to the claim area, so be patient. Maybe they do it on purpose to get you to try the slot machines conveniently located nearby. Carts are available for a small fee in case you packed your entire wardrobe.

Getting Mobile: Renting a Car

Just past the baggage claim are the rental-car counters. All the usual suspects are here—Alamo, Allstate, Avis, Budget, Enterprise, Hertz, National, and Thrifty, among others. For more information on getting a good deal when you rent a car in advance, see chapter 4, "Tying Up the Loose Ends." Appendix C in this guide provides a list of companies and their toll-free phone numbers.

Once you do all the paperwork at the counter, the rental agent will direct you outside, where you catch a shuttle bus to the car lots. Each company has its own buses that run regularly, but make sure to ask the counter agent to notify the driver that you will be waiting. From the airport, it's only about a five-minute trip to your car.

Driving into Town

For general tips on driving around Las Vegas, see chapter 8, "Getting Around." But for now, let's get you into town and headed for your hotel.

If you're driving into town, you'll probably be coming in on **Interstate 15,** the major north-south freeway that runs right through the city. The exit you take depends on where you're staying, so check the recommendations below:

➤ **If you're staying on the South Strip:** Traveling north on I-15, exit at Tropicana Avenue and turn right at the stop light. The Strip is less than a half-mile to the east—trust me, you'll see it. Southbound travelers should take the same exit but follow the signs for Tropicana Avenue East. If you're hungry, you'll soon come across every fast-food franchise you could imagine within blocks.

Time-Savers

When you leave the airport, follow the signs to the 215 freeway. This is a newly completed road that makes it incredibly easy to drive to and from McCarran. It adds a few miles to your trip, but it's still a lot faster than going out of the airport into city-street traffic. The 215 will lead you to I-15, which you take north to the Strip exits or downtown.

➤ **If you're staying on the Center Strip:** Northbound drivers should exit at Flamingo Road and turn left at the light. Coming south, you can exit at either Flamingo Road-East or Spring Mountain Road and turn right. (At press time, there was word that a major construction project was about to begin at the Spring Mountain Road exit, so it may be best to avoid it and choose Flamingo Road-East for a while.)

➤ **If you're staying on the North Strip:** Coming from the north or south, exit at Sahara and head east. The Strip is about three-fourths of a mile away.

➤ **If you're staying in the Paradise Road area:** Take the Flamingo Road exit and head east. You'll cross the Strip and go about another mile to Paradise Road. You're right around the 4000 block with higher numbers to the south (turn right) and lower numbers to the north (turn left).

➤ **If you're staying downtown:** From I-15, the quickest route is to take the freeway offshoot that runs past downtown. The interchange is a bit tricky (locals call it the Spaghetti Bowl), with the freeway carrying three different numbers: 515, 95, and 93. Whatever you want to call it, take it south and exit at Casino Center Boulevard. This will dump you right into the heart of downtown, with Fremont Street crossing two blocks ahead and Las Vegas Boulevard (which eventually becomes the Strip) three blocks to the left.

How to Get Where You're Going If You Didn't Rent a Car

If you chose to skip the rental car, you have three ways of getting from the airport to your hotel.

Catch a Cab

Past the rental-car counters is the main exit. Just outside these doors is the taxi stand. A warning: If a couple of flights have arrived at roughly the same time, the line for a cab can be enormous, with waiting times of up to 20 minutes. Basic taxi fare is $2.20 for the first mile, $1.50 for each additional mile, plus time penalties if you get stuck in traffic. These fares are governed by the state and should be the same for every company. 10 to 15 percent is adequate to tip the cab driver, but if you're sharing a fare, you should do 10 percent per person or group.

You really shouldn't ever have to call for a cab, since they are usually waiting outside the airport and all major hotels 24 hours a day. However, if you happen to wander into less-traveled territory, these are the major cab companies in town:

Dollars & Sense

All taxis will carry up to five people, so while you're stuck waiting on line at the taxi stand, strike up a conversation with the other people around you to see if anyone is headed in your direction and is willing to split the fare with you.

ABC ☎ 702/736-8444

Ace ☎ 702/736-8383

Checker ☎ 702/873-2000

Desert ☎ 702/386-9102

Henderson ☎ 702/384-2322

Star ☎ 702/873-2000

Western ☎ 702/736-8000

Whittlesea ☎ 702/384-6111

Yellow ☎ 702/873-2000

Dollars & Sense

Here are a few examples of what you can expect to pay for a cab from McCarran to various parts of the city. Keep in mind that these are just estimates, and your actual fare may vary a bit depending on traffic and different routes taken.

To South Strip area	$9.50–$10.50
To Center Strip area	$9.50–$12
To North Strip area	$11–$13
To downtown area	$16–$20
To Paradise Road area	$7–$12

Jump on a Shuttle

At the same place where you pick up a taxi or the rental-car buses, you'll find shuttle buses that run regularly to and from the Strip and downtown. These large, comfortable buses can be a bargain if you're by yourself or with one other person, since they charge about $3.50 per person for a trip to the Strip or Paradise Road areas and $4.75 per person to go downtown. (If there are more than two people in your group, however, you can take a cab for less.) You also have to hope that the people on your bus are going to your hotel or one close by, or otherwise you'll be riding and waiting through a lot of extra stops. (My luck usually makes my hotel the last stop on the trip.)

There are several companies that operate these services, but **Bell Trans** (☎ **702/385-5466**) is the biggest and most reliable. Look for large shuttle vans with the rates posted on the sides cruising the airport.

Get on the Bus

The bus should only be your last resort. **Citizen's Area Transit (CAT),** ☎ **702/CAT-RIDE,** runs regular service to and from the airport. The fare is $1.50 per person and 50¢ for seniors and children. Take CAT only if you are truly broke or desperate. If you're lugging a heavy load, just remember that even if the bus stops right in front of your hotel, you may have a long walk from the bus stop to the door (remember, distances in Vegas can be deceiving).

The no. 108 bus departs from the airport and will take you to the Stratosphere, where you can transfer to the 301, which stops close to most Strip- and Convention Center–area hotels.

The no. 109 bus goes from the airport to the Downtown Transportation Center at Casino Center Boulevard and Stewart Avenue.

Schedules and routes vary, so call for information. For more truly solid arguments against using CAT even for getting around the city after you've settled in, check out chapter 8.

The Strip, Downtown & All Around: Figuring Out Las Vegas

As I mentioned earlier, this is a very spread-out city, but the areas you'll probably be staying in are very centralized and easy to navigate.

There are three main neighborhoods, which I've discussed before (see chapter 5, "Pillow Talk: The Lowdown on the Las Vegas Hotel Scene," for the pros and cons of staying in each one). There's **the Strip,** where all the big hotels and resorts are located; **downtown,** where you'll find Glitter Gulch and the Fremont Street Experience; and **the Paradise Road area,** which is home to the convention center and some smaller, non-casino hotels. I'm including a few other neighborhoods that may be of some interest to you if you're staying for more than a few days or are planning future trips.

The best analogy to help put it all into perspective is this: Las Vegas is shaped sort of like a crooked Santa Claus cap. The Strip is one side of the cap, Paradise Road is the other, and downtown is the fuzzy ball on top. Chew on that one for a moment. Or, better still, there's about a bajillion maps in this book to help you get your bearings. I labeled or bulleted everything I discuss, so you won't feel lost for a minute.

The Strip

The Strip, A.K.A. Las Vegas Boulevard South, is the heart of Vegas. That's where first-time visitors will spend most of their time, and with good reason—this is where most of the major attractions, hotels, and casinos (including New York New York, Caesars, and Circus Circus) are located.

The Strip acts as the center of town, so addresses are all measured from there (100 West is a block west of the Strip, 100 East is a block east, and so on). If you're worried about getting around, keep in mind that the bulk of the action occurs on the southern end of the Strip.

Downtown

Also known as *Glitter Gulch,* this is the oldest section of town. It's located just to the south and east of where I-15 and the 515/95/93 freeways come together. Las Vegas Boulevard runs right into Fremont Street (now a pedestrian walkway with no auto traffic allowed), where most of the area's big hotels are located.

Bordering neighborhoods are questionable in terms of safety, so stick to the well-traveled, brightly lit parts.

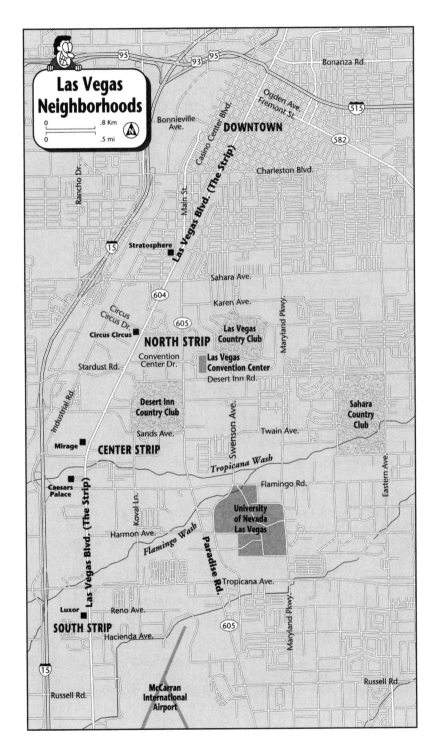

Las Vegas
Neighborhoods

0   .8 Km
0   .5 mi

95   93   95

Bonanza Rd.

515

Ogden Ave.
Fremont St.

Casino Center Blvd.

Bonnieville
Ave.

DOWNTOWN

582

Rancho Dr.

Charleston Blvd.

Main St.

Las Vegas Blvd. (The Strip)

15   Stratosphere

Sahara Ave.

Karen Ave.

604

Maryland Pkwy.

Circus
Circus Dr.

605

Las Vegas
Country Club

Circus Circus

NORTH STRIP

Convention
Center Dr.

Las Vegas
Convention Center

Stardust Rd.

Desert Inn Rd.

Industrial Rd.

Desert Inn
Country Club

Sahara
Country
Club

Swenson Ave.

Sands Ave.

Twain Ave.

Mirage

CENTER STRIP

Eastern Ave.

Tropicana Wash

Caesars
Palace

Flamingo Rd.

Koval Ln.

University
of Nevada
Las Vegas

Las Vegas Blvd. (The Strip)

Harmon Ave.

Flamingo Wash

Paradise Rd.

15

Luxor

Reno Ave.

Tropicana Ave.

605

SOUTH STRIP

Maryland Pkwy.

Hacienda Ave.

Russell Rd.

Russell Rd.

McCarran
International
Airport

Paradise Road

This section refers to Paradise Road and the area surrounding it. It's a major north-south artery that runs from the airport to its intersection with the Strip (which mostly runs parallel about a half mile to the west) at the Stratosphere Tower. There are a few large hotels and attractions here, but mostly you'll find smaller, non-casino hotels and a lot of restaurants. The Las Vegas Convention Center is also in this area.

Between the Strip & Downtown

If you take Las Vegas Boulevard north, it will lead you to downtown. Between the Strip and downtown is where you'll find most of the wedding chapels (the best are described in chapter 13, "More Fun Stuff to Do"). Unless you're actually getting married, this area is really only good for its high silliness and kitsch factor ("Joan Collins was married here!").

Dollars & Sense

The Maryland Parkway is another major north-south artery about 2 miles west of the Strip and 1 mile west of Paradise Road. Virtually every major (and minor) retailer and food chain has an outlet on this road—you'll find Sears, J.C. Penney, Toys R Us, and all the big pharmacy/drug stores. This can be valuable if you need to pick up something like shampoo or a pair of comfortable shoes and don't feel like paying the exorbitant prices charged in hotel stores. To get there from the Strip, travel east (away from I-15) on any major road (Flamingo, Tropicana, Sahara) about 2 miles.

East Las Vegas

This is one of the areas where locals go to gamble. There are several big hotel/casinos along Boulder Highway near Flamingo Road, such as **Sam's Town Hotel and Gambling Hall,** 5111 Boulder Hwy. (☎ **800/634-6371**). I don't recommend staying in this neighborhood, simply because most of the places you'll want to see are too far away—it's about 7 or 8 miles to the Strip. However, if you're staying for more than a few days and want to explore, it might be worth your while. Take Flamingo Road east from the Strip to get here.

Henderson

Henderson is a small town just southeast of Las Vegas—maybe a 20-minute car ride from the Strip if traffic is good. Here, you'll find some fun, family-oriented attractions, like the Clark County Heritage Museum and factory tours of Ethel M. Chocolates. (These and other attractions are described more fully in chapter 13.) To get to Henderson from the Strip, take Las Vegas Boulevard south to Sunset Road and head east. Most of what you'll want to see is around the intersection of Sunset Road and the 95 freeway.

Street Smarts: Where to Get More Information Once You're Here

Every major hotel has tourist information at its reception, show, or sightseeing desk. These hotels will be able to tell you about special events, concerts, or shows in town that you may have missed during your research.

Most show desks at the big hotels can make reservations for you at any show in town—not just the ones in that particular hotel.

Reception or sightseeing desks can often provide you with detailed maps and directions to anywhere you want to go.

There's also the concierge desk, where you can usually get good dining tips or advice on the cheapest place to find a bottle of aspirin. (The only caveat is to remember that they are probably prejudiced toward their personal or professional favorites, so you may not be getting an unbiased opinion.)

In addition, you can check with the **Las Vegas Convention and Visitors Authority**, 3150 Paradise Rd., Las Vegas, NV 89109 (☎ **800/332-5333** or 702/

Bet You Didn't Know

Illusionists Siegfried and Roy have sawed a women in half more times than anybody else in the world.

892-0711) or the **Las Vegas Chamber of Commerce**, 711 E. Desert Inn Rd., Las Vegas, NV 89109 (☎ **702/735-1616**). Ask the Chamber of Commerce for its *Visitor's Guide,* which contains extensive listings for accommodations, attractions, excursions, children's activities, and more. They can also answer all your Las Vegas questions (including those about weddings and divorces).

I'm in Trouble. What Do I Do?

Already? You just got here!

Well, if something does go drastically wrong, there are two social-service organizations in town designed to help you out. The **Traveler's Aid Society** has an office at McCarran Airport (☎ **702/798-1742**), which is open daily from 8am to 5pm. They can help reunite families separated while traveling, feed stranded people without cash, or offer emotional counseling, just to name a few of their services.

Similar services are available through **Help of Southern Nevada**, 953-53B E. Sahara Ave., Suite 208 (at Maryland Parkway in the Commercial Center; ☎ **702/369-4357**), Monday through Friday from 8am to 4pm.

Chapter 8

Getting Around

In This Chapter

➤ Getting behind the wheel

➤ Taking a taxi

➤ Hopping a bus or trolley

➤ Hoofing it

There are city buses, but no subways or rail lines. You're going to wind up doing one of four things: driving, taking a cab, taking a bus or trolley, or pounding the pavement. In this chapter, you'll get an idea of the pros and cons of each of these alternatives, plus some tips that might save you time and money.

Using Your Own Wheels

In Vegas, driving is really the way to go. It's just a matter of practicality and convenience. You can do and see more in the city when you're mobile and not relying on taxis, buses, or your feet to get somewhere. Of course, practical as having a car is, there are also some drawbacks to consider.

Pros

The added mobility and freedom involved with traveling by car is probably the biggest reason to spring for a rental car. The Strip is really too spread out for walking the entire length, downtown is too far away for a cheap cab ride, and the bus service is ineffective at best.

Cars are also cheaper than taking cabs everywhere, especially if you want to get out and explore. Parking in some major cities like New York or San Francisco is always a concern, but that's not a worry here. All the major hotels have free self-parking and most have free valet service (see below for more details).

Dollars & Sense

I know it's tempting to go all out when renting a car in Las Vegas. After all, what could be cooler than cruising the Strip in a convertible or luxury sedan? But although the right car might make you look cool, it's just going to be sitting in a parking lot most of the time. Save the money for the casinos; get something small and cheap. Trust me, you don't really need to impress the valet parking attendants.

Cons

Your primary worry when driving is the traffic, which is especially bad on and around the Strip. I once took a drive from the southernmost Strip hotel, the Luxor, to the northernmost, the Stratosphere. It took me almost 30 minutes to cover the 4 miles. *Do the math, folks; that's an average of about 8 miles an hour.*

Road construction is also a big drawback—Vegas seems to be in a perpetual state of catch-up in dealing with the huge numbers of tourists that have descended. The roads are always ripped up for some "improvement" project or another, and this only adds to the traffic problems. Plus, there are the stoplights, which seem to take forever. Finally, gas prices are higher here than in most of the rest of the country—as much as 15¢ per gallon higher than the average.

Tourist Traps

There are lots of gas stations at the Tropicana Avenue exit just west of the freeway. Unless you're running on fumes, avoid them. Their prices are substantially higher than those at other places in town.

Park It Here

Free valet parking—need I say more?

This has got to be one of the greatest things about driving in Las Vegas. The big hotels all have signs that will direct you to the valet service at the main entrances where you get a claim check. When you're ready to leave, turn in the claim ticket so that your car can be brought back, and all it will cost you is a $1–$2 tip for the attendant. (In hot weather, they'll usually even turn on the air conditioning for you so the car is cool when you get in. Nice, huh?) The only drawback to using the service is that retrieving your car can take a while, especially if the hotel is busy. Expect a 5- to 20-minute wait.

Time-Savers

If time is of the essence (or if you're overly protective of your car or too cheap to pay the tip), you might want to use the free (in most places) self-parking instead of valet parking at the major hotels. The newer hotels have parking structures that will even allow you to find some shade. Just be warned that many times, these self-park areas are quite a hike from the casinos and showrooms.

Downtown hotels vary on their parking policies. Most will charge for self-parking but offer validation in the casinos, which will make it free. Again, use the valet services where available to save yourself the hassle.

Avoiding Gridlock

As I mentioned, driving in Las Vegas can be a nightmare when it comes to the traffic. Over the course of my oh-so-frequent visits, however, I have found a few alternative routes that can save you time and stress.

North-South Alternatives to the Strip

You don't want to get stuck in bumper-to-bumper traffic on the Strip every time you need to get somewhere, so here are some alternate routes for traveling north-south:

➤ **I-15:** This major interstate runs parallel to the Strip and is easily accessible from Tropicana, Flamingo, and Sahara Avenues with limited access on Spring Mountain. If you need to get from one end of the Strip to the other, or especially if you are going downtown, this route is your best bet. The only exception is during morning and evening rush hours, when you can finish reading *War and Peace* in the time it takes to get from one place to another.

➤ **Industrial Road:** This is my favorite fast route for getting from one Strip location to another. It's located just west of the Strip and runs all the way from Tropicana to Sahara Avenues. The city has recently reconfigured and re-paved what used to be a meandering two-lane road to a smooth, four-lane mini-highway. A lot less traffic and fewer stoplights make this the best-kept secret for Vegas driving.

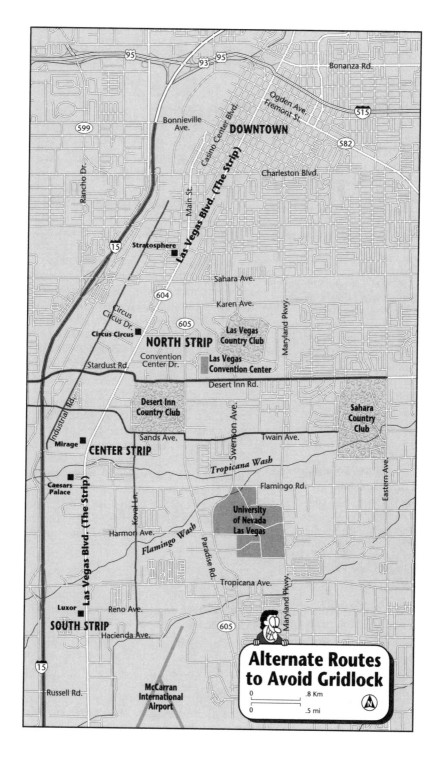

Alternate Routes to Avoid Gridlock

0 — .8 Km
0 — .5 mi

➤ Koval Lane: Koval runs parallel to the Strip on the east side between Las Vegas Boulevard and Paradise Road. It only runs from Tropicana to Sands, so it isn't good for end-to-end Strip runs, but short trips are a lot faster.

Lesser-Known Routes East-West Across Town

The major east-west arteries, such as Flamingo and Tropicana, can get congested, too, so here are some alternatives that generally move faster:

Bet You Didn't Know

Americans love to gamble, and according to a recent survey, they spend nearly as much on gambling (6 percent of the gross national product) as they do on groceries (8 percent).

Time-Savers

If you're in a hurry, avoid driving the Strip at all costs. Even during the day, the traffic is nightmarish, and at night, it approaches gridlock. Use any of the parallel streets or I-15 to save time.

➤ **Spring Mountain/Sands/Twain:** It's one street with three different names, depending on where you are, and it crosses the Strip next to Treasure Island and Paradise Road near the Fairfield Inn. There are fewer stoplights and less traffic here than you'll find on other major east-west routes like Flamingo Road or Tropicana Avenue. At press time, a major construction project was getting underway at Spring Mountain and I-15, with plans to put in new off-ramps and a railroad-crossing overpass. If you see anything that remotely looks like a bulldozer in this vicinity, avoid the area at all costs. It'll be a mess.

➤ **Desert Inn Road:** This is another terrific project engineered by the city. This street has been changed into a six-lane, divided freeway (with no traffic lights) that begins at Paradise Road on the east and ends at Valley View just west of I-15. There is limited access to and from the Strip, so this is best used for getting from one side to the other without the hassle of Las Vegas Boulevard, I-15, or crosswalks filled with tourists.

Rules of the Road

Despite what you might have heard about states in the West being free and loose with their speed limits and traffic laws, Las Vegas police and the Nevada Highway Patrol go strictly by the book. Here are a few general rules:

➤ Speed limits are comparable to those in the rest of the United States, with 35–45 mph common on many major streets, 25–35 mph on side streets, and 55–70 mph on the freeways.

➤ Right turn on red is permitted (and often angrily encouraged by the driver behind you if you don't take advantage of it).

➤ Left turns at major intersections are mostly "green arrow only." Up to three lanes of traffic can turn at the same time.

➤ U-turns are allowed at intersections where there is no sign strictly forbidding it.

And If You Get Lost...

The Stratosphere Hotel may not be doing too well business-wise, but it sure has revolutionized driving for tourists in Las Vegas. At 110 stories, this appropriately-named structure is the tallest building west of the Mississippi River and can be seen from just about every place in town. It's more than twice as tall as any other building in Las Vegas. If you get lost while driving, take a minute to scan the horizon and find the Stratosphere Tower. Head toward it, and you'll find yourself at the northern end of the Strip and Paradise Road and only five minutes from downtown.

Yo! Taxi!

If you plan on spending all or most of your time in one general area, traveling by taxi is a viable option. However, if you plan on venturing outside the immediate neighborhood, it'll wind up costing you a bundle.

Pros

There are cabs everywhere in Vegas, so finding one is usually not a problem. Even at 4am, you'll find a line of them outside most major hotels and the airport. Although I can't vouch for every driver, car, and company, the taxis I've taken have all been clean, and the drivers professional and courteous.

Cons

The biggest downside is the price. A friend and I were once too tired to walk back from the southern end of the Strip to our hotel in the center section. We hailed a cab and immediately got stuck in nighttime traffic—and that meter's ticking even when you're not moving. To go about 2 miles cost us almost $15 with tip. Anyway, if you plan to rely on cabs, be sure to budget some extra dough to cover them.

Tourist Traps

Taxi fares are regulated by the state of Nevada and should be the same for all companies: $2.20 for the first mile and $1.50 for each additional mile, plus time penalties. Be sure that the rates are prominently displayed in the cab before letting the driver start the meter.

See chapter 7, "Getting Your Bearings," for more details on cab companies and average fares.

Magic Bus or Bucket of Bolts?

Don't do it. How's that for objective travel writing?

Citizen's Area Transit (CAT), ☎ **702/CAT-RIDE,** is the city bus service, and I think it stinks. I wouldn't dream of telling you to rely on it for your transportation needs.

It is cheap, I'll give them that. At $1.50 for adults and 50¢ for kids and seniors, this is a pretty good bargain.

The drawbacks, on the other hand, are enough to fill a book of their own, but since I have other things to cover here, I'll stick to the biggies.

The service, on the whole, is unreliable—schedules apparently mean very little.

The routes don't always make sense, either. Suppose that you want to get from the airport to the MGM Grand, which is less than 2 miles away. You have to take the #108 bus all the way up Paradise Road to the Stratosphere Tower, transfer to the #301, and ride that all the way back down the Strip. The bus makes you travel more than 8 miles, and if you get there in less than 2 hours, it would be a miracle.

Finally, it seems that a great number of people don't share my misgivings about the bus system, which unfortunately results in buses that are crowded to the point that they can't stop to take on additional passengers. I've actually seen a bus pass a crowded bench without even slowing down when the next one wasn't scheduled for another 45 minutes.

But hey, it's your choice.

Traveling by Trolley

A little less aggravating and even cheaper than the bus system is the **Las Vegas Strip Trolley** (☎ **702/382-1404**), which runs from 9:30am to 2am. It's basically a bus designed to look like a trolley car, and it goes up and down the Strip, stopping in front of every major hotel and casino. There's also a trolley that runs from the Stratosphere Hotel into downtown. The fare is $1.30 per ride; children under five years old ride free. Exact change is required.

The entertainment factor of these trolleys is a plus—you'll get to hear amusing Vegas facts from the driver as you travel. In addition, the fares are low and the routes are convenient.

On the down side, trolleys, like city buses, are often as crowded as cattle cars and will pass right by the stops if full. There are several of them running at the same time, but because there is no definable schedule to speak of, your wait time could be interminable.

Put One Foot in Front of the Other

Once you get into a centralized neighborhood (Center Strip, downtown, and so on), it's fairly easy to walk from one hotel to the next. It's certainly easier than retrieving a car every time. However, if you want to get out of one area and into another neighborhood, you won't want to walk the distances unless you're one of those marathon types.

Pros & Cons

Obviously, the biggest plus is that walking is free. All it's going to cost you is the price of a pair of comfortable shoes. If you're okay with staying in one basic area, it's a good alternative.

A major negative is the weather, which can be brutally hot during the day and exceptionally chilly at night. This is something to consider when you're looking down the street and saying, "Oh, it's not that far!" Another thing to keep in mind is that the sidewalks often have as much traffic as the streets do, especially during peak holiday or convention times.

Of special note for parents: Keep in mind that sex is a big industry in Las Vegas. To promote their enterprises, many strip clubs and escort services place people on the sidewalks to hand out flyers and magazines that you might not want your children to see. It's easy to just say "no," but many people will take the brochures and then discard them on the ground where anyone, including your 8 year old, can get a look at them.

Tips on Hoofin' It

Comfortable shoes are an absolute must for Las Vegas—and even if you have a rental car, you'll be doing a lot of walking. Men should stick with well-ventilated athletic shoes or well-padded loafers, and women should avoid anything with a heel. I don't really recommend sandals in Las Vegas, partly because of the hot sun (sunburned feet are a bummer), but also because the sidewalks can be cluttered with trash, broken glass, or the equivalent.

Also remember, when walking in Vegas, be sure to carry plenty of water (the casinos will let you bring it in).

Objects Next Door May Be Farther Away Than They Appear

I don't know, maybe it's the desert that makes distances so deceiving, but getting from point A to point B always seems to take much longer than you think it will, so make sure that you budget your time accordingly.

Bet You Didn't Know

Las Vegas has an average of 310 sunny days a year and an average rainfall of around 4 inches. In other words, you can pretty safely plan on leaving your umbrella at home.

101

Here's an example. I was staying on one of the top floors of Treasure Island and had to go two doors down to Caesars Palace for a meeting at the south casino entrance. I figured, *It's two hotels down; it'll only take 10 minutes*, and planned my schedule accordingly. Unfortunately, I had to make it down the long hall to the elevators, down the 30-some-odd floors, through the Treasure Island casino throng to the Mirage monorail, across the divide to the front door of the Mirage, inside and through that casino mob to the moving sidewalk, down to the Strip and then up the Caesars' moving sidewalk, through the Forum Shops, and all the way across the Caesars casino. I did it in just less than 25 minutes. The moral of the story is to give yourself extra time, even if you're just going next door.

Walking the Easy Way: People Movers!

And for those moments when you just don't think you can wiggle your toes, let alone lift your feet off the ground, don't worry. There are so many monorails, trams, and moving sidewalks underfoot that you can literally get from one spot to another without moving a muscle.

The monorails listed below are totally free of charge—take advantage of them and enjoy the ride!

➤ **MGM Grand to Bally's Monorail:** Adjacent to the main entrance at the MGM Grand is the boarding platform for a monorail that will take you up the street to Bally's shopping arcade. It's a great trick for getting from the South to the Central Strip.

➤ **Treasure Island to Mirage Tram:** Yes, the two hotels are right next to each other, but there is no quicker way to get from one to the other. Pick up the tram at the back of Treasure Island between the hotel and parking structure, and it will deliver you practically to the front door of the Mirage.

➤ **Mirage/Caesars Palace People Movers:** If you exit the Mirage past the white tigers, you'll find a moving sidewalk that will take you out to the Strip. Walk a few steps, and you can jump on the Caesars Palace moving sidewalk that will take you inside the Forum Shops or casino. It works the other way around, too!

➤ **Luxor/Excalibur Monorail/People Movers:** An enclosed, air-conditioned moving sidewalk was recently completed to move things along between these two mega-hotels. This is in addition to the monorail that has been around for years.

Even more of these people movers are in the works, with proposed monorails between the Mirage, Bellagio, and Monte Carlo and moving sidewalks between the upcoming Project Paradise and Luxor.

Part 4

The Best Restaurants in Las Vegas

Fine dining in Las Vegas used to mean wearing a tie to McDonald's. Happily, this is no longer the case. As the city goes relentlessly upscale, the array of restaurants and the cuisine they serve are moving up as well. Some of the world's most famous chefs have come to Vegas to launch high-profile restaurants, and virtually every hotel has at least one gourmet dining room, ensuring that you can find an elegant meal—provided you're willing to pay for it.

On the other hand, Las Vegas's famed bargains are still here, including those famous buffets and cheap meal deals—a 99¢ shrimp cocktail or a $4.95 prime-rib dinner. The quality of the food might not be the same as in those fancy restaurants, but if all you need is fuel on a budget and generous helpings, you'll find plenty of options.

And in between, you'll find a sufficiently wide variety of menus, prices, and sur-roundings to satisfy any craving. Theme restaurants? Sushi bars? Diners serving cheeseburgers at 3am? Vegas has 'em all.

ALL-U-CAN EAT
SPAGHETTI
AND MEATBALLS

Chapter 9

The Lowdown on the Las Vegas Dining Scene

In This Chapter

➤ Trends and local faves

➤ Finding the food

➤ Prices and policies

➤ Finding fast food and quick meals

➤ Eating on a tight budget

As tempting as it may be to spend all your time in front of a slot machine, you still have to eat every now and then—if only so that you don't collapse in a heap right before you win that big jackpot. In some of the larger hotels, you could hang out for a week and never eat in the same place twice. But there's more to Las Vegas dining than what you'll find adjacent to a casino.

What's Hot

Las Vegas, still young and unencumbered by tradition, seems to be searching for an identity when it comes to the restaurant scene. It's not like New Orleans, where you *have* to try famous Creole cooking, or San Francisco, where you've *gotta* have Chinatown dim sum. Las Vegas can't boast of a famous cheese steak or indigenous ethnic specialty, but some trends are emerging.

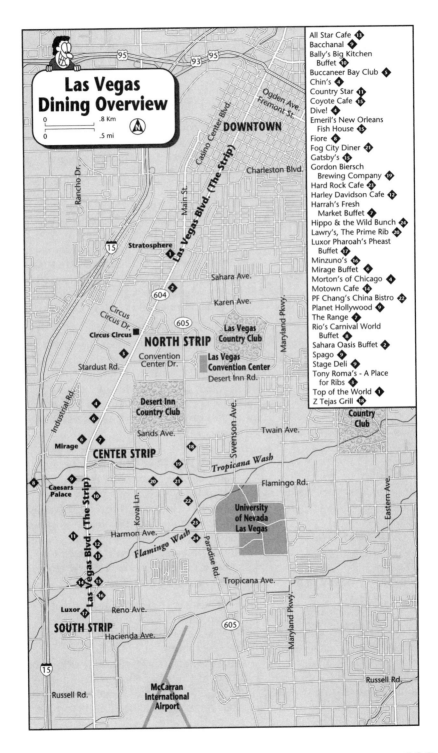

Las Vegas Dining Overview

0 — .8 Km
0 — .5 mi

All Star Cafe 13
Bacchanal 9
Bally's Big Kitchen
  Buffet 10
Buccaneer Bay Club 5
Chin's 4
Country Star 11
Coyote Cafe 15
Dive! 7
Emeril's New Orleans
  Fish House 15
Fiore 8
Fog City Diner 21
Gatsby's 15
Gordon Biersch
  Brewing Company 19
Hard Rock Cafe 23
Harley Davidson Cafe 12
Harrah's Fresh
  Market Buffet 7
Hippo & the Wild Bunch 24
Lawry's, The Prime Rib 20
Luxor Pharoah's Pheast
  Buffet 17
Minzuno's 16
Mirage Buffet 6
Morton's of Chicago 4
Motown Cafe 14
PF Chang's China Bistro 22
Planet Hollywood 9
The Range 7
Rio's Carnival World
  Buffet 8
Sahara Oasis Buffet 2
Spago 9
Stage Deli 9
Tony Roma's - A Place
  for Ribs 3
Top of the World 1
Z Tejas Grill 18

DOWNTOWN

NORTH STRIP

Las Vegas
Country Club

Las Vegas
Convention Center

CENTER STRIP

Country
Club

University
of Nevada
Las Vegas

SOUTH STRIP

McCarran
International
Airport

Trend #1: Well, We're Movin' on Up

A few years ago, foodies in search of a gourmet meal in elegant surroundings found themselves literally and figuratively in the middle of the desert. But all that has changed. These days, with everyone rushing to capture high-end dollars, high-gloss joints are mushrooming. Food snobs may still turn up their noses at the choices, but most of us regular folks will be impressed.

Wolfgang Puck has opened a **Spago** here, and **Emeril's** is Emeril Lagasse's latest venture. Even the hotels are getting in on the action: you've got **Gatsby's (MGM Grand), Fiore (Rio), Coyote Cafe (MGM Grand),** and **Buccaneer Bay Club (Treasure Island),** just to name a few.

Trend #2: You Gotta Have a Theme

The most successful hotels in town all have some sort of identifiable theme: Luxor does Egypt, Treasure Island does the pirate thing, and New York New York does... well, New York. It's no small wonder that theme restaurants are popping up all over town, too. How's this for starters: the **Hard Rock Cafe** (rock and roll), **Planet Hollywood** (movies and celebrities), the **Motown Cafe** (Detroit 1960s R&B), the **All Star Cafe** (sports celebrity), **Country Star** (country and western music), and the **Harley Davidson Cafe** (motorcycle mania).

Here's my take on this trend: Some wags say that once you've been to a theme restaurant like the Hard Rock Cafe, you'll never need to go again, because they're indistinguishable. Personally, I think their unique memorabilia can endlessly entertain the truly devoted, and if you've got kids along, they're pretty sure to be pleased. But one thing's not arguable: They are uniformly overpriced! (Eight bucks for a hamburger?!) One thing these theme restaurants are not is high on value.

Tourist Traps

All theme restaurants have adjoining gift shops where you can buy logo items or memorabilia. If you're looking for souvenirs or gifts for the folks at home, look elsewhere. Prices are often high at these shops, and the merchandise is not exactly unique.

Trend #3: The Chain Gang

National chain restaurants have descended on Las Vegas. Sure, you've always been able to find a **Denny's,** but now, as in most major metropolitan and suburban areas, Las Vegas offers the familiar foods of **Tony Roma's, Chili's Grill and Bar,** and **Lawry's The Prime Rib,** just to name a few.

One thing I've noticed at national chain restaurants in Las Vegas is that their prices are sometimes higher than those in other cities. In addition, some big chains that offer special meals don't offer them at their Vegas branches. In other words, if you're looking for a meal with the words "grand slam" in it, you aren't going to find it.

Trend #4: A Smorgasbord of Buffets

Every major hotel (and some minor ones) has a buffet, and it seems as if they're getting bigger and more expensive every time I visit. There are still few inexpensive ones in town ($3–$7), but just as everything is moving upscale here, so are the buffets. A Las Vegas vacation isn't really complete without at least one visit to a buffet (buffets have been an institution since the 1940s, when the El Rancho Hotel offered an all-you-can-eat spread for a buck!).

Location! Location! Location!

It used to be all about the Strip—and with good reason. There are literally hundreds of restaurants, buffets, and food stands along that one 4-mile stretch of road. If you want to sample a variety of foods on your trip but don't want to have to hop all over town to find them, I'd still tell you to stick close to the Strip. It has any type of food you can think of and quite a few you never dreamed of.

But many of the notable new hot spots are popping up elsewhere, especially on Paradise Road, which is now quickly becoming something of a Restaurant Row. Downtown is trying hard to play catch-up with the rest of the city; you'll find some scattered gems here and there.

The focus on the Strip and Paradise Road means that few visitors to Vegas venture out to discover the places serving up some of the best food in town. **The Liberty Cafe**, dishing up some of the best hamburgers and milkshakes in town, is only a few blocks from the Strip—but it's hidden inside a pharmacy. I've included many of these finds in the next chapter.

The Price Is Right

There's something for every budget in Las Vegas. You can easily feed a family of four for under 20 bucks or quickly blow $200 on dinner for two.

Quite frankly, the amount of money you spend on food depends on whether you can be satisfied with the likes of a Denny's or Sizzler. If you're like most of us and *eat* rather than *dine*, you're not going to have any trouble finding value in Las Vegas. Everyone is different, but I think that $30 to $50 per person, per day, is more than adequate for three solid, recommendable meals. You can do it for less if you want to pinch pennies, and if you plan on hitting all the high-priced theme restaurants, you can do it for a lot more.

Dollars & Sense

The farther away from tourist areas you get, the better the food bargains you'll find.

Taxes & Tipping

Sales tax in Las Vegas is 7 percent, which applies to food as well as merchandise, so remember that a $40 filet mignon is in fact a $42.80 filet mignon.

Your guideline for tipping for wait staff should be 15 percent of the check for satisfactory service, but going up to 20 percent is not unreasonable for extraordinary service (it's easier to figure out the math, too). Most buffets are self-serve as far as food is concerned, but the wait staff still serves drinks. A couple of dollars is an adequate tip for this service, while $5 or so might suffice for a large party.

Dressing the Part: What to Wear

For the most part, Las Vegas is a very informal town. You'll see people in jeans at even the best restaurants. There are still a few holdouts that require jackets and forbid all-American denim, so bring at least one nice outfit. A general rule of thumb is *if you have to call to make a reservation, ask about a dress code while you're on the phone.* If you don't have to make reservations, don't worry about what you're wearing.

A Few Notes on the Listings

Price Categories

The pricing system for meals at the restaurants listed in this chapter is based on the average cost of a dinner entree (à la carte). Here is how the restaurants are rated:

$$$$$	Very Expensive	Main courses all over $20
$$$$	Expensive	Most main courses $15–$19
$$$	Moderate	Most main courses $10–$14
$$	Inexpensive	Most main courses $5–$9
$	A Mind-Blowing Deal	

Location

Once again, I've divided the Strip into three sections: South, North, and Center. The borders of these areas correspond to those set up in chapter 6, "Hotels A to Z."

Also keep in mind that a *Paradise Road* designation means that the restaurant is *near* Paradise Road but not necessarily *on* it.

I've also included a few stand-out places that are not in any of the definable neighborhoods. These restaurants are given an *off-the-beaten-track* designation; it will be worth your while to go find them.

Parking

Unless otherwise noted, the restaurants listed are in the hotel/casinos, all of which have free self parking and valet parking.

Light Bites & Munchies for When You're on the Run

Maybe you're not in the mood for a full-scale meal. Maybe you don't have time before your 7:30 show reservations. Perhaps you just want something to nibble on to tide you over until that extravagant dinner you have planned. Or possibly, you blew too much money on video poker and now you're short on dough. If that's the situation you're in, many of the restaurants in chapter 10, "Making Your Restaurant Choice," won't do.

What are your options? A lot of the big hotels have food courts similar to what you'll find in your local mall, though. Often, the prices are slightly higher than what you're used to paying for similar fare at home, but not to the point of being outrageous. Below, you'll find a few of the better places in various neighborhoods. No matter where you are, one of these should be nearby.

On the South Strip

If you're on the south end of the Strip, **MGM Grand Hotel/Casino** has a Farmer's Market–style food court—but the casino area you have to go through to get there is so immense that I don't recommend it. Instead, go across the street to the **Monte Carlo Resort & Casino,** 3770 Las Vegas Blvd. S. (☎ **702/730-7777**), which has a food court featuring Haagen-Dazs, Nathan's Hot Dogs, the Golden Bagel, Sbarro, and the ubiquitous Golden Arches. It's open (varying from stand to stand) from 6am to 3am. You'll find it between the lobby (which is at the back of the hotel's first floor) and casino (at the front).

Bet You Didn't Know

In 1953, the Sands buried a time capsule on its grounds containing Sugar Ray Robinson's boxing gloves, Bing Crosby's pipe, and a wax impression of Jimmy Durante's nose, among other treasures.

Or right next door at **New York New York,** 3790 Las Vegas Blvd. S. (☎ **702/740-6969**), you'll find a bunch of (surprise!) New York–theme eateries located just inside the doors as you enter from the Brooklyn Bridge. They're scattered throughout the Greenwich Village and Times Square re-creations.

Farther down the street is the **Luxor,** 3900 Las Vegas Blvd. S. (☎ **702/262-4000**), which has a coffee house, Heidi's Yogurt, Nathan's Hot Dogs, Mickey D's, Swenson's ice cream, and Little Caesar's Pizza.

On the Center Strip

For those wandering the Center Strip, try **La Piazza Food Court, in Caesars Palace,** 3570 Las Vegas Blvd. S. (☎ **702/731-7110**), which has a Haagen-Dazs and a number of non-chain offerings. You can satisfy a wide variety of cravings here: chomp on sushi, Chinese stir-fry, deli, rotisserie chicken, smoked fish, or burritos. Or take advantage of the salad bar and fresh bakery. The food quality is leaps and bounds above that of the typical food court and has prices to reflect it ($7 to $15, which is still a reasonable deal). Hours vary at each place, but collectively, the food court is open from 8:30am to 11pm Sunday through Thursday and from 9am to midnight on Fridays and Saturdays. You'll find it opposite the entrance to the Forum Shops at the northern end of the casino. You could also wander through the **Forum Shops,** which is a glorified mall with some smaller food outlets.

Bet You Didn't Know

Former President Ronald Reagan performed at the Last Frontier in 1954. Those who saw him said he was a pretty good song-and-dance man.

On the North Strip

If you're casino hopping at the northern end of the Strip, your best bet is to check out the **Mardi Gras Food Court at the Riviera,** 2901 Las Vegas Blvd. S. (☎ 702/ 734-5110). It's adjacent to the main casino entrance. You'll find a Burger King, Panda Express, Pizza Hut, and other stands that sell everything from Mexican to Philippine food. Hours are different at each outlet, but are between 8am and 2am.

Inside the Tower Shops at the **Stratosphere Las Vegas,** 2000 Las Vegas Blvd. S. (☎ 702/380-7777), are chains like McDonald's, Nathan's Hot Dogs, the Rainforest Cafe, and Haagen-Dazs, plus a pizzeria, coffee house, and dessert places. Hours vary but are comparable to that of other food courts. If you come in through the main entrance, you should see a set of stairs and escalators directly in front of you. Take these to the second level, and voilà!

Downtown

If you're downtown, just cruise the **Fremont Street Experience**, an outdoor pedestrian mall that has an assortment of food vendors operating from carts or tucked between the casinos.

The Best Meal Deals in Town

Las Vegas is famous (or infamous, perhaps?) for its budget meals served in casino restaurants. Rest assured that that 69¢ shrimp cocktail probably isn't of the highest quality, but people chow down on these bargain meals all the time and seem perfectly content to save a few bucks on food that can be dropped at the blackjack table.

It's almost impossible to list specifics, since they change weekly, but here are a few places that offer bargain-basement food prices:

➤ **El Cortez Emerald Room**, 600 E. Fremont St., downtown
(☎ **702/385-5200**). A $1 bacon-and-egg breakfast. I kid you not.

➤ **Holiday Inn Casino Boardwalk Cyclone Coffee Shop**, 3750 Las
Vegas Blvd. S., on the South Strip at Harmon (☎ **702/735-2400**). An
all-you-can-eat fish fry for the low, low price of just $2.49.

➤ **Imperial Palace Coffee Shop**, 3535 Las Vegas Blvd. S., on the
Center Strip just north of Flamingo Ave. (☎ **702/731-3311**). A nighttime prime-rib special for $2.95. Get outta here!

➤ **Westward Ho Snack Bar**, 2900 Las Vegas Blvd. S., on the North
Strip next to Circus Circus (☎ **702/796-3300**). Have they got a deal
for you: full breakfasts from $1.99.

These places might not necessarily be serving what I've listed here, but they
usually offer some sort of special. The best way to find others is to read the
signs in front of the various casinos. They always advertise their current meal
deals.

Chapter 10

Making Your Restaurant Choice

In This Chapter

➤ Easy-to-use indexes of restaurants by price, location, and cuisine

➤ Reviews of my favorite restaurants

Loosen your belts and pick up your forks: It's time to eat. I've started this chapter off with indexes you can use to figure out which are the best bets for your particular tastes and needs. I've indexed by location, so you can find a good restaurant in the area that's most convenient for you; by price, so you can budget yourself; and by cuisine, so you can satisfy your cravings.

After that, it's on to my picks of the best restaurants in town, listed alphabetically so that they'll be easier for you to refer back to; each name is followed by its price range, what part of town it's in, and the type of cuisine you'll find there.

Price Categories

The price categories used in this chapter are based on the average cost of a dinner entree (à la carte):

$$$$$	Very Expensive	Main courses more than $20
$$$$	Expensive	Most main courses $15–$19
$$$	Moderate	Most main courses $10–$14
$$	Inexpensive	Most main courses $5–$9
$	A Mind-Blowing Deal	

Quick Picks: Las Vegas Restaurants at a Glance
Restaurant Index by Location

South Strip

All Star Cafe $$$

Country Star $$$

Coyote Cafe $$$$$

Emeril's New Orleans Fish House $$$$$

Gatsby's $$$$$

Harley Davidson Cafe $$$

The Luxor Pharoah's Pheast Buffet $$

Mizuno's $$$$$

Motown Cafe $$$

Center Strip

Bacchanal $$$$$

Bally's Big Kitchen Buffet $$

Buccaneer Bay Club $$$$

Chin's $$$$

Dive! $$$

Fiore $$$$$

Harrah's Fresh Market Buffet $$

The Mirage Buffet $$$

Morton's of Chicago $$$$$

Planet Hollywood $$$

The Range $$$$$

Rio's Carnival World Buffet $$

Spago $$$$

Stage Deli $$$

North Strip

Tony Roma's—A Place for Ribs $$$

Top of the World $$$$$

Downtown

Hugo's Cellar $$$$$

Limericks $$$$

Main Street Station Garden Court Buffet $$

Paradise

Fog City Diner $$$

Gordon Biersch Brewing Company $$$

Hard Rock Cafe $$$

Hippo & the Wild Bunch $$$

Lawry's The Prime Rib $$$$$

PF Chang's China Bistro $$$

Z Tejas Grill $$$

Off the Beaten Track

Garlic Cafe $$$$

Ginza $$$

Liberty Cafe $

Mediterranean Cafe & Market $

Pamplemousse $$$$$

Romano's Macaroni Grill $$$

Viva Mercados $$$

113

Restaurant Index by Price

$$$$$

Bacchanal (Center Strip)

Coyote Cafe (South Strip)

Emeril's New Orleans Fish House (South Strip)

Fiore (Center Strip)

Gatsby's (South Strip)

Hugo's Cellar (Downtown)

Lawry's The Prime Rib (Paradise Road)

Mizuno's (South Strip)

Morton's of Chicago (Center Strip)

Pamplemousse (Off the Beaten Track)

The Range (Center Strip)

Top of the World (North Strip)

$$$$

Buccaneer Bay Club (Center Strip)

Chin's (Center Strip)

Garlic Cafe (Off the Beaten Track)

Limericks (Downtown)

Spago (Center Strip)

$$$

All Star Cafe (South Strip)

Country Star (South Strip)

Dive! (Center Strip)

Fog City Diner (Paradise Road)

Ginza (Off the Beaten Track)

Gordon Biersch Brewing Company (Paradise Road)

Hard Rock Cafe (Paradise Road)

Harley Davidson Cafe (South Strip)

Hippo & the Wild Bunch (Paradise Road)

The Mirage Buffet (Center Strip)

Motown Cafe (South Strip)

PF Chang's China Bistro (Paradise Road)

Planet Hollywood (Center Strip)

Romano's Macaroni Grill (Off the Beaten Track)

Stage Deli (Center Strip)

Tony Roma's—A Place for Ribs (North Strip)

Viva Mercados (Off the Beaten Track)

Z Tejas Grill (Paradise Road)

$$

Bally's Big Kitchen Buffet (Center Strip)

Harrah's Fresh Market Buffet (Center Strip)

The Luxor Pharoah's Pheast Buffet (South Strip)

Main Street Station Garden Court Buffet (Downtown)

Rio's Carnival World Buffet (Center Strip)

$

Liberty Cafe (Off the Beaten Track)

Mediterranean Cafe & Market (Off the Beaten Track)

Restaurant Index by Cuisine

American

All Star Cafe ($$$/South Strip)

Buccaneer Bay Club ($$$$/Center Strip)

Dive! ($$$/Center Strip)

Fog City Diner ($$$/Paradise Road)

Hard Rock Cafe ($$$/Paradise Road)

Harley Davidson Cafe ($$$/South Strip)

Hippo & the Wild Bunch ($$$/Paradise Road)

Liberty Cafe ($/Off the Beaten Track)

Planet Hollywood ($$$/Center Strip)

Top of the World ($$$$$/North Strip)

Regional American

Country Star ($$$/South Strip/Southern & Barbecue)

Emeril's New Orleans Fish House ($$$$$/South Strip/Cajun & Creole)

Gordon Biersch Brewing Company ($$$/Paradise Road/California)

Motown Cafe ($$$/South Strip/Southwestern, Southern, & Cajun)

Spago ($$$$/Center Strip/California)

Stage Deli ($$$/Center Strip)

Tony Roma's—A Place for Ribs ($$$/North Strip)

Steak/Seafood

Lawry's The Prime Rib ($$$$$/Paradise Road)

Limericks ($$$$/Downtown)

Morton's of Chicago ($$$$$/Center Strip)

The Range ($$$$$/Center Strip)

Buffets & Brunches

Bally's Big Kitchen Buffet ($$/Center Strip)

Harrah's Fresh Market Buffet ($$/Center Strip)

The Luxor Pharoah's Pheast Buffet ($$/South Strip)

Main Street Station Garden Court Buffet ($$/Downtown)

The Mirage Buffet ($$$/Center Strip)

Rio's Carnival World Buffet ($$/Center Strip)

Mexican & Southwestern

Coyote Cafe ($$$$$/South Strip)

Viva Mercados ($$$/Off the Beaten Track)

Z Tejas Grill ($$$/Paradise Road)

Asian

Chin's ($$$$/Center Strip)

Gatsby's ($$$$$/South Strip)

Ginza ($$$/Off the Beaten Track)

Mizuno's ($$$$$/South Strip)

PF Chang's China Bistro ($$$/Paradise Road)

Other International

Bacchanal ($$$$/Center Strip/Continental)

Fiore ($$$$/Center Strip/Italian & Provincial)

Garlic Cafe ($$$$/Off the Beaten Track/International)

Hugo's Cellar ($$$$$/Downtown/International)

Mediterranean Cafe ($/Off the Beaten Track/Greek)

Pamplemousse ($$$$$/Off the Beaten Track/French)

Romano's Macaroni Grill ($$$/Off the Beaten Track/Italian)

My Favorite Las Vegas Restaurants A to Z

All Star Cafe

$$$. South Strip. AMERICAN.

This entry into the theme restaurant sweepstakes features memorabilia from major sports stars (Andre Agassi, Wayne Gretsky, Shaquille O'Neal, Tiger Woods, and so on) and the games they play. The menu sticks with traditional all-American specialties like hamburgers, hot dogs, and pastas. They're satisfying but a little expensive for what you're getting. Best for dedicated sports fans and kids.

3785 Las Vegas Blvd. S. (in the Showcase Mall next to the MGM Grand Hotel/Casino). ☎ *702/795-8326. Reservations accepted for parties of 10 or more only.* **Main courses:** *$6–$18. DC, DISC, JCB, MC, V.* **Open:** *Sun–Thurs 11am–midnight, Fri–Sat 11am–1am.*

Bacchanal

$$$$$. Center Strip. ITALIAN.

This is the quintessential over-the-top Vegas dining experience: a Roman (food) orgy. Costumed "wine goddesses" dance and lounge about while Zeus, Cleopatra, and of course, Caesar put in appearances. Against a palatial setting, dinner is a sumptuous multicourse feast with free-flowing wine and champagne—so who cares what kind of food they serve? If you do, it's primarily steakhouse fare, like beef filets, roast lamb, and various types of seafood. Dessert is, as would be expected, a spectacle. Silly Vegas fun all the way.

In Caesars Palace, 3570 Las Vegas Blvd. S. ☎ *702/731-7110. Reservations required.* **Prices:** *The fixed-price meal is $69.50 (includes all courses, but not tax and tip).* **Open:** *Tues–Sat 6–11pm, with seatings at 6, 6:30, 9, and 9:30pm.*

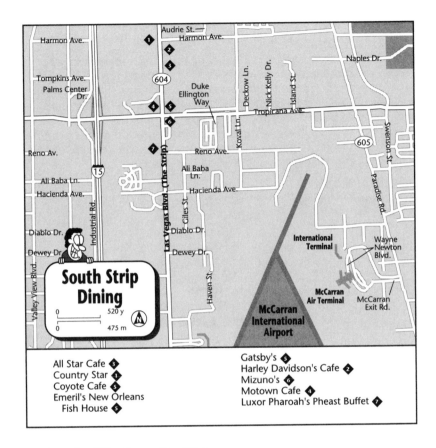

All Star Cafe ◆③
Country Star ◆①
Coyote Cafe ◆⑤
Emeril's New Orleans
    Fish House ◆⑤

Gatsby's ◆⑤
Harley Davidson's Cafe ◆②
Mizuno's ◆⑥
Motown Cafe ◆④
Luxor Pharoah's Pheast Buffet ◆⑦

Bally's Big Kitchen Buffet

$$. Center Strip. BUFFET.

This is not one of those cheap chow-downs where quality is an afterthought. You'll feel that your money was well spent when you see the fresh and expertly prepared spread. Traditional salads, fruits, and vegetables are accompanied by interesting entrees like peppercorn steak or barbecued chicken. The Sterling Sunday Brunch, at $50 a head, is expensive but lavish by any standard, with caviar and champagne served. The dinner buffet often features Chinese selections.

In Bally's Las Vegas, 3645 Las Vegas Blvd. S. ☎ *702/739-4111. Reservations not accepted.* **Buffet prices:** *breakfast $8.95, brunch $9.95, dinner $12.95, Sunday brunch $9.95. AE, CB, DC, DISC, MC, V.* **Open:** *Mon–Sat 7am–2:30pm, Sun 9:30am–2:30pm, daily 4:00–10:30pm.*

Buccaneer Bay Club
$$$$. Center Strip. AMERICAN/CONTINENTAL.

This Treasure Island restaurant is a standout and a great place to splurge. There are some funky choices thrown in among the traditional favorites, and the service is impeccable. And the setting—well, it's something you'll only see in Las Vegas. The meandering pirate-theme layout offers intimate dining and a chance to watch a swashbuckling pirate battle (waged every 90 minutes) from the windows. You can order well-prepared, straightforward American and continental dishes or get a little more adventurous with some delicious offerings, like the quail appetizer or the Colorado buffalo prime rib.

In Treasure Island, 3300 Las Vegas Blvd. S. ☎ *702/894-7350. Reservations required, especially for window tables.* **Main courses:** *$16–$26. AE, CB, DC, DISC, JCB, MC, V.* **Open:** *Daily 5–10:30pm.*

Extra! Extra!

If you've got the kids in tow, call ahead to find out if restaurants offer children's menus and prices. Depending on the age of your children, you should also want to inquire about high chairs and booster seats (for babies and toddlers), coloring books (for toddlers), or muzzles for unruly teenagers (just kidding). If I were you, I'd make a beeline for **Planet Hollywood** ($$$/Center Strip), **Hippo & The Wild Bunch** ($$$/Paradise Road), or **The Luxor Pharoah's Pheast Buffet** ($$/South Strip).

Time-Savers

If you happen to be in town during a major convention, avoid the restaurants on Paradise Road. These are nearest to the convention center, and they'll be packed to the rafters.

Chin's
$$$$. Center Strip. CHINESE.

This place is an institution. The consistently excellent food has been drawing tourists and locals alike for more than two decades (and that's an eternity in Vegas). This isn't your average take-out joint. Chin's is gourmet all the way, bringing a deft touch to old standbys such as orange chicken or barbecued pork. Especially notable is the strawberry chicken—lightly breaded fillets under a warm strawberry sauce. Amazing! An understated, elegant atmosphere and terrific service complete the package.

3200 Las Vegas Blvd. S. (in the Fashion Show Mall). ☎ *702/733-8899. Reservations recommended.* **Main courses:** *$10–$12 for lunch, $12–$28 for dinner. AE, MC, V.* **Open:** *Mon–Sat 11:30am–10pm, Sun noon–10pm.*

Country Star
$$$. South Strip. SOUTHERN.

Put on your cowboy boots and line dance your way into this spot, where the theme is country-western music. You'll find lots of fun displays of clothes, records, and bric-a-brac from the likes of Reba McEntire, Dolly Parton, and Merle Haggard, to name a few. Music videos play constantly. The atmosphere is not quite as boisterous and relentless as the vibe at the Hard Rock Cafe. The Deep South–influenced food (think barbecue and chicken-fried steak) is better than what's served up at most theme restaurants, if a little pricey for what it is. Really good BBQ sauce, too!

3724 Las Vegas Blvd. S. (at Harmon Ave.). ☎ *702/740-8400. Reservations accepted for large parties only.* **Main courses:** *$5–$21. DC, DISC, JCB, MC, V.* **Open:** *Sun–Thurs 11am–midnight, Fri–Sat 11am–1am.*

Coyote Cafe
$$$$$. South Strip. SOUTHWESTERN.

This is actually two restaurants in one: an upscale Grill Room and an informal Cafe. Menus in both rooms are Southwestern in flavor (with some Mexican, Cajun, and Creole touches here and there) and offer an innovative and contemporary flair. The chef has a sure hand, with creations such as the *painted soup*—so-called because the black bean and smoked Cheddar concoction is "painted" with chipotle and garnished with salsa fresca and chili powder. I recommend the lively Cafe area (with lighter fare) for its fun atmosphere and cheaper prices; you can also get a spicy Southwestern breakfast here.

In the MGM Grand Hotel/Casino, 3799 Las Vegas Blvd. S. ☎ *702/891-7349. Reservations recommended for Grill Room, not accepted for Cafe.* **Main courses:** *Grill Room $17–$32, Cafe $8–$18. AE, CB, DC, DISC, JCB, MC, V.* **Open:** *Grill Room—daily 5:30–10pm, Cafe—daily 8am–11pm.*

Dive!
$$$. Center Strip. SANDWICHES.

This theme restaurant emerges from director Steven Spielberg's imagination with a decor suggesting the inside of a (pure fantasy) submarine. There are portholes, sonar screens, working periscopes, and a high-tech video simulation of a sub dive every hour. Kids will love it. Oh, and by the way, they serve food, too—mostly submarine sandwiches, of course.

3200 Las Vegas Blvd. S. (in the Fashion Show Mall). ☎ *702/369-DIVE. Reservations accepted for large parties only.* **Sandwiches:** *$6.95–$13.95. AE, CB, DC, DISC, MC, V.* **Open:** *Sun–Thurs 11:30am–10pm, Fri–Sat 11:30am–11pm.*

119

Emeril's New Orleans Fish House
$$$$$. South Strip. SEAFOOD/CAJUN.

Pow! That's how celebrity chef Emeril Lagasse approaches his kitchen—with spicy enthusiasm and creative touches that make you sit up and take notice. The selections are terrific, all dressed up with a taste of the Big Easy (as Emeril would say, "Let's kick it up a notch!"). There's a Cajun spin on everything from ahi steak to the freshest mussels, clams, and oysters. Try the legendary lobster "cheesecake" or barbecued shrimp. The non-fish food includes poultry, beef, and vegetarian choices that are equally inventive and tasty. A sinful dessert menu (don't miss the banana cream pie) completes the package.

*In the MGM Grand Hotel/Casino, 3799 Las Vegas Blvd. S. ☎ 702/891-7374. Reservations required. **Main courses:** $12–$18 for lunch, $18–$49 for dinner. AE, CB, DC, DISC, MC, V. **Open:** Daily 11am–3pm and 5:30–10:30pm.*

Bacchanal ⬥	Harrah's Fresh Market Buffet ⬥	The Range ⬥
Bally's Big Kitchen Buffet ⬥	Mirage Buffet ⬥	Rio's Carnival World Buffet ⬥
Buccaneer Bay Club ⬥	Morton's of Chicago ⬥	Spago ⬥
Fiore ⬥	Planet Hollywood ⬥	Stage Deli ⬥

Fiore
$$$$$. Center Strip. ITALIAN.

The food at Fiore is superb, and the attention to detail in the decor and service provides a memorable experience from start to finish. It's a beautiful room, with exquisitely appointed tables, but you might choose to dine on the terrace. The dishes are sophisticated yet hearty; the barbecued Atlantic salmon in honeyed hickory sauce is a winner, as are the creations that emerge from the wood-burning pizza ovens. Wine lovers will enjoy choosing from among the more than 400 selections, and hand-rolled cigars are available after dinner for a smoke on the terrace. Not for the budget conscious or those who prefer Italian cuisine to be spaghetti and meatballs.

In the Rio Hotel & Casino, 3700 W. Flamingo Rd. ☎ **702/252-7702.** *Reservations recommended.* **Main courses:** *$26–$48. AE, CB, DC, DISC, MC, V.* **Open:** *Daily 5–11pm.*

Fog City Diner
$$$. Paradise Road. AMERICAN.

This is a fun, trendy, upscale incarnation of the classic roadside diner. Those old comfort food standbys are given a creative, contemporary twist: plain old meatloaf is blackened with tomato chutney gravy; mashed potatoes have the zing of garlic. Fish lovers will gravitate toward the seasonal selections, clam chowder, and Pacific Northwest oysters, all billed as the freshest in Las Vegas. Indecisive types can try the grazing plate, which offers small portions of a variety of entrees.

325 Hughes Center Dr. (off Flamingo just west of Paradise). ☎ **702/737-0200.** *Reservations recommended.* **Main courses:** *$7–$16. AE, CB, DC, DISC, MC, V.* **Open:** *Sun–Thurs 11:30am–10pm, Fri–Sat 11:30am–11pm.*

Garlic Cafe
$$$$. Off the Beaten Track. INTERNATIONAL.

Garlic lovers should make a pilgrimage to this unique restaurant, where garlic livens up a wide array of dishes that range the globe for inspiration—from Thailand to Jamaica, Japan, Hungary, the U.S., and beyond. You can decide how much garlic you want (on a scale of 1 to 5 heads) in each dish, and the wait staff will help make sure you don't overwhelm the food or yourself. Entrees are huge and amusingly named (Salmon in Garfunkel Crust). After-dinner mints, anyone?

3650 S. Decatur Blvd. (west of the Strip at Spring Mountain Rd.). ☎ **702/221-0266.** *Reservations recommended.* **Main courses:** *$10–$28. AE, DC, MC, V.* **Open:** *Daily 5–10pm.*

Extra! Extra!

For a knockout view, check out **Top of the World** ($$$$$/North Strip). The food may not live up to the view, but it's an amazing sight to be 100 stories over the Strip. Runners-up include **The Range** ($$$$$/Center Strip), where large picture windows also overlook the Strip, and the **Buccaneer Bay Club** ($$$$/Center Strip), where you get to scope out a live–action pirate battle.

Gatsby's
$$$$$. South Strip.

If money is no object, look no farther. This is simply the finest restaurant in town. Chef Terence Fong takes familiar dishes and elevates them to a new level by insisting on the freshest seasonal ingredients and bringing subtle but exciting innovations to their preparation. Simple ahi tuna is made memorable by getting an Asian accent, with a sesame seed crust and a spicy wasabi butter. The menu offers sumptuous choices, including dishes prepared with Maine lobster, the finest foie gras, and beluga caviar. Desserts are magical as well, including five different flavors of soufflés, each one more triumphant than the next. A full multicourse dinner with wine can easily run you $100 a head.

In the MGM Grand Hotel/Casino, 3799 Las Vegas Blvd. S. ☎ ***702/891-7337.*** *Reservations recommended; jackets suggested for men.* **Main courses: $30–$58.** *AE, CB, DC, DISC, MC, V.* **Open:** *Wed–Mon 6–10:30pm.*

Ginza
$$$. Off the Beaten Track. JAPANESE.

This lovely little restaurant with traditional Japanese decor has been around for almost 20 years, offering an extensive (and extremely fresh) selection of sushi. What could a *Vegas roll* possibly be? It's salmon, tuna, yellowtail, and avocado rolled with seaweed in sesame-studded rice and deep-fried—delicious. Other options include tempura vegetables; sukiyaki; and a variety of beef, chicken, and seafood entrees.

1000 E. Sahara Ave., between State St. and the Maryland Pkwy. ☎ ***702/ 732-3080.*** *Reservations accepted for large parties only.* **Main courses: $13–$18.** *AE, MC, V.* **Open:** *Tues–Sun 5pm–1am.*

Gordon Biersch Brewing Company
$$$. Paradise Road. CALIFORNIA.

The draw here is California cuisine served in a casual brew-pub atmosphere (think stainless steel beer vats). Among the starters are *satays* (seafood, beef, and more on skewers), creative pizzas from a wood-burning oven, and stir-fry for starters. Dinner entrees are along the lines of beer-basted meatloaf, seared king salmon, charred tuna steak, and filet mignon. Don't miss the garlic

French fries—yum! Portions are plentiful and tasty, and the German-style lagers, brewed on-site, wash it all down perfectly.

3987 Paradise Rd. (just north of Flamingo). ☎ *702/312-5247. Reservations not accepted.* **Main courses:** *$11–$16. AE, DISC, MC, V.* **Open:** *Sun–Thurs 11:30am–10pm, Fri–Sat 11:30am–11pm; bar open until 2am, with live bands on weekends.*

Hard Rock Cafe
$$$. Paradise Road. AMERICAN.

From Elvis to Jimi Hendrix to Kurt Cobain, the music is the message at this theme restaurant, a shrine to all things rock 'n' roll. The requisite memorabilia include guitars, gold records, and costumes galore. It's not much different from any of the other Hard Rocks around the world, so if you've seen one, this won't come as much of a surprise. Expensive but respectable burgers rule here, but there are a few tasty salads to lighten the fare. Kids can't get enough.

4475 Paradise Rd. (at Harmon Ave.). ☎ *702/733-8400. Reservations not accepted.* **Main courses:** *$5–$14. AE, DC, MC, V.* **Open:** *Sun–Thurs 11am–11:30pm, Fri–Sat 11am–midnight.*

Harley Davidson Cafe
$$$. South Strip. AMERICAN.

Another theme restaurant enterprise, this one's dedicated to all things Harley, featuring motorcycle memorabilia, gift items, and an all-American menu with everything from burgers, sandwiches, and hot dogs to barbecue and pasta. There are a few unique items, and the desserts are all-out decadent (chocolate-chip Toll House–cookie pie). The prices are on the high side for what you get, and the music's blaring, but that's no different than the deal at any of the other theme restaurants in town. Live big- (or semi-big) name bands like the Monkees perform on occasion. There's also a bar, gift shop, and Harley slot machines.

3725 Las Vegas Blvd. S. (at Harmon). ☎ *702/740-4555, Internet www.harley-davidsoncafe.com. Reservations accepted only for parties of 10 or more.* **Main courses:** *$6–$18. AE, DC, DISC, MC, V.* **Open:** *Sun–Thurs 11:30am–midnight (bar open until 1am), Fri–Sat 11:30am–1am (bar open until 2am).*

Harrah's Fresh Market Buffet
$$. Center Strip. BUFFET.

Harrah's buffet is all new (as of 1997) and features individual serving stations instead of one endlessly long buffet line. Unique specialties include seafood, pastas, and Asian, Mexican, and American dishes (including Cajun/Creole and traditional meatloaf with mashed potatoes). The farmer's market decor is a bit overdone for my taste, but the quality and quantity of the food is a cut above average, and the staff is extremely friendly.

In Harrah's Las Vegas, 3475 Las Vegas Blvd. S. ☎ *702/369-5000. Reservations not accepted.* **Buffet prices:** *breakfast $6.99, lunch $8.99, dinner $11.99. AE, DC, DISC, MC, V.* **Open:** *Daily 7–11am, 11am–3:30pm, and 4–10pm.*

North Strip Dining

0 — 440 y
0 — 402 m

Chin's ❹
Dive! ❹
Morton's of Chicago ❹
Sahara Oasis Buffet ❷
Tony Roma's-A Place for Ribs ❸
Top of the World ❶

Hippo & the Wild Bunch

$$$. Paradise Road. AMERICAN.

This place is a hoot. Step into a vibrant, whimsical jungle world populated by wacky animal sculptures. It's loud and festive, with rock music, a wait staff on roller skates, and even a balloon artist making hats and animals for guests. Kids adore it! As the evening wears on, it becomes a grown-up night-club. They could get away with serving so-so food here, but it's surprisingly good. The wide-ranging menu includes pizza, pot stickers, and Southwestern dishes, plus some mighty fine burgers.

4503 Paradise Rd. (at Harmon Ave.). ☎ *702/731-5446. Reservations not accepted.* **Main courses:** *$6–$14 (children's menu $2–$3). AE, CB, DC, DISC, MC, V.* **Open:** *Sun–Thurs 11am–3am, Fri–Sat 11am–5am.*

Hugo's Cellar

$$$$$. Downtown. INTERNATIONAL.

A red rose is given to the female guests upon arrival—just one of the many nice touches that make you feel pampered here. Step through the romantic bar area, and join a mostly local crowd in the dining room. The menu is fairly standard; don't come looking for much innovation. But there are nice touches, such as the salads prepared at your table and the chocolate-dipped fruits that cap off the meal (the prices below look awfully high, but these extras are included). The lovely, cozy wood-and-brick room and the flawless service add up to make this a good choice for a romantic dinner.

In the Four Queens, 202 Fremont St. ☎ ***702/385-4011***. *Reservations required.* ***Main courses:*** *$24–$35. AE, DC, DISC, MC, V.* ***Open:*** *Daily 5:30–10:30pm.*

Lawry's The Prime Rib
$$$$$. Paradise Road. STEAK-HOUSE.

Lawry's practically invented prime rib, and they sure know how to do it right. The elaborate meal presentation includes 50 years' worth of traditional touches, like the spinning salad bowl (too hard to explain, but trust me) and the metal carving carts piled high with meat for you to select from. There are other things on the menu these days (fresh fish, for example), but people come here for a seriously satisfying carnivorous experience. You should, too, if you like prime rib.

Extra! Extra!

When your ears are ringing from the ca-ching of slot machines and you want a nice place for quiet conversation, head for **Morton's of Chicago** ($$$$$) and **Chin's** ($$$$) on the Center Strip or **Hugo's Cellar** ($$$$$) downtown.

4043 Howard Hughes Pkwy. (just west of Paradise Rd.). ☎ ***702/893-2223***. *Reservations recommended.* ***Main courses:*** *$19–$30. AE, DC, DISC, JCB, MC, V.* ***Open:*** *Sun–Thurs 5–10pm, Fri–Sat 5–11pm.*

Liberty Cafe
$. Off the Beaten Track. DINER.

Small, showing its age a bit, and decidedly down to earth—isn't that what a 24-hour diner is supposed to be? Take a seat in a vinyl booth or at the counter, and try one of the best burgers in town plus an old-fashioned creamy milkshake. Or how about meatloaf, ground-round steak, or biscuits and gravy? It's all good, it's unbelievably cheap, and it's a welcome relief from the manufactured theme restaurants and pretentious dining rooms that dominate this town.

1700 S. Las Vegas Blvd. (inside the Blue Castle Pharmacy, just north of the Stratosphere Tower). ☎ ***702/383-0101***. *Reservations not accepted.* ***Main courses:*** *Nothing over $7. No credit cards.* ***Open:*** *Daily 24 hours.*

Limericks
$$$$. Downtown. STEAKHOUSE.

This is a classic steakhouse: comfortable, hearty, and plush. You'll sit in luxurious booths that occupy a sort of Olde English drawing room. The portions are beyond generous, and the T-bones, prime rib, and filet mignon are so tender they melt in your mouth. No surprises here, nothing stuffy or trendy—just solid food in a comfortable atmosphere.

In Fitzgerald's Casino Holiday Inn, 301 E. Fremont St. ☎ ***702/388-2400***. *Reservations recommended.* ***Main courses:*** *$14–$21. AE, DISC, MC, V.* ***Open:*** *Daily 5:30–10:30pm.*

The Luxor Pharoah's Pheast Buffet
$$. South Strip. BUFFET.
This is a great value and offers better-than-average buffet food. It's all set in an amusing "archaeological dig." All the standards are here (salads, fresh fruit, a carving station with turkey and ham), plus some interesting twists, like Mexican, Chinese stir-fry, and Italian pastas. A huge, meandering layout amongst the King-Tut's–tomb decor can be confusing, and be prepared for long lines at peak dining times; try to come during off-hours after the rush has died down.

In the Luxor, 3900 Las Vegas Blvd. S. ☎ *702/262-4000. Reservations not accepted.* **Buffet prices:** *breakfast $5.99, lunch $6.49, dinner $8.99. AE, DC, DISC, MC, V.* **Open:** *Daily 7am–11pm.*

Main Street Station Garden Court Buffet
$$. Downtown. BUFFET.
A buffet is a buffet is a buffet, right? Well, actually, Main Street stands out. It has succeeded in rising above the rest with a beautiful dining room (high ceilings and actual windows!—a rarity in Vegas) plus original food. Selections are prepared at stations that include barbecue and soul food, Chinese and Hawaiian specialties, and wood-fired, brick-oven pizzas. On Friday nights, there's a seafood buffet that features lobster and other fresh fish.

In the Main Street Station, 200 N. Main St. ☎ *702/387-1896. Reservations not accepted.* **Buffet prices:** *breakfast $4.99, lunch $6.99, dinner $8.99, Friday seafood buffet $12.99, Sunday champagne brunch $7.99. AE, CB, DC, DISC, MC, V.* **Open:** *Daily 7–10:30am, 11am–3pm, and 4–10pm. Sunday brunch 7am–3pm.*

Mediterranean Cafe & Market
$. Off the Beaten Track. GREEK/MIDDLE EASTERN.
This is a wonderful little gem—an authentic, family-owned Middle Eastern restaurant offering great value and terrific food with no glitz and neon in sight. The *gyros* (lamb and beef in a pita) are fresh and delicious, and the menu features other favorites, like phyllo pie served with a side of hummus, and chicken and vegetable kabobs. Eat here and then get some to take home at the adjoining market.

4147 S. Maryland Pkwy. (at Flamingo Rd.). ☎ *702/731-6030. Reservations not accepted.* **Main courses:** *Nothing over $5. AE, MC, DISC, V.* **Open:** *Daily 8am–10pm.*

The Mirage Buffet
$$$. Center Strip. BUFFET.
It's not surprising that one of the best hotels in town would also have one of the best buffets. It costs a little more than some of the others, but you dine in a lovely garden setting and choose from a magnificent array of selections that are uniformly head and shoulders above the cheaper competition in quality. The enormous salad bar, with more than 25 types of salads, and the

dessert table, laden with sweet temptations, are especially notable. Sunday brunch adds free champagne, smoked salmon, and fruit-filled crepes for starters.

In the Mirage, 3400 Las Vegas Blvd. S. ☎ *702/791-7111. Reservations not accepted.* **Buffet prices:** *breakfast $7.50, lunch $8.95, dinner $12.95, Sunday brunch $13.95. Children ages 4–10 eat for half price, and children under 4 eat free. AE, CB, DC, DISC, MC, V.* **Open:** *Mon–Sat 7am–9:30pm, Sun 8am–9:30pm.*

Mizuno's
$$$$$. South Strip. JAPANESE.
Skilled chefs wield their knives with amazing speed and dexterity at the table grills (complete with a light show flashing overhead). Their deft preparations command everyone's attention in this stunning restaurant, where the decor includes antique Japanese scrolls and shoji screens. Choose from teppanyaki prepared steak, filet mignon, shrimp, lobster, chicken, or vegetable tempura— all flavorful and prepared right before your eyes.

In the Tropicana Resort & Casino, 3801 Las Vegas Blvd. S. ☎ *702/739-2222. Reservations recommended.* **Full dinners:** *$15–$39. AE, CB, DC, MC V.* **Open:** *Daily 5–10:30pm.*

Morton's of Chicago
$$$$$. Center Strip. STEAKHOUSE.
Thick, juicy, tender steaks and the occasional celebrity sighting are the primary draws here. The decor gives it an exclusive-club feel, which is why you may see a movie star or Siegfried & Roy slicing into the succulent prime rib. Maine lobster, swordfish, oregano chicken, lamb chops, and veal are all on the menu. You'll devour the basket of warm onion bread instantly, but try to save room for a miniature soufflé to top off your feast.

3200 Las Vegas Blvd. S. (in the Fashion Show Mall). ☎ *702/893-0703. Reservations recommended.* **Main courses:** *$18–$30. AE, CB, DC, JBC, MC, V.* **Open:** *Mon–Sat 5:30–10:30pm, Sun 5–9:30pm.*

Motown Cafe
$$$. South Strip. REGIONAL AMERICAN.
Yes, another theme production, this one celebrates the Detroit music scene of the 1960s and early 1970s. Martha Reeves & the Vandellas, Diana Ross, The Jackson 5—their memorabilia is here and their classic hits provide the background music while you dine on perfectly ordinary but satisfying burgers, fries, Cajun/Creole dishes, or light Southwestern fare. As with other theme restaurants, it's a little high-priced for what you get. After dinner, they crank up the tunes for dancing into the wee hours.

In New York New York, 3790 Las Vegas Blvd. S. ☎ *702/895-9653. Reservations not accepted.* **Main courses:** *$6–$17. AE, DISC, MC, V.* **Open:** *Sun–Thurs 8am–11pm, Fri–Sat 8am–midnight.*

Pamplemousse
$$$$$. Off the Beaten Track. FRENCH.

An intimate French bistro in the middle of Vegas? Stranger things have happened. It's a lovely and charming hideaway, where the fare is hearty, traditional French country favorites, accompanied by an excellent selection of wines. The menu changes daily, but look for crispy duck breast or an elegant rack of lamb; most dishes are created with wonderful, rich sauces. The service is outstanding.

400 E. Sahara Ave. (just east of Paradise Rd.). ☎ *702/733-2066. Reservations required.* **Main courses:** *$18–$25. AE, CB, DC, DISC, MC, V.* **Open:** *Two seatings nightly, 6–6:30pm and 9–9:30pm.*

PF Chang's China Bistro
$$$. Paradise Road. CHINESE.

Part of a small chain, this restaurant offers fantastic Chinese food in a lively bistro setting. I recommend starting your meal with the spiced chicken, vegetable lettuce wraps, or Peking ravioli stuffed with ground pork. Entrees run the gamut from lemon pepper shrimp to Malaysian chicken, but even the basics like Mongolian beef and sweet-and-sour pork are delicious. The portions are more than generous, and the service is among the best in town. Highly recommended.

4165 S. Paradise Rd. (just south of Flamingo). ☎ *702/792-2207. Reservations not accepted.* **Main courses:** *$8–$13. AE, DC, DISC, MV, V.* **Open:** *Sun–Thurs 11:15am–11pm, Fri–Sat 11:15am–midnight.*

Planet Hollywood
$$$. Center Strip. AMERICAN.

By now, you've surely heard of this chain of theme restaurants owned by action mega-stars Arnold Schwarzenegger and Sylvester Stallone (among others). There's a lot of movie and TV memorabilia (including Barbara Eden's genie bottle!), always a boisterous young crowd, and a menu that actually offers interesting choices, like blackened shrimp and the famous Captain Crunch Chicken (yep, it's what it sounds like). It's overpriced and overwhelming, but hey, that's Hollywood for you, and your kids won't let you skip it.

In Forum Shops at Caesars Palace, 3500 Las Vegas Blvd. S. ☎ *702/791-STAR. Reservations not accepted.* **Main courses:** *$8–$20. AE, DC, MC, V.* **Open:** *Sun–Thurs 11am–midnight, Fri–Sat 11am–1am.*

The Range
$$$$$. Center Strip. STEAKHOUSE.

In my opinion, this the best steakhouse in town. The warm copper-and-mahogany interior is classy and plush yet not intimidating, and panoramic windows offer incredible views of the Strip below. The menu is limited to what the kitchen does best—chicken, seafood, salads, and of course, wonderful, tender steaks. Side dishes are served family style—a neat touch. Try not to miss the five-onion soup appetizer (baked in a large onion with cheese) or the chicken quesadillas.

*In Harrah's Las Vegas, 3475 Las Vegas Blvd. S. ☎ 702/369-5000. Reservations highly recommended. AE, CB, DC, DISC, MC, V. **Main courses:** $19–$27. **Open:** Daily 5:30–11pm.*

Bet You Didn't Know

Arnold and Sly are taking their theme restaurant to the next level with plans for the Planet Hollywood Hotel & Casino, a 3,000-room resort designed to compete against the Hard Rock. It'll be located on the Strip next to the Desert Inn and is slated for a 1999 opening.

Rio's Carnival World Buffet
$$. Center Strip. BUFFET.

Locals consistently vote this the best buffet in town. There's an incredible selection—food stations include barbecue and ribs, stir-fry, Mexican, Chinese, sushi and teppanyaki, Italian, and diner food (burgers and hot dogs). It's all fresh and well prepared. Some people love the festive carnival decor (here and in the rest of the hotel), but I find it too rowdy and a little much for my taste.

*In the Rio Hotel & Casino, 3700 W. Flamingo Rd. ☎ 702/252-7777. Reservations not accepted. **Buffet prices:** breakfast $5.55, lunch $7.77, dinner $9.99, weekend brunch $7.99. AE, CB, DC, MC, V. **Open:** Mon–Fri 7–10:30am, 11am–3pm, and 3:30–10pm; Sat–Sun 7am–10pm.*

Romano's Macaroni Grill
$$$. Off the Beaten Track. ITALIAN.

The moderately priced Italian food here is better than what you'll find at the high-rent places and a lot less pretentious in presentation. A warm ambiance enhances selections like thin-crust pizzas, pastas, chicken, and fresh-baked breads. They've got a full bar and a large wine list, and an excellent array of desserts.

*2400 W. Sahara Ave. (just west of I-15 on your right). ☎ 702/248-9500. Reservations not accepted. **Main courses:** $5–$17. AE, CB, DC, DISC, MC, V. **Open:** Sun–Thurs 11am–10pm, Fri–Sat 11am–11pm.*

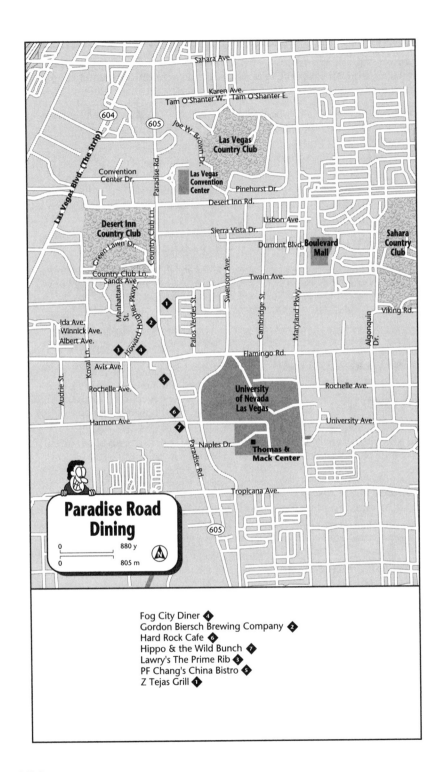

Fog City Diner ⬥
Gordon Biersch Brewing Company ⬥
Hard Rock Cafe ⬥
Hippo & the Wild Bunch ⬥
Lawry's The Prime Rib ⬥
PF Chang's China Bistro ⬥
Z Tejas Grill ⬥

Spago
$$$$. Center Strip. CALIFORNIA.

Celebrity chef Wolfgang Puck brought his famed L.A. restaurant to Vegas a few years ago and immediately raised the bar for dining excellence in town. Smoked salmon pizza, Chinois chicken salad, scallops, and crispy Chinese-style duck are among your choices, all lovingly prepared and presented. The vaguely industrial decor and high prices lend an air of pretentiousness to the proceedings in the dining room, so perhaps the European-style sidewalk cafe out front is a better bet.

In the Forum Shops at Caesars Palace, 3500 Las Vegas Blvd. S. ☎ *702/ 369-6300. Reservations recommended for the dining room, not accepted for the cafe.* **Main courses:** *$14–$28 in the dining room, $9–$17 in the cafe. AE, CB, DC, DISC, MC, V.* **Open:** *Dining room—Sun–Thurs 6–10:30pm, Fri–Sat 5:30–11pm; cafe—daily 11am–1am.*

Stage Deli
$$$. Center Strip. DELI.

This outpost of a New York City legend retains all its flair even way out here in the desert. They actually fly in the fresh-baked breads, meats, bagels, lox, and pickles from the Big Apple daily, so you're getting the real deal here. There's a huge (and I do mean *huge*) menu with all the standard deli offerings, like pastrami, knishes, and matzo-ball soup. The graffiti-strewn walls add urban authenticity. Great for a quick, inexpensive breakfast, too!

Bet You Didn't Know

During a heat wave in the summer of 1953, the Sands moved a roulette table into the swimming pool so gamblers could play in comfort.

In the Forum Shops at Caesars Palace, 3500 Las Vegas Blvd. S. ☎ *702/893-4045. Reservations accepted for large parties only.* **Main courses:** *$6–$14. AE, DC, DISC, MCB, MC, V.* **Open:** *Sun–Thurs 7:30am–10:30pm, Fri–Sat 7:30am–midnight.*

Tony Roma's—A Place for Ribs
$$$. North Strip. AMERICAN.

This is an outpost of a nation-wide chain, and the chain itself voted the Stardust branch the best of its 140 locations in terms of service, food quality, and cleanliness. If you've ever been to a Tony Roma's, you'll know what to expect, but for the uninitiated, it's all about barbecue: shrimp, chicken, burgers, and their signature baby-back ribs. Forget about your cholesterol count and indulge. Desserts are a variety of freshly baked pies, and there's also a full bar. There's another branch downtown at 200 E. Fremont St. (inside Sam Boyd's Fremont Hotel & Casino; ☎ **702/385-6257**).

In the Stardust Resort & Casino, 3000 Las Vegas Blvd. S. ☎ *702/732-6111. Reservations not accepted.* **Main courses:** *$8–$13. AE, CB, DC, DISC, MC, V.* **Open:** *Sun–Thurs 5–11pm, Fri–Sat 5pm–midnight.*

131

Extra! Extra!

When you're so hungry you could eat a horse, head to any of the buffets mentioned earlier and pile it on. My favorites are at **The Mirage** and **Harrah's Las Vegas,** both on the Center Strip, and at **Main Street Station,** downtown. If you'd rather have waiter service, check out the monster portions at **PF Chang's China Bistro** ($$$/Paradise Road).

Top of the World
$$$$$. North Strip. AMERICAN.

Talk about a room with a view! This place is over 100 stories up and revolves slowly to give diners breathtaking vistas of the entire city, day or night. And make no mistake—that's the reason to come, because the food isn't nearly as exciting as the sea of neon lights below. It's terribly expensive and not at all memorable. Exceptions are the appetizers (Southwestern spring rolls, bruschetta) and desserts (the 9-inch tall chocolate Stratosphere Tower re-creation is a silly and delicious must). The panorama makes it worthwhile, but just barely.

At the top of Stratosphere Las Vegas, 2000 Las Vegas Blvd. S. ☎ *702/380-7777. Reservations required.* **Main courses:** *$13–$30. AE, CB, DC, DISC, JCB, MC, V.* **Open:** *Sun–Thurs 11am–11pm, Fri–Sat 11am–midnight.*

Viva Mercados
$$$. Off the Beaten Track. MEXICAN.

This is one of the best Mexican restaurants in town, but unlike most guacamole-and-sour cream joints, they serve surprisingly healthy fare. Everything's cooked in canola oil, and there are lots of vegetarian and seafood selections. There are 11 varieties of salsa, from extremely mild to call-the-fire-department hot. Definitely worth the 10-minute drive from the Strip.

6182 W. Flamingo Rd (about 3 miles west of the Strip on your right). ☎ *702/ 871-8826. Reservations not accepted.* **Main courses:** *$8–$17. AE, DISC, MC, V.* **Open:** *Sun–Thurs 11am–10pm, Fri–Sat 11am–11pm.*

Z Tejas Grill

$$$. Paradise Road. TEX-MEX.
Great Tex-Mex food and an intimate and comfortable Southwestern interior make this a solid alternative to the omnipresent steaks and seafood. There's a wide-ranging menu that focuses heavily on spicy chicken and beef dishes (including a surprising grilled Jamaican jerk chicken), plus a full bar offering margaritas made from scratch. Pop in for happy hour with half-priced appetizers and discounted drinks.

Bet You Didn't Know

Bandleader Xavier Cugat and Spanish bombshell singer Charo were the first couple to exchange vows at Caesars Palace, two days after its opening in 1966.

3824 S. Paradise Rd. (between Twain Ave. and Corporate Dr.). ☎ *702/732-1660. Reservations recommended.* **Main courses:** *$7–$17. AE, CB, DC, DISC, JCB, MC, V.* **Open:** *Daily 11am–11pm.*

Part 5

Ready, Set, Go! What to See & Do in Las Vegas

Yes, it's true. There's more to do in Las Vegas than drop coins into a slot machine.

Ultimately, this city is one big amusement park with a healthy dose of resort pampering thrown in for good measure. Don't believe me? Where else can you ride a roller coaster, play a few hands of blackjack, watch a live pirate battle, go bowling, take a simulator ride through ancient Egypt, play with a dolphin, practice your golf swing, get a massage, shop 'til you drop, and get married? I could go on... and will, in this section of the book. I'll give you tips on how to gamble, cover all the top attractions, tell you where to shop, and suggest all kinds of fun stuff to do in the coming chapters.

Don't overlook your very own hotel as a gen-u-ine sightseeing attraction. The hotels themselves constitute a large part of the fun in Vegas. Even if your hotel doesn't have, say, a volcano erupting out front, you can occupy many a (free) hour just walking around and gawking at the lights, the action, and the people. You'll probably want to check out the action at neighboring hotels, too. If so, just flip back to Part 2, "Finding the Hotel That's Right for You," for a rundown of what the various hotels have to offer. You've never seen gimmicks, gadgets, shows, entertainment, and architecture like this.

Chapter 11

How to Gamble Like a Pro

In This Chapter

➤ Playing the most popular games

➤ Basic gambling etiquette

➤ My favorite casinos

Okay, it's time to ante up and get serious.

Las Vegas is all about gambling, and you want to give it a whirl and try your luck. But you've never been to Vegas before, and you don't know all the rules of the games. You don't want to look clueless at the craps table, and you don't want to lose your shirt. But that doesn't mean you can't learn and catch some of the fun yourself.

Entire books have been written about the nuances of all the games (and if you're interested, a good bet—no pun intended—is *The Complete Idiot's Guide to Gambling Like a Pro*). But if you're not that serious-minded about it and you just want to know the basics, I'll tell you what you need to know to play the most popular games.

First Things First

Before you walk into a casino, there are a few basic rules and important facts that you need to know.

Age

You have to be at least 21 years old to even enter a casino area, much less play the games. If you're traveling with kids, you'll have to find a baby-sitter or childcare center at your hotel if you plan on spending any significant time at the tables or slots. If you're one of the lucky ones who looks younger than your years, carry a valid driver's license with you, because casino officials and cashiers will card you. If you're under 21, it's not like trying to sneak into a bar. Just a few years ago, there was a major news story involving a man who hit a huge slot machine jackpot only to have it taken away from him when the casino found out he was only 17.

Clubs
Most hotels offer free enrollment in their slot and gaming clubs. You're issued a card that you insert into a special reader on slot machines or turn in at gaming tables. Every time you place a bet or pull the handle, points are awarded to your account that can later be traded in for discounts on meals, shopping, and accommodations. If you gamble enough, you may even get a free room. Check at the main cashier cage in any casino to find out the details on their clubs.

Drinking & Smoking
All of the large casinos and most of the small ones will offer you free drinks (alcoholic or not) if you're gambling. Some even offer free packs of cigarettes (although some casinos have no-smoking sections). Cocktail servers roam about, so just flag one down if you're thirsty. Be warned, though, that once you place your order, they take their time getting your drink back to you. They'll tell you it's because of the long distances they have to cover to the kitchens and back, but the suspicious among us suspect that they just want you to keep pumping quarters into that slot machine while you wait.

Cheating
Don't do it, don't try it, don't even think about it.

Take a glance at the ceiling when you walk into any casino, and you'll see innocuous little black domes or opaque glass panels everywhere. These disguise the cameras that cover every square inch of the place, and somebody is always watching. The management also has a floor staff and undercover operators (is that really a 72-year old lady sitting next to you?) trying to catch you doing anything out of the ordinary. Save the cheating for income-tax time (note to IRS agents: just kidding).

Be Prepared to Lose
I'm sorry to say it, but losers outnumber winners in any casino. If they didn't, the place wouldn't stay in business very long. Casinos in the Las Vegas area rake in somewhere in the neighborhood of $6 to $7 billion dollars annually, so you get the picture. Only take as much gambling money as you can really afford to lose. Once you set aside your bankroll for the casinos, consider it gone. If you actually come home with some of it left, consider yourself lucky.

Gambling Is Just a Game

The key to successful gambling cannot be found in any strategy book or streak of good luck. It's a state of mind. No matter how much you're winning or losing, try to remember that gambling is strictly entertainment, not a way to make money. If you're looking for an investment opportunity, consider the stock market (a different form of gambling altogether), not a slot machine.

Bet You Didn't Know

A law banning gambling in the state of Nevada went into effect in 1910. It even forbade flipping a coin. Although it remained in effect until 1931, illegal gambling halls sprouted up in Las Vegas within weeks of the law.

Slot Machines: The One-Armed Bandits

In the early days of casino gambling, slot machines weren't a big deal. They were relegated to the edges of casino rooms if they were present at all. (In fact, legend has it that they were invented to give wives something to do while their husbands played the table games.) These days, of course, the majority of the floor space is taken up by slot machines. Casinos make more money from them than from all the other games combined. There are more than 120,000 slot machines in Clark County!

A slot machine is actually a computer with a highly specialized program that randomly decides how much and how often you will win on any given play. Most of the time, the computer decides that you lose, but occasionally it decides that you win, and then you'll hear the coins raining down into the little bin below.

How They Work

It's pretty simple, really: Put in a coin and pull the handle. Each machine has at least three mechanical reels loaded with symbols (7s, fruit, animals, you name it) that spin after you pull the handle or push a button. The object (usually) is to get three matching symbols on the *pay line*. If they come up, you win. Each machine has a chart on the front explaining what the different winning combinations pay.

But There Are So Many Different Types!

Slot machines will take coins away from you in just about any denomination. Nickel machines are usually the lowest limit (although a few penny slots still exist), followed by those that take dimes (rare), quarters, half-dollars, dollars, and $5. The high-limit machines can cost you anywhere from $10 to $500 or more for a single pull of the handle.

A sample slot machine.

If you play a second coin, a winning combination will win on either the top or the center payline.

With only one coin in, you have to line the symbols up on this center payline.

When you play three coins, a winning combination on any payline wins.

Tourist Traps

Vast amounts of money are always on display in Vegas, and crooks find lots of easy marks. Don't be one of them. At gaming tables and slot machines, men should keep their wallets well-concealed and out of the reach of pickpockets, and women should keep purses in view and on their laps at all times. Thieves are just waiting for you to become so entranced with your game that you let your guard down, so don't let it happen.

Once you have chosen your playing level (based on how big your budget is and how adventurous you are), you have to decide between progressive and so-called *flat-top* machines. Flat-top machines have a fixed high-end limit of how much you can win. Hit three 7s, for example, and you win 1,000 coins but never any more or less. Progressive machines offer unlimited high-end winnings as the jackpot grows each time you put a coin in. Here those three 7s could win you different amounts, depending on how much money has

139

accumulated in the jackpot. Most progressive slots are located in *carousels*—groups of machines that contribute to one central jackpot and are easily distinguishable by the large electronic signs above them displaying how large the jackpot is. I've recently seen machines with individual progressive jackpots. Play these, and you don't have to worry about the guy sitting next to you winning the big prize.

Dollars & Sense

The lower the denomination required to play a slot machine, the less often you'll hit the jackpot. Nickel machines pay off less frequently than quarter machines, for example, which pay off less frequently than dollars, and so on. Most people (almost 75 percent) who play slots use the quarter machines.

Playing and jackpot levels are the only constants. After that, all bets are off (if you'll pardon the pun). You have machines that take 2 coins, 3 coins, or 45 coins at a time. Some have more than one set of reels. Some include bonus wheels that spin and award you extra dough. But it's not all that complicated; if you study a machine carefully for just a moment before you play it, you'll see all the rules and your possible winnings.

Hitting the Jackpot

So you're sitting there bleary eyed, mindlessly pumping quarters into a machine, when suddenly you see the big jackpot come up. Bells and sirens will often blare just in case you weren't paying attention. But then you realize that there's no money raining down in the bin. Relax. Most machines have payout limits; any jackpot that exceeds the limit is paid in cash by an attendant. I once was next to a woman who hit a $7,500 jackpot at The Mirage, and she was surrounded by casino officials within seconds.

Also be aware that any jackpot of $1,200 or more is automatically reported to the IRS by the casino. Yes, that is considered income and is taxable. (You can also deduct losses but only if you have winnings. It's basically a wink and a nod between the IRS and casinos. Win $2,000? Then claim $2,000 in losses.) So maybe instead of trying for that one big jackpot, you should go after a bunch of smaller ones.

Tips & Tricks

I'm no expert, but I still have a few hints for you to take with you to the slot machines. These are not guaranteed to make you a penny, but when I stick to them, I usually do pretty well.

➤ **Be prepared to walk away:** If you sit down at a slot machine and it isn't paying anything within the first 5 to 10 pulls, walk away. Odds are that it isn't going to get any better.

➤ **Play the max:** I always, without exception, put in the maximum number of coins allowed (usually two or three per pull), especially if I'm playing a progressive machine. The more you put in, the more you'll win, and most machines, progressive or not, offer higher payout odds on maximum bets. Put in one quarter, get three cherries, and you'll get two quarters back, for example. The odds there are 1:1. However, put in three quarters, hit those same three cherries, and you get nine quarters as a payoff. This makes the odds 1:3. In addition, the big jackpots on some flat-tops and most progressives can only be won if you put in the maximum number of coins.

➤ **Look for busy carousels:** As you walk around the casino, you'll see banks of machines (carousels) that are empty and those that are packed with people winning. There's usually a reason why those carousels are empty—it's because the machines aren't paying well. Take your time to find a carousel where lots of people have lots of money in their coin returns. There's no guarantee that you'll do better here, but the odds are a little better.

➤ **Investigate progressive payouts:** If you see a bank of progressive slots, ask an attendant or change person what the jackpot starts at and when it usually hits. Most of the time, they will be happy to give you this "insider" information. If a progressive slot carousel jackpot starts at $10,000, usually hits before it reaches $15,000, and is currently at $14,500, then sit down and start playing! If it's only at $10,500, then that means somebody recently won and it probably won't hit again anytime soon.

Time-Savers

Instead of wandering around from machine to machine looking for that special vibe, ask the floor or change attendants if they know of a certain area that is doing well. Technically, they aren't supposed to tell you this, but many often do—especially those in the change areas above slot carousels.

➤ **Use credits and set boundaries:** Most slot machines offer you the choice of using coins or credits. Suppose that you drop in two quarters and hit a 20-coin jackpot on your first pull. The machine will either spit out 20 quarters or put 20 credits on an electronic meter. I often use the credits instead of putting in more coins from my initial stash, because it's easier to keep track of how much you're winning or losing—but I set a limit. In this scenario, for example, I have 20 credits and I tell myself that if it gets down to 10 credits, I'll stop, cash out, and walk away up 8 quarters. If the meter gets up to 30 credits, I'll raise my lower limit to 15 or 20 credits, and so on. This way, you always know you'll come out a winner.

Video Poker

This is another popular machine that allows you to play a hand of regular poker on a video screen as opposed to playing at a card table. Ever played poker on your computer at home? Same thing, only you get real money here if you win.

These machines are basically glorified slot machines, only with a poker hand on a video display instead of mechanical reels. Most machines will let you play from one to five coins per hand, and your winnings go up accordingly.

Put in your coins, press the DEAL button, and five virtual-reality cards pop up. Select the cards you want to keep with HOLD buttons, and press DEAL again for your replacement cards. You only have one chance to draw for a winning poker hand. The machine doesn't have a hand of its own, so you aren't competing against it. You're just trying to get a hand that's high enough to win something.

Winning Hands

Most video-poker machines have a minimum of *jacks or better* to win. This means that out of five cards, you have at least two jacks of any suit (the ace is always the highest card value, and the two is the lowest). If you've never played poker, consult the following chart to learn more about poker hands:

One pair	Out of your five cards, you have two that are alike. Most video-poker games require a pair of jacks as the minimum before they'll pay.
Two pair	Two pairs of matching card values—for example, two 5s and two 8s.
Three of a kind	Three cards out of your five have to have matching values (for example, three kings).

Continues

142

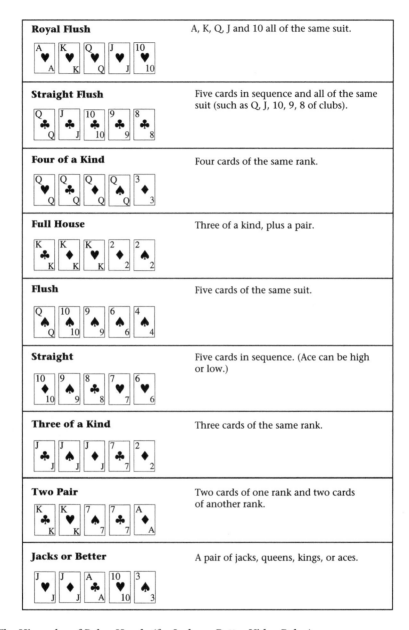

The Hierarchy of Poker Hands (for Jacks or Better Video Poker).

Continued

Straight	All five of your cards have to be in sequential order. It doesn't matter what suit they are; they don't have to match. The lowest possible straight is 2-3-4-5-6, and the highest is 10-J-Q-K-A.
Flush	Five cards of the same suit, regardless of value (for example, five diamonds).
Full house	A combination of one pair and three of a kind (two aces and three 7s, for example).
Four of a kind	Pretty simple to figure out but hard to get. Four of the five cards will have the same face value (4-4-4-4-9, for example).
Straight flush	Five cards in sequential order, all in the same suit, such as the 5-6-7-8-9 of spades.
Royal flush	The ultimate poker hand is the highest possible straight flush. If you wind up with the 10-J-Q-K-A of all spades, clubs, diamonds, or hearts, you win big time.

Tips & Tricks

Just like slot machines, video poker comes in many different denominations, although quarter and dollar machines are the most prevalent. Progressive video poker is popping up everywhere, but most still offer a fixed (flat-top) payout. You'll also find a huge range of add-ons that may include a wild card, a *double-down feature* (where you double your money on a winning hand), or special bonuses for certain hands. Beginners should probably stick to the basic games that offer payouts starting with *jacks or better* until you're used to the concept. There's also something called an *8/5 machine*, which refers to the amount of payout on a full house or flush, with eight coins paid for the former and five for the latter. The 8/5 machines are the most prevalent and offer the best odds. Here are a couple of other helpful tips for playing video poker:

➤ **Remember your payout minimums:** A pair of 8s, for example, isn't going to win you anything on a jacks-or-better machine. Drawing three cards to try to get another eight (for a winning three of a kind) means that you only have two chances to get it right (there's only two more 8s in the deck). If you have an ace and jack with those two 8s however, you can keep the high cards and draw for a possible pair. Here, you have six chances of getting a winning hand (three more aces and three more jacks).

➤ **Don't go for the glory at the expense of a sure thing:** You are dealt the A-K-10 of spades and the jacks of hearts and diamonds. It may be tempting to go for the royal flush by keeping the A-K-10, but the odds of your getting it are around 1 in 40,000. Keep your sure-thing pair of jacks and try to build on that. This is only one example, but it applies to any situation where you have to dump a winning hand for the mere possibility of a better one.

Blackjack

Blackjack is probably the most popular card game in gambling; most of the tables in casinos are devoted to it. It's very simple to learn the basics and develop a strategy, but there are a few quirks of playing in a casino that you have to be aware of.

In short, you compete against the dealer to get as close to 21 points per hand without going over. Numbered cards are worth their face value, face cards are worth 10 (J-Q-K), and the ace is worth either 1 or 11 points (your choice).

The primary differences between games are the number of decks used and the minimum bets allowed. You'll find from one to six decks per game, and table minimums from $1 to $500 per hand, although $5 per hand is the most common.

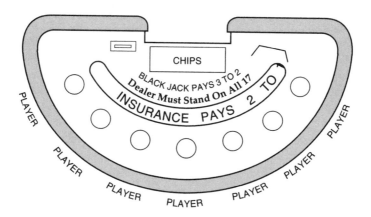

Basic Rules

After placing your bet on the table, the dealer gives you two cards, usually face up, and then deals himself (or herself, as the case may be) two cards: one face up and one face down. Blackjack is called if your two cards equal 21 (a 10 or face card plus an ace); you win automatically.

145

If the dealer has a 10 or an ace showing, he will check his hidden card. If he has a blackjack, everyone loses.

If you don't have 21, you are allowed as many additional cards as you want to try to reach 21. You lose if you go over.

Once you've gone as high as you can (or want to), the dealer will reveal his hidden card and attempt to beat your score. If he does, you lose; if he doesn't, you win. If you tie, it's called a *push*, and nobody wins or loses.

There can be up to six or seven other people at the table, but you are only playing against the dealer.

Important Casino Dos and Don'ts

Casino blackjack is played with chips, not cash, for betting. Chips come in different denominations, and you can buy them at the main cashier or at the table itself.

Most casino blackjack games require the dealer to draw to at least 17. In other words, the dealer has to keep taking cards until her hand totals 17 or higher. This is important to remember when devising your own strategy.

Once you've placed a bet on the table and cards are being dealt, don't touch your bet. This is a big no-no.

Most Vegas blackjack games use six decks of cards all mixed together in a *shoe*, which is a special card dispenser. The cards are dealt face up. *Don't touch them!* The dealer is the only one allowed to handle the cards in these games, and you'll get scolded if you do. There are a few single-deck games around, and these are usually dealt by hand face down. In this case, you are allowed to touch the cards (they're face down, so you have to). In either case, signal for an additional card by making a light scratching motion toward yourself on the table with your hand or cards if you're holding them. This is sort of a non-verbal way of saying *gimme another one*. If you don't want to draw, wave your hand once above your cards (*no more*), or if you're holding your cards, tuck them face down on the table gently under your bet.

Tourist Traps

Many of the casinos in the downtown area are small affairs not affiliated with any hotel. You'll often see employees standing out front trying to lure you inside with the promise of "free" stuff. Almost without exception, it isn't worth it, so avoid these places.

Basic Strategy

If your two cards total 17 or above, don't draw. Your chances of getting a higher hand are slim. If you have a two-card total of 11 or less, draw a card—there's no way you can go over 21 with one additional card. It's when you have 12 to 16 points, regardless of how many cards you have, that it starts to get a bit tricky. This is where the dealer's single upturned card is important. If you fall into that 12-to-16–point range and the dealer has a 7 or higher showing, you should probably draw a card. Chances are that the dealer has a 10-point card hidden, and you'll lose if you don't draw a card. If the dealer has a 6 or lower card showing, she'll probably have to draw (to reach at least 17), and there's a good chance of her going over 21. Consider staying, even with a hand as low as 12. Following are some basic blackjack strategy charts to help you at the tables:

BASIC STRATEGY *										
The Dealer is Showing:	2	3	4	5	6	7	8	9	10	Ace
Your Total is: 4–11	H	H	H	H	H	H	H	H	H	H
12	H	H	S	S	S	H	H	H	H	H
13	S	S	S	S	S	H	H	H	H	H
14	S	S	S	S	S	H	H	H	H	H
15	S	S	S	S	S	H	H	H	H	H
16	S	S	S	S	S	H	H	H	H	H

S=Stand　　　　H=Hit　　　　O=Optional

SOFT HAND STRATEGY *										
The Dealer is Showing:	2	3	4	5	6	7	8	9	10	Ace
You Have: Ace, 9	S	S	S	S	S	S	S	S	S	S, H
Ace, 8	S	S	S	S	S	S	S	S	S	
Ace, 7	S	D	D	D	D	S	S	H	H	S
Ace, 6	H	D	D	D	D	S	H	H	H	H
Ace, 5	H	H	D	D	D	H	H	H	H	H
Ace, 4	H	H	D	D	D	H	H	H	H	H
Ace, 3	H	H	H	D	D	H	H	H	H	H
Ace, 2	H	H	H	D	D	H	H	H	H	H

S=Stand　　　　H=Hit　　　　D=Double Down

"Insurance" is offered when the dealer has an ace showing. You are allowed to place an additional bet of up to half your original wager (for example, if you bet $10.00, you can wager up to $5.00 on an insurance bet). If the dealer has 21, you lose your original bet but are paid 2:1 on your insurance bet, and therefore you come out even (for example, you lose your $10.00 bet but gain an additional $5.00 on the insurance bet). If the dealer does not have 21, you lose your insurance bet, and the game proceeds as usual. Most people consider this a "sucker bet" since the odds are that the dealer won't have 21. Most of the time you will lose your insurance bet and then may lose your original bet as well. I advise against taking this option.

Another option you have at most blackjack tables is to "double down." This bet is placed after you are dealt your first two cards but before any additional cards are dealt. You must double the amount you bet by placing additional chips on the table (for example, if you bet $10.00 originally, you put out another $10.00 in chips). What you are wagering is that one additional card will give you a high enough hand to win—but you only get one card. Since the odds are that your one additional card will be worth 10 points (a 10 or a face card), this option is best exercised when your first two cards total 10 or 11 and the dealer has a low card showing. If you get what you're hoping for, you'll wind up with 20 or 21 and will probably win the hand, doubling your entire bet. If all you get is a four (for instance), you don't get another card to boost your point total and will probably lose it all.

Yet another option is called "splitting." You are allowed to do this when the first two cards you are dealt are of the same value (for example, two eights or kings). To split this hand, separate the two cards and put out an additional bet equal to your original bet. The dealer will then treat each card as a separate hand, and you are allowed to draw as many cards as you like to get as close to 21 as possible. Whichever hand beats the dealer wins double that bet whether it be both hands or just one. Hands that don't beat the dealer lose the bet. When to split your hand is a matter of debate, but most people agree that two aces or two eights should always be split into separate hands. The odds are in your favor that you'll wind up with two better hands than the one you would have had otherwise.

DOUBLING DOWN										
The Dealer is Showing:	**2**	**3**	**4**	**5**	**6**	**7**	**8**	**9**	**10**	**Ace**
Your Total is: 11	D	D	D	D	D	D	D	D	D	H
10	D	D	D	D	D	D	D	D	H	H
9	H	D	D	D	D	H	H	H	H	H
H=Hit					**D=Double Down**					

SPLITTING STRATEGY										
The Dealer is Showing:	**2**	**3**	**4**	**5**	**6**	**7**	**8**	**9**	**10**	**Ace**
You Have: 2, 2	H	H	SP	SP	SP	SP	H	H	H	H
3, 3	H	H	SP	SP	SP	SP	H	H	H	H
4, 4	H	H	H	H	H	H	H	H	H	H
5, 5	D	D	D	D	D	D	D	D	H	H
6, 6	H	SP	SP	SP	SP	H	H	H	H	H
7, 7	SP	SP	SP	SP	SP	SP	H	H	H	H
8, 8	SP	SP	SP	SP	SP	SP	SP	SP	SP	SP
9, 9	SP	SP	SP	SP	SP	S	SP	SP	S	S
10, 10	S	S	S	S	S	S	S	S	S	S
Ace, Ace	SP	SP	SP	SP	SP	SP	SP	SP	SP	SP

S=Stand   H=Hit   SP=Split   D=Double Down

Dollars & Sense

While playing blackjack, be sure to ask the dealer or the pit boss (the employee overseeing a group of tables) about restaurants, shows, and attractions in that particular hotel. You'll often get complimentary meals or tickets or discounts if you've been playing for a while.

Tips & Tricks

Blackjack is an easy game to play and can be a lot of fun under the right conditions:

➤ **Look for a fun dealer:** Before sitting down at a table, watch the dealer to see if he or she is one of the stone-faced, boring ones, or if there's some life and energy there. A fun dealer will chat, offer advice, and generally make the entire experience more enjoyable.

➤ **Look for a fun table:** Same concept as above, only this one concerns your tablemates. If everyone is sitting there with a sour expression on their faces, concentrating mightily on their cards, you may have too serious a table. Find a table where the people are laughing and talking, and you'll have a better time.

➤ **Set aside a minimum:** Keep two piles of chips—one for betting and one for saving. Every time you win a hand, set aside part of your winnings (maybe half?) into the savings pile and don't touch it, no matter how bad your luck gets. If you exhaust your betting pile, walk away and you'll still have money left.

Roulette

Lots of people have seen roulette wheels, but few ever sit down to play. That's too bad, because it's easy to learn and can be a lot of fun to play.

A ball is spun on a wheel with 38 numbers (0, 00, and 1 through 36). The zeros are green, and the other numbers are either red or black but divided evenly. Bets are placed on the *field*, which is a grid layout on the table showing all the numbers and a variety of different combinations. *Inside bets* are those placed on the 0 through 36 number part of the field. *Outside bets* are placed in the boxes surrounding the numbers and include red, black, even, odd, 1 through 18, 19 through 36, first 12, second 12, third 12, and the columns bets. You are betting which number will come up when the ball settles into a slot on the wheel.

Standard roulette Wheel.

How to Bet

Lay cash or chips down on the table, and you are given special roulette chips. Each player at the table has a different color of chips, so it's easy to keep track of which are yours. Bets are allowed even after the ball begins spinning, but once it starts to fall toward the numbers, bets are cut off.

Inside bets are complicated to play and to explain, so for the purpose of this instructional, I'm going to stick to the outside bets with one exception. Outside bets don't pay as much, but beginners should probably stay with them at first.

Standard roulette Table.

150

➤ **Odd-Even:** If you place a bet in the Odd field and an odd number comes up on the wheel (17, 23, and so on), you win double your money. If it comes up as an even number, you lose. Even numbers win for bets placed in the Even field. If either zero or double zero comes up, you lose bets placed in either field.

➤ **Red-Black:** A bet placed here will win if the number comes up in the color you bet. A red number will double your money if you bet on red, but you lose if you placed a black bet. The opposite happens when you bet on black. Zero or double zero causes you to lose.

➤ **1–18, 19–36:** If you've bet either of these boxes and the winning number falls within the range listed, you've just doubled your money. Suppose that you bet on 1–18 and the number 15 comes up on the wheel; you've won. If the number 32 comes up, you've lost. Either zero will cause you to lose these bets.

➤ **First 12, second 12, third 12:** This is similar to the 1–18 and 19–36 bets, only a little more specific. Bet on the first 12, and if any number between 1 and 12 hits, you get paid triple your bet, but any other number is a loser. The same concept goes with second 12 (numbers 13–24) and third 12 (numbers 25–36).

➤ **Column bets:** At the end of the Inside fields are three boxes that are marked *2 to 1*. If you put money here, you're betting that the winning number on the wheel will be one of the numbers in the column above that box. If it is, then you triple your bet. If it isn't, you lose it all.

➤ **Single-number bets:** This is the one inside bet that you may want to try. Place your chips on any single number on the field (17 or 34, for example), and if that number comes up, you win 35 times your bet. This is fun to play, and the winnings can be big, but the odds are *way* against you.

Tips & Tricks

Here's some commonsense advice for first-timers:

➤ **Look for single-zero roulette:** As mentioned earlier, most tables and wheels have zero and double zero. A few have only the single zero. If you can find one of these tables, play it, because your odds are slightly better with fewer possible numbers on the wheel.

➤ **Stick with the outside bets:** It's tempting to place all your money on your one single lucky number. It can be exciting, but the problem is that you'll most likely lose. The outside bets may not be as glamorous and don't pay as out as much, but your money will go farther and the odds are a lot better.

Keno

Your local lotto was derived from an ancient Chinese game, and keno is the same basic concept. It's definitely not fast paced, but it can be good for a diversion while you're sitting in a hotel restaurant or lounge.

*Sample
keno card.*

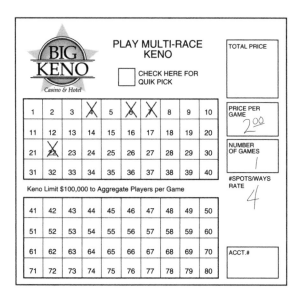

Twenty numbers are drawn from a field of 1 through 80. Various bets are placed on which numbers will come up, and if enough of your numbers do, you win.

Most hotel coffee shops and lounges will have large boards with the 80 numbers displayed. They're also scattered throughout the casinos. On the tables or at the bar, you'll find keno tickets. You place a bet by filling out the ticket and giving it to the *runner*, who will take it to the keno lounge. The ticket shows the 80 numbers (called *spots*) and has boxes for the amount of your bet and the number of sequential games you want to play.

Possible bets and the money you can win from them vary wildly from casino to casino, but the most common are 6-, 7-, 8-, 9-, and 10-spot bets. If you play a 6-spot game, for example, you mark 6 numbers on the ticket and hand it in. Just like the lotto, if your 6 numbers come up, you win. If 5 of the 6 are selected, you'll win, but substantially less than you would have with all six numbers. Four numbers will likely pay even money, and 3 or less are losing tickets.

One important note is that you have to cash in winning tickets before the start of the next game, or you lose it all. If you can't find a keno runner, take it to the keno cashier right away to get paid.

There are many more complex ways to play a keno ticket involving groupings and splits… it's all much more than you need to know if you just want something to do while eating a cheeseburger. Just pick your lucky numbers and go. My one bit of advice is that fewer spots mean better odds. It's a lot easier to get 6 out of 6 than it is to get 10 out of 10. Plus, if you get 5 numbers on a 6-spot ticket, you'll win something, whereas 5 on a 10-spot will probably get you zippo. You don't win as much on a lower spot ticket, but you could win more often.

Craps

You may have heard that craps is really complicated—if so, you've heard right. I don't even understand the whole thing, and I've read entire books on the subject. It can be a little intimidating, but it is possible to play a simple game. Basically, bets are placed on what number will come up on a pair of dice thrown. Bets can be placed even if you're not the one throwing the dice.

Whoever has the dice is called the *shooter*. The shooter's first roll is called *coming out*. The object is to get a 7 or 11 on the first roll in any combination (2-5, 5-6, and so on). That's an automatic winner. A roll of 2, 3, or 12 is called *crapping out* and is an automatic loser. If any other number comes up, (4, 5, 6, 8, 9, or 10), this becomes the *point*, and the object of the game switches a little. Now the goal is to roll the point number again before a 7 is rolled. If a 7 comes up before the point, then the shooter has *crapped out*. Bets are placed on various parts of the gaming table as described below:

The Pass Line Bet

This is where beginners should stay. Place your initial bet on the "pass" line, and you are betting that the player will not crap out. A roll of 7 or 11, or establishing a point number and rolling it before a 7, will win double your bet. For example, you place your bet on the pass line. Once it's there, you can't touch it until you win or lose. The shooter rolls a 4. This is now the point. The next roll is a 5 and then a 10. Finally on the fourth throw, the shooter rolls a 4 and you win. If that fourth throw had turned up a 7, you would have lost.

The Don't Pass Bar Bet

Exactly the opposite of the above. You're betting the shooter will crap out. A roll of 7 or 11, or establishing and then making a point number will cause you to lose a Don't Pass bet. If the shooter rolls a 2, 3, or 12, or doesn't make his point, then you win.

The Come Bet

This bet is placed *after* a point number has been established. For instance, say the shooter throws a 5 on his first throw. That is the point, and placing a bet in the "Come" field is now just like a Pass Line bet above. You are wagering that the next throw of the dice will be 7 or 11. If it is, you win. If the next throw is a 2, 3, or 12, you lose. If it is any other number, the bet is moved into the corresponding box (4, 5, 6, 8, 9, or 10) where it remains until the shooter either rolls the number again (you win) or rolls a 7 (you lose).

The Don't Come Bet

The pessimists' version of the Come bet: You win if the throw is 2, 3, or 12 and lose if it is a 7 or 11. If any other number appears (4, 5, 6, 8, 9, or 10), you win if a 7 is thrown before that number is repeated but lose if it does not.

The Place Bet

Put your wager in this field above any number, and you are betting that this number will be rolled before a 7 appears on the dice. These bets may be increased, decreased, or removed entirely at any time during play.

The Hard Way, Big 6/8, Field & Proposition Bets

These bet are the boxes that comprise the rest of the gaming table. If you win, the payoffs can be large, but they are, according to most people, not worth the effort since the odds are against you in every single case. The Hard Way bets are wagering that 4, 6, 8, or 10 will be rolled as shown (double 2, 3, 4, or 5 depending on which box you choose) before it is thrown in any other combination or before a 7 appears. The Big 6 and Big 8 bets say that a 6 or 8 will be thrown before a 7 appears—the same as a Place bet above but with lower payback odds. The next two bets are based on one roll of the dice and are to be avoided. A Field bet wagers that the next throw of the dice will be a 2, 3, 4, 9, 10, 11, or 12 which are the seven least likely numbers that will appear. Proposition bets say that the next roll will be either 2, 3, 7, 11, or 12 (there's a box for each) or any craps (2, 3, or 12).

Basic Strategy

Stick with the Pass Line and Come bets at first. These are the easiest to play and offer the best odds.

Advanced Strategy

There's a lot more to this game than what I've described here including "playing the odds" (side bets that are placed on the point number), Buy bets, and Lay bets. If you're interested in learning more about the intricacies of craps, check out the section below called, "How to Learn More."

Tips & Tricks

I'm not much of a craps player, but here is what I've learned:

➤ If you can find a table with any room, just stand and watch for awhile. Even if you think you didn't understand what you've just read about the game, it will all become a lot clearer once you see it in action.

➤ It's a lot of fun to be the one throwing the dice, but it's a lot easier to bet and watch your money if you let someone else do the work.

➤ Avoid the Hard Way and one-roll bets like the plague. You'll almost always lose.

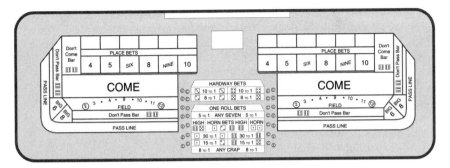

Standard craps table.

Number Rolled	How Many Ways to roll the Number?	True Odds	Winning Combinations
Two	1	35 to 1	⚀·⚀
Three	2	17 to 1	⚀·⚁·⚁·⚀
Four	3	11 to 1	⚀·⚂·⚂·⚀·⚁·⚁
Five	4	8 to 1	⚀·⚃·⚃·⚀·⚁·⚂·⚂·⚁
Six	5	6.2 to 1	⚀·⚄·⚄·⚀·⚁·⚃·⚃·⚁·⚂·⚂
Seven	6	5 to 1	⚀·⚅·⚅·⚀·⚁·⚄·⚄·⚁·⚂·⚃·⚃·⚂
Eight	5	6.2 to 1	⚁·⚅·⚅·⚁·⚂·⚄·⚄·⚂·⚃·⚃
Nine	4	8 to 1	⚂·⚅·⚅·⚂·⚃·⚄·⚄·⚃
Ten	3	11 to 1	⚃·⚅·⚅·⚃·⚄·⚄
Eleven	2	17 to 1	⚄·⚅·⚅·⚄
Twelve	1	35 to 1	⚅·⚅

Here's how the 36 combinations stack up.

Other Games People Play

The games I've gone through are the most popular but certainly not the only ones in town. In addition, you have *standard poker* (just like video poker, only with real players and real cards), *baccarat* (a complex card game similar to blackjack), *mini-baccarat* (the same thing, only a little simpler), *pai-gow poker* (a Chinese take on seven-card stud poker), *let-it-ride* (another poker-based card game), *wheel of fortune* (just like it sounds, only without the puzzle or Vanna White), and *sports betting* on just about any game in the world (stop in your hotel's Sports Book—the area of a casino where sports betting occurs—and place a wager, then sit down and celebrate or bemoan your team's performance on a nearby TV).

How to Learn More

What I've told you in this chapter will help you get started on the most popular games, but to learn more, I recommend three valuable resources:

Bet You Didn't Know

Visitors on a trail ride once brought a horse into the crowded casino of the Thunderbird Hotel. They put a pair of dice between his lips at the craps table, and he threw a natural seven.

➤ **Hotel gaming lessons:** Every casino offers free lessons on any table game from blackjack to craps to baccarat and everything between. They're very helpful and usually taught in an easy-to-understand manner right at the table so that you can see what's going on instead of trying to visualize it from a book.

➤ *The Complete Idiot's Guide to Gambling Like a Pro:* Yes, you heard me right. Writer/researcher Susan Spector has teamed with gambling expert Standford Wong to present a comprehensive yet amazingly simple guide that will take you through every detail of even the most complex games. Look for it in your local bookstore.

➤ **Casino games for your computer:** There are thousands of computer games out there that simulate and teach you the rules of casino gambling. If you're hooked up to the web or any of the subscriber services like AOL, simply search for "games" or "casino games" and you'll probably find a bunch of shareware programs that you can easily download. If not, then head to your local computer store, which will definitely have a few games for you to purchase.

My Money's Burning a Hole in My Pocket. Where Shall I Go to Gamble?

You will not lack for opportunities to gamble. Trust me on that. You can start with the slot machines at the airport baggage carousel and keep going at restaurants, coffee shops, bars, and so on. I won't take up your time by listing every single casino in town; suffice it to say that every hotel on the Strip has a gigantic casino with all the games you could ever want to play. Here are a few of my favorites.

If You're a Serious Gambler...

The Mirage, 3400 Las Vegas Blvd. S. (☎ 702/791-7111), is my favorite place to gamble. The Polynesian-theme casino is large and surprisingly quiet, allowing for minimal distractions from your quest to get rich quick.

Even more high class is the **Las Vegas Hilton,** 3000 Paradise Rd. (☎ 702/732-7111), with a medium-sized gambling area filled with Austrian crystal chandeliers and marble galore (but see also what they've come up with in the section below).

Perhaps the most elegant joint of all is the casino at the **Desert Inn Country Club Resort & Casino,** 3145 Las Vegas Blvd. S. (☎ **702/733-4444**). It's relentlessly chic, with fewer slot machines than average, which makes for a sedate environment.

If You Want to Do Some Not-So-Serious Gambling...

Harrah's Las Vegas, 3745 Las Vegas Blvd. S. (☎ **702/369-5000**), has redone its casino in a European carnival theme that creates a festive atmosphere. Check out the *party pits*—gambling-table areas where dealers are encouraged to break from the stern-faced tradition by wearing funny hats and celebrating wins.

The casino at **The Hard Rock Hotel & Casino,** 4455 Paradise Rd. (☎ **702/693-5000**), is a masterpiece of Vegas silliness. The craps tables are shaped like grand pianos, some slot machines have guitar necks for handles, and the gaming chips have faces of famous rock stars on them. Be prepared for blaring rock music, though.

Caesars Palace, 3570 Las Vegas Blvd. S. (☎ **702/731-7110**), offers serious luxury for serious gamblers, but lovers of the absurd will have a great time here, too. After all, the cocktail waitresses are wearing togas, and faux marble Roman statues keep an eye on the proceedings.

In summer, **Tropicana Resort & Casino,** 3801 Las Vegas Blvd. S. (☎ **702/739-2222**), offers swim-up blackjack in its beautiful tropical pool area. Need I say more?

The crowning achievement in gambling fun is the new Spacequest Casino at the **Las Vegas Hilton,** 3000 Paradise Rd. (☎ **702/732-7111**). It's designed as a twenty-fourth–century space station with large windows that offer a view of earth (and orbiting space shuttles, taxi cabs, and Hilton limos). The slot machines here don't have handles—instead, you pass your hand through a bar of light to trigger the mechanism. Highly ridiculous in a really good way. (Be sure to visit the bathrooms, which will give you an instant urinalysis while you use the facilities.)

If You Want to Do Some Cheap Gambling...

If you want to gamble but don't have much dough to spend, you'll have to head downtown to make your money last the longest.

Binion's Horseshoe Casino, 128 E. Fremont St. (☎ **800/237-6537**), is Old Las Vegas at its best, with flocked wallpaper and dark wood surrounding the gaming areas, where you'll find blackjack tables with a $1 minimum ($3–$5 is the standard).

157

A few blocks down the street is the **El Cortez Hotel & Casino,** 600 E. Fremont St. (☎ **702/385-5200**), offering roulette with minimum bets as low as 10¢ and 25¢ craps.

And if you *really* want to stretch a dollar, go one block north of Fremont at 4th Street to find the **Gold Spike,** 400 E. Ogden Ave. (☎ **702/384-8444**). The casino is almost hilariously stuck in the 1970s, with worn shag carpeting and fake-wood paneling, but this is the only place I know of that has penny slot machines.

Chapter 12

The Top Attractions A to Z

Las Vegas has something for everyone, whatever your tastes, whatever your budget. However, Vegas being Vegas, the attractions here are not quite the same as what you'll find in other destinations. For example, New York City has the Statue of Liberty, Egypt has the Sphinx, and Paris has the Eiffel Tower. Las Vegas has... the Statue of Liberty, the Sphinx, and (in a few years) the Eiffel Tower—but these knockoffs are more gimmicks than actual attractions, so they don't really count in my book. No, what separates Las Vegas from other destinations—besides the gambling, the mammoth theme hotels, the lavish shows, and the Elvis impersonators, that is—is the preponderance of theme parks, simulator rides, off-the-wall museums, and free street-side extravaganzas. When you finally pry your fingers from the slot machine, rest assured you'll find plenty of action-packed fun and quirky amusements to occupy your time.

If you have the kiddies in tow, this chapter should be of special interest to you, since a lot of what's described here will keep them entertained.

Keep in mind that the shows described below are separate from the big, splashy, dare I say, Vegas-style production shows—those are covered in chapter 15, "The Shows A to Z."

A Few Notes on Logistics

I've included here only the most entertaining or unusual sights in town—the real must-sees.

Even working from just this list, there's much more than you could possibly see and do unless you're planning a really long trip, so I suggest that you whip out a pen and scribble your own interest rating beside each listing on a scale of 1 to 5.

1 I absolutely cannot miss this attraction!

2 I'm very interested in this attraction.

3 This is something that I'd like to do if there's time.

4 Only if I'm really bored.

5 You couldn't drag me!

For the sake of consistency, I'm sticking with the South, North, and Central Strip neighborhoods which parallel those set up in the hotel and restaurant chapters. Remember that a Paradise Road designation means that the attraction is located somewhere near Paradise Road and not necessarily on it. As in other chapters, I use the Off The Beaten Track designation for places that are located outside the defined neighborhoods but are worth the extra time and mileage.

If your time in Las Vegas is limited, try to plan the attractions you want to see by neighborhood, instead of running all over town. If you stick to one area at a time, you'll maximize your sightseeing opportunities.

All the attractions listed below offer free valet or do-it-yourself parking, unless otherwise noted.

Should I Just Take a Guided Tour?

There aren't many organized sightseeing tours in Vegas, but the ones I've uncovered are very reasonably priced. Also, a good tour guide will fill you in on entertaining and historical tidbits that you wouldn't get, wandering around by yourself.

The most reputable company around offers one of the most interesting tours: **Grayline** (☎ **702/384-1234**) will take you on a 7½-hour journey around town that includes the Strip, Fremont Street, a visit to the top of the Stratosphere Tower, and a lunch buffet. The all-inclusive price is $28 for adults, $26 for seniors and children 10 to 16, and $24 for children under 10.

Las Vegas Tour and Travel (☎ **702/739-8975**) offers similar tours and can even arrange a nighttime helicopter ride for the adventurous (and wealthy).

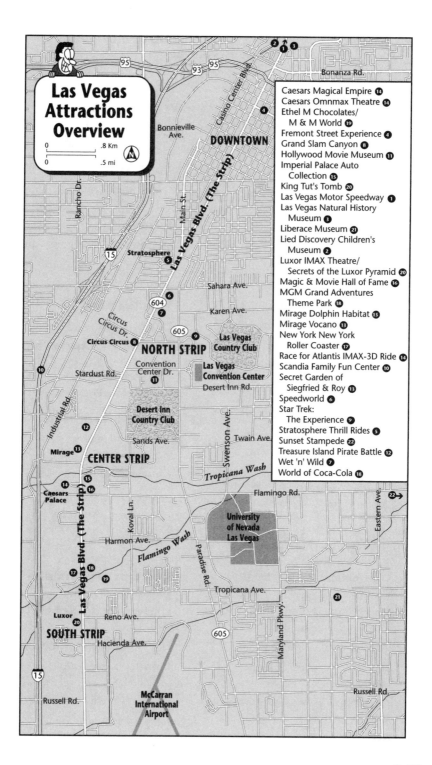

Las Vegas Attractions Overview

0 ————— .8 Km
0 ————— .5 mi

DOWNTOWN

Bonnieville Ave.

Caesars Magical Empire ⑭
Caesars Omnmax Theatre ⑭
Ethel M Chocolates/
  M & M World ⑲
Fremont Street Experience ④
Grand Slam Canyon ⑧
Hollywood Movie Museum ⑪
Imperial Palace Auto
  Collection ⑮
King Tut's Tomb ⑳
Las Vegas Motor Speedway ①
Las Vegas Natural History
  Museum ③
Liberace Museum ㉑
Lied Discovery Children's
  Museum ②
Luxor IMAX Theatre/
  Secrets of the Luxor Pyramid ⑳
Magic & Movie Hall of Fame ⑯
MGM Grand Adventures
  Theme Park ⑱
Mirage Dolphin Habitat ⑬
Mirage Vocano ⑬
New York New York
  Roller Coaster ⑰
Race for Atlantis IMAX-3D Ride ⑭
Scandia Family Fun Center ⑩
Secret Garden of
  Siegfried & Roy ⑬
Speedworld ⑥
Star Trek:
  The Experience ⑨
Stratosphere Thrill Rides ⑤
Sunset Stampede ㉒
Treasure Island Pirate Battle ⑫
Wet 'n' Wild ⑦
World of Coca-Cola ⑱

Rancho Dr.

Stratosphere ⑤

Sahara Ave.

Karen Ave.

Circus Circus Dr.

Circus Circus ⑧

NORTH STRIP

Las Vegas Country Club

Las Vegas Convention Center

Convention Center Dr.

Stardust Rd.

Desert Inn Rd.

Desert Inn Country Club

Industrial Rd.

Sands Ave.

Mirage ⑬

CENTER STRIP

Swenson Ave.

Twain Ave.

Tropicana Wash

Caesars Palace

Flamingo Rd.

University of Nevada Las Vegas

Eastern Ave.

Kovai Ln.

Harmon Ave.

Flamingo Wash

Paradise Rd.

Luxor ⑳

Reno Ave.

Tropicana Ave.

SOUTH STRIP

Hacienda Ave.

Maryland Pkwy.

Russell Rd.

McCarran International Airport

Russell Rd.

Quick Picks: Las Vegas Attractions at a Glance
Index by Location

South Strip

Ethel M. Chocolates/M&M World

King Tut's Tomb and Museum

Luxor IMAX Theater/Secrets of the Luxor Pyramid

MGM Grand Adventures

New York New York Roller Coaster

World of Coca-Cola

Center Strip

Caesars Magical Empire

Caesars OMNIMAX Theatre

Carnaval Fantastique

Forum Shops at Caesars Palace Fountain Shows

Imperial Palace Auto Collection

Masquerade Village Show in the Sky

The Mirage Volcano

Race for Atlantis IMAX 3D Ride

The Secret Garden of Siegfried and Roy/Mirage Dolphin Habitat

Treasure Island Pirate Battle

North Strip

Grand Slam Canyon Theme Park

Speedworld

Stratosphere Tower and Thrill Rides

Wet 'n' Wild

Paradise Road

Hollywood Movie Museum

Star Trek: The Experience

Downtown

Fremont Street Experience

Off the Beaten Track

Liberace Museum

Lied Discovery Children's Museum

Index by Type of Attraction

Amusement Park/Thrill Rides

Grand Slam Canyon Theme Park

MGM Grand Adventures

New York New York Roller Coaster

Stratosphere Tower and Thrill Rides

Wet 'n' Wild

Museums/Memorabilia Exhibits

Ethel M. Chocolates/M&M World

Hollywood Movie Museum

Imperial Palace Auto Collection

King Tut's Tomb and Museum

Liberace Museum

Lied Discovery Children's Museum

World of Coca-Cola

The Secret Garden of Siegfried and Roy/Mirage Dolphin Habitat

Shows/Entertainment

Caesars Magical Empire

Carnavale Fantastique

Fremont Street Experience

Forum Shops at Caesars Palace Fountain Shows

Masquerade Village Show in the Sky

The Mirage Volcano

Treasure Island Pirate Battle

Theaters & Simulation Rides

Caesars OMNIMAX Theatre

Luxor IMAX Theater/Secrets of the Luxor Pyramid

Race for Atlantis IMAX 3D Ride

Speedworld

Star Trek: The Experience

Las Vegas Attractions A to Z

Caesars Magical Empire
Center Strip

This is tremendous fun and worth every penny (although it costs a *lot* of pennies). Ancient Rome is the theme here. After you arrive, you are assigned to a group (of no more than 24 people), and a Roman guard leads you and your group to a private room for dinner and an interactive magic show. Afterward, you are free to wander through the catacombs, where you can see more magic shows or a light-and-laser show; make requests from *Invisabella*, the ghostly player piano; have a drink at one of the bars and more. You can stay as long as you like, but to see everything once, allow at least three hours.

In Caesars Palace, 3570 Las Vegas Blvd. S. ☎ *702/731-7110.* **Admission:** *$65–$75 (includes three-course meal and wine); children pay half price (must be at least 10 years of age).* **Open:** *Daily 4:30–11:30pm.*

Caesars OMNIMAX Theatre
Center Strip

If you've never been to one of these kinds of theaters, you'll want to check this out. Inside a large geodesic dome, reclining seats offer a panoramic view of the 57-foot curved screen, all the better to take in the 3D, 70mm films shown here in an 89-speaker surround-sound environment. Films change regularly, but they all offer almost-like-the-real-thing events, like riding a roller coaster, plunging over a waterfall, or climbing Mt. Everest. Folks prone to motion sickness might want to pass this one by.

In Caesars Palace, 3570 Las Vegas Blvd. S. ☎ *702/731-7110.* **Admission:** *$7 adults; $5 children 2–12, seniors, hotel guests, and military personnel.* **Open:** *Box office open daily 9am–11pm; show times vary.*

163

Dollars & Sense

If you are spending a lot of time (or money) gambling in one casino, check with the dealer or casino attendant to find out if you can get a discounted (or free) admission to the hotel's attractions. A simple "How much is it to get into (fill in the blank)?" may get you a free pass if you're dumping money into their coffers via the casino.

Carnaval Fantastique
Center Strip
In the new Carnaval Court at Harrah's, aerealists perform "death-defying" acts accompanied by lasers, lights, sound effects, and fireworks under a faux big-top. This is another roadside attraction designed to entertain passersby and hopefully lure them into the casino afterward. It's free, so why not?

In Harrah's Las Vegas, 3475 Las Vegas Blvd. S. ☎ *702/369-5000.* **Admission:** *Free.* **Open:** *Shows nightly every hour, starting at dusk.*

Ethel M. Chocolates/M&M World
South Strip
Calling all chocoholics. This four-story retail and exhibit space, brought to you by the company that makes M&Ms, Milky Way, Snickers, and more is devoted to the four basic food groups: milk chocolate, dark chocolate, white chocolate, and chocolate truffles. Although the space is more gift shop than museum, it's still fun to wander around here—plus they give free samples! There's also a free shuttle running to the factory in Henderson that leaves every hour between 10:30am and 4:30pm.

3785 Las Vegas Blvd. S. (inside the Showcase Mall just north of Tropicana). ☎ *800/4-ETHELM.* **Admission:** *Free.* **Open:** *Sun–Thurs 10am–midnight, Fri–Sat 10am–1am.*

Dollars & Sense

On a strict budget? Lost all your money in the slots? No problem. There are lots of inexpensive diversions in town to keep you amused (and away from the casinos). Many of the free publications in town, such as *What's Up Magazine* and *Showbiz* include coupons for discount admissions to attractions. In addition, some hotels have people at the front door passing out coupons for discounted admission to the hotel's attractions.

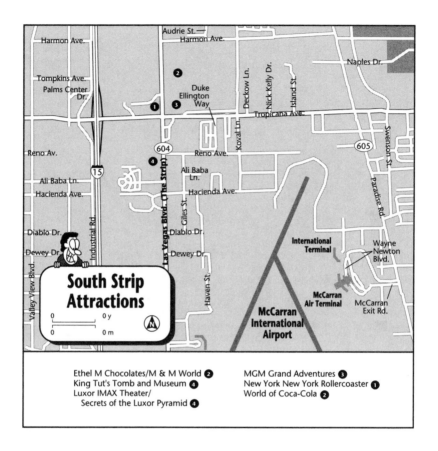

Ethel M Chocolates/M & M World ❷
King Tut's Tomb and Museum ❹
Luxor IMAX Theater/
 Secrets of the Luxor Pyramid ❹

MGM Grand Adventures ❸
New York New York Rollercoaster ❶
World of Coca-Cola ❷

Kids The Forum Shops at Caesars Palace Fountain Shows

Center Strip

You'll have to see this one to believe it. Every hour on the hour, the statues in two giant marble fountains in this snazzy hotel shopping arcade come to life! Near the Strip entrance, a statue of Bacchus in the Festival fountain begins to move and speak to the accompaniment of lasers, water, and smoke. In the Roman Great Hall (at the end of the new expansion), the Atlantis fountain uses hydraulics, projection-screen TVs, and fire effects to entertain the crowd.

The Forum Shops at Caesars Palace, 3500 Las Vegas Blvd. S. ☎ 702/893-4800. **Admission:** *Free.* **Open:** *Shows hourly Sun–Thurs 10am–11pm, Fri–Sat 10am–midnight.*

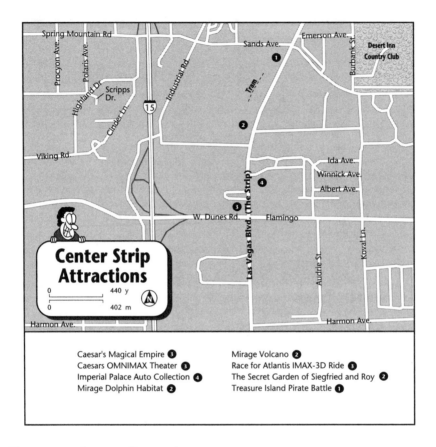

Caesar's Magical Empire ❸
Caesars OMNIMAX Theater ❸
Imperial Palace Auto Collection ❹
Mirage Dolphin Habitat ❷

Mirage Volcano ❷
Race for Atlantis IMAX-3D Ride ❸
The Secret Garden of Siegfried and Roy ❷
Treasure Island Pirate Battle ❶

Fremont Street Experience
Downtown

This high-tech light-and-laser show is not to be missed. Above the five-block, open-air pedestrian mall on Fremont Street is a 90-foot steel-mesh canopy equipped with more than 2 million lights. At night, a five- to seven-minute light-and-laser show flashes overhead, accompanied by concert hall–quality sound. Shows rotate throughout the night and seasonally (the Christmas show is a lot of fun). Aerialists and live bands perform between shows on some nights. Just before this book went to press, the city announced a multimillion dollar expansion of the Fremont Street Experience that will extend the light show down the side streets that are currently blocked by the pedestrian mall.

On Fremont St., between Main St. and Las Vegas Blvd. ☎ *702/678-5777, Internet www.vegasexperience.com.* **Admission:** *Free.* **Open:** *Nightly, with shows every hour, on the hour, from dusk to midnight.*

Grand Slam Canyon Theme Park
North Strip

This miniature amusement park under a giant pink dome might be a good place to head on a hot day. There's a double-loop roller coaster, a water flume, laser tag, and a few other rides—plus a separate video/carnival game arcade, food stands, and a "dinosaur bone" excavation area for the smaller kids. Both kids and adults will have their fill of this place after a few hours.

In Circus Circus, 2889 Las Vegas Blvd. S. ☎ *702/734-0410. Admission: All-day ride pass $15.95 if you're above 4 feet tall, $13.95 if not. Per-ride prices $2 for children's rides, $4 for family rides, and $5 for thrill rides. Open: Sun–Thurs 10am–6pm, Fri–Sat 10am–10pm.*

Hollywood Movie Museum
Paradise Road
Debbie Reynolds herself (on film) shows you pieces of her massive movie memorabilia collection, including costumes and props from movies such as *Showboat, Ben Hur, Cleopatra,* and *Gigi,* accompanied by clips showing their use in the films. A small walkthrough museum contains Barbra Streisand's *Funny Girl* dress, Marilyn Monroe's famous subway dress from *The Seven-Year Itch,* and the ruby slippers from the *Wizard of Oz,* among other items.

In the Debbie Reynolds Hotel & Casino, 305 Convention Center Dr. ☎ *702/7-DEBBIE. Admission: $7.95 adults, $5.95 children 5–12. Open: Mon–Fri 10am–10pm, with tours every hour, on the hour.*

Tourist Traps
Las Vegas amusement parks are not huge places, and in most instances, you can cover all the rides in an hour or two. Unless you plan on doing every ride over and over, consider paying the per-ride fees instead of purchasing an all-day ride pass.

Imperial Palace Auto Collection
Center Strip
You don't have to be a car buff to enjoy this extensive collection of classic automobiles and trucks. It includes cars once owned by JFK, Eisenhower, Hitler, and Hirohito, among others from the political world; and Elvis, Liberace, and W.C. Fields, to name a few from the entertainment world. Allow one to two hours to tour the collection.

In the Imperial Palace, 3535 Las Vegas Blvd. S. ☎ *702/731-3311. Admission: $6.95 adults, $3 seniors and children under 12, free for children under 5 and AAA members. Open: Daily 9:30am–11:30pm.*

King Tut's Tomb and Museum
South Strip

This is a complete, full-scale reproduction of the great Egyptian king's tomb, meticulously laid out according to historical records. Everything was re-created with painstaking detail, with the replicas hand-crafted in Egypt. This isn't the real thing, obviously, but it comes close, for which you have to give someone credit. Audio tours are available in a variety of languages.

In the Luxor, 3900 Las Vegas Blvd. S. ☎ *702/262-4000.* ***Admission:*** *$4.* ***Open:*** *Sun–Thurs 9am–11pm, Fri–Sat 9am–11:30pm.*

Liberace Museum
Off the Beaten Track

Whether you're a fan of the outrageous performer or not, this "museum" is a must for Vegas visitors. Bejeweled costumes, pianos, cars, furniture, and knick-knacks fill multiple buildings, all celebrating the camp silliness that was Liberace. There's also his 50-pound, $50,000 rhinestone and a gift shop full of cheaper rhinestone-encrusted items. It's silly fun, so don't take it too seriously. An hour or two is plenty of time to see it all.

1775 E. Tropicana Ave. (at Spencer St. about 3 miles west of the Strip on the right). ☎ *702/798-5595.* ***Admission:*** *$6.95 adults, $4.50 seniors over 60, $3.50 students, $2 children 6–12, free for children under 6.* ***Open:*** *Mon–Sat 10am–5pm, Sun 1–5pm.*

Dollars & Sense

Some hotels offer free shuttles to outlying attractions. Check with the concierge or tour desk to find out what your hotel can do for you.

Lied Discovery Children's Museum
Off the Beaten Track

Great for toddlers and young children, this bright, airy, interactive science museum is fun and educational. Your young ones can encase themselves in a soap bubble, play in a miniature radio station or grocery store, and learn about nutrition from a cardboard snake. Drop-in art classes are offered on weekend afternoons. Teenagers will probably think this place is a big yawn, but small children will find it a terrific diversion, and adults will enjoy it, too.

833 Las Vegas Blvd. N. (about 1[1/2] miles north of Fremont). ☎ *702/382-5437.* ***Admission:*** *$5 adults, $4 children 12–17, $3 children 3–11.* ***Open:*** *Tues–Sat 10am–5pm, Sun noon–5pm.*

Luxor IMAX Theater/Secrets of the Luxor Pyramid
South Strip

The Luxor IMAX is a state-of-the-art theater that projects a standard two-dimensional or high-tech three-dimensional film onto a giant seven-story screen. You'll wear a 3D headset that includes built-in speakers for total environment immersion. Movies change regularly, so call ahead to find out what's playing. Those with a fear of heights can request a lower-level seat.

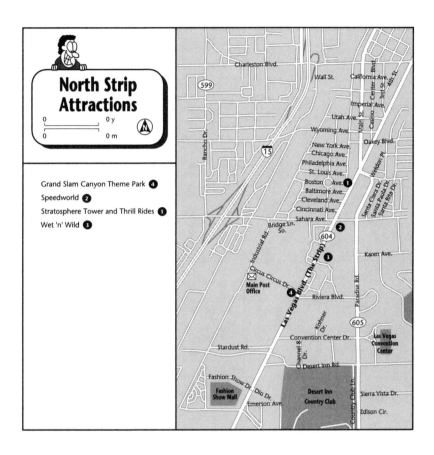

North Strip Attractions

0 y
0 m

Grand Slam Canyon Theme Park ❹
Speedworld ❷
Stratosphere Tower and Thrill Rides ❶
Wet 'n' Wild ❸

Secrets of the Luxor Pyramid is a two-part show that starts with an interactive video introducing you to the adventure story about an archaeological expedition beneath the Luxor pyramid. It concludes with a simulator ride that mimics flight through a dangerous catacomb using video, sound, and motion technology (the seats move). If you're prone to motion sickness, you may choose a non-motion version, but even that can get to you.

Both parts take about an hour.

In the Luxor, 3900 Las Vegas Blvd. S. ☎ *702/262-4000.* **Admission:** *$7 for 2D films, $8.50 for 3D films. Secrets of the Luxor Pyramid: $4 for episode 1, $5 for episode 2. A combined ticket for both episodes of Secrets and passes to the IMAX Theater is $19.* **Open:** *Sun–Thurs 10am–11pm, Fri–Sat 10am–11:30pm. Show times vary, depending on the length of the film.*

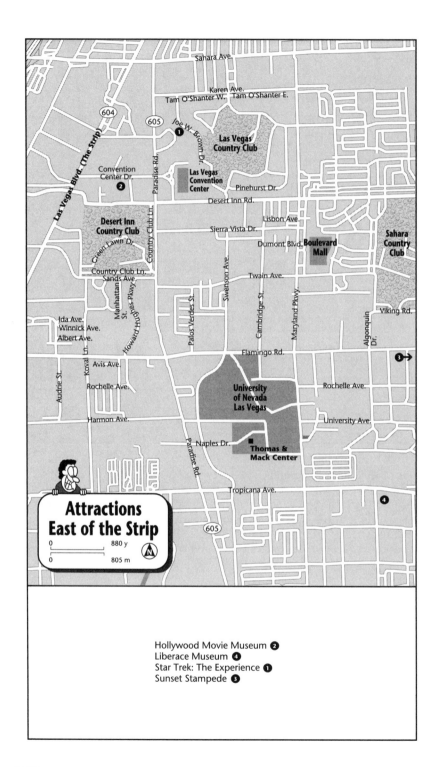

Attractions
East of the Strip

Hollywood Movie Museum ❷
Liberace Museum ❹
Star Trek: The Experience ❶
Sunset Stampede ❸

Bet You Didn't Know

The Moulin Rouge Hotel-Casino was built in 1955 in an effort to cater to African-Americans who were not welcome in the major Strip hotels. The original building still exists on Martin Luther King, Jr. Boulevard just west of downtown, and plans are in the works to restore it as a historical site.

Masquerade Village Show in the Sky
Center Strip
Here's another free hotel show, this one in the carnival-themed Rio Hotel & Casino. In this extravaganza, giant Mardi Gras–style floats filled with singers, dancers, and musicians travel on tracks in the ceiling two stories above the floor, while on an adjacent stage, there are more performers and gigantic animal puppets. If you're not content with merely watching, you can actually pay to get in costume and ride one of the floats.

In the Rio Hotel & Casino, 3700 W. Flamingo Rd. (just east of I-15). ☎ *702/252-7777.* **Admission:** *Free to view, $12.95 to participate.* **Open:** *Shows every 2 hours, Sun–Tues noon–10pm, Thurs–Sat 1–11pm.*

MGM Grand Adventures
South Strip
Except on hot days, this parking lot–turned–theme park is a pleasant enough way to spend a few hours—especially if you're a teenager. The outdoor amusement park has the prerequisite roller coaster and other attractions, although the park seems to have more food stands and T-shirt emporiums than rides. The best thrill will cost you extra: The Sky Screamer is sort of a giant slingshot that makes you feel like you're flying.

Behind the MGM Grand Hotel/Casino, 3799 Las Vegas Blvd. S. ☎ *702/891-7777.* **Admission:** *Entry only (no rides) $2. Entry plus unlimited rides $9–$11. Sky Screamer $22.20 for one person, $17.50 each for two people, $12.50 each for three people.* **Open:** *Daily; hours vary seasonally.*

The Mirage Volcano
Center Strip
OK, so it's not a real volcano, but it's still pretty cool anyway. Flames, lights, water, and sound simulate an eruption for the sidewalk crowd. The show lasts only a few minutes, but the price is right—free! Get there at least 10 minutes before the spewing starts for the best vantage point near the main driveway entrance.

In front of The Mirage, 3400 Las Vegas Blvd. S. ☎ *702/791-7111.* **Admission:** *Free.* **Open:** *Eruptions take place every 15 minutes from dusk to 1am.*

171

Kids New York New York Roller Coaster
South Strip

Apparently, the designers of New York New York didn't think their little Big Apple looked busy enough, so they threw in a roller coaster. It's designed to look like a New York City cab, and it plummets, loops, and rolls in and around the hotel's re-created New York skyline. A unique feature of the ride is the Barrel-Roll Drop, which turns you upside down and then drops you straight toward the ground. Not for the faint of heart. Enter through the second-level arcade and be prepared for a long line.

In the New York New York, 3790 Las Vegas Blvd. S. ☎ 702/740-6969. Admission: $5. Open: Sun–Thurs 10:30am–10:30pm, Fri–Sat 10:30am–midnight.

Tourist Traps

Many people are amazed that Vegas hotels offer such extravagant shows—for free! The bottom line is that most of these shows last only a few minutes, and the hotels are hoping you'll spend time before or after the show dumping some dough in the casino. Avoid the temptation by setting aside separate times for gambling and sightseeing.

Kids Race for Atlantis IMAX 3-D Ride
Center Strip

Virtual-reality motion-simulator rides seem to be the rage these days, and The Forum Shops have a giant-screen version with the latest technology. After you strap on your 3D headset with built-in speakers, you'll think you're on a wild chariot race through the lost city of Atlantis. This is being billed as the biggest and the best ride of its kind, so if this is your thing, you should love it.

The Forum Shops at Caesars Palace, 3500 Las Vegas Blvd. S. ☎ 702/733-9000. Admission: $9.50 adults, $6.75 children under 12. Open: Sun–Thurs 10am–11pm, Fri–Sat 10am–midnight. The ride lasts 20 minutes once you get inside.

Kids The Secret Garden of Siegfried and Roy/Mirage Dolphin Habitat
Center Strip

The Secret Garden is a small zoo where rare lions, tigers, leopards, and the like from Siegfried and Roy's show live while they aren't on stage. Not a lot of people take the time to visit this, and it's a shame. Guests get earphones so they can listen to prerecorded facts and fun tidbits about the animals. The Dolphin Habitat allows you to play with and learn about our flippered friends. Playing "catch" with a dolphin is an undeniable thrill. There's also a gift shop and cafe. Allow at least two hours, but you can stay as long as you like.

Behind The Mirage, 3400 Las Vegas Blvd. S. ☎ *702/791-7111.* **Admission:** *$10 (except Wed, when it's $5 for the Dolphin Habitat only). Free for children under 11.* **Open:** *Daily 10am–5:30pm (Secret Garden closed Wed).*

🌟Kids **Speedworld**
North Strip

This isn't your standard racing video game. It's a wild, eight-minute motion-simulator ride that puts you in replicas of Indy race cars (three-fourths the size of the real cars) and lets you career through the Las Vegas Motor Speedway or around (and even inside) the hotels on the Strip and downtown. The cars mimic the experience of racing—down to the wind in your hair and the required pit stops if you crash. Adjacent 3D motion theaters take you on similar races as a group experience.

In the Sahara Hotel & Casino, 2535 Las Vegas Blvd. S. ☎ *702/737-2111.* **Admission:** *Indy-car simulator $8 (you must be at least 48 inches tall and less than 300 pounds to ride), 3D simulator $5.* **Open:** *Mon–Thurs 10am–10pm, Fri–Sun 10am–midnight.*

Star Trek: The Experience
Paradise Road

Attention, all personnel! You won't want to miss this one. Your Star Trek "Experience" kicks off with a self-guided tour of Star Trek memorabilia and clips from the TV and movie series. Next, you are "beamed aboard" The Enterprise (I can't tell you how, but it's cool). There are full re-creations of the bridge and a shuttlecraft, on which you experience a state-of-the-art motion simulator ride. Gift shops and eateries are adjacent. You don't have to be a die-hard Trekkie to enjoy this, but it would probably help.

In the Las Vegas Hilton, 3000 Paradise Rd. ☎ *702/732-5111.* **Admission:** *$9.95.* **Open:** *Daily 11am–11pm.*

Stratosphere Tower and Thrill Rides
North Strip

The indoor and outdoor observation decks of this 110-story tower offer unbelievable views of Las Vegas and a big chunk of southern Nevada. Thrill-seekers (or the seriously demented) can try the **Let It Ride** roller coaster, which whirls around the outside (!!) of the tower—over 1,000 feet in the air—or experience the **Big Shot,** an open car that rockets up 160 feet to the tip of the tower and drops back down in a bungee effect. Only for the truly adventurous.

In Stratosphere Las Vegas, 2000 Las Vegas Blvd. S. ☎ *702/380-7777.* **Admission:** *$6 for tower access, $5 for the roller coaster, $6 for the Big Shot, $14 for tower access and both rides. Minimum height for rides is 48 inches.* **Open:** *Tower: Sun–Thurs 9am–1am, Fri–Sat 9am–2am. Rides: Sun–Thurs noon–midnight, Fri–Sat noon–1am (weather permitting).*

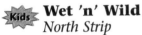 Treasure Island Pirate Battle
Center Strip

Here's the lowdown, matey: It's a live-action battle (with actors and stunt-people) between a full-scale British frigate and a pirate ship on Buccaneer Bay, an 18th-century port village. I'm not kidding. It has cannons and explosions and sword fights with soldiers and pirates swinging on ropes and falling into the water. It all ends with one of the ships sinking grandly into the bay—but I won't tell you which one. It's free, but get there at least 30 minutes before show time for a good viewing spot—preferably on the gangplank that leads into the casino.

In front of Treasure Island, 3300 Las Vegas Blvd. S. ☎ ***702/894-7111.*** **Admission:** *Free.* **Open:** *Battles every 90 minutes 4–11:30pm.*

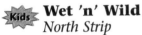 Wet 'n' Wild
North Strip

If you need to cool off, try this 26-acre water park filled with thrill rides (like a 45-mph drop into a "bottomless" pool), water slides and chutes (including the world's fastest and highest), wave pools, and white-water rafting just for starters. You can also work on your tan in an adjacent waterfall sunbathing area. There's even video and arcade games if one kid wants to get wet and the other doesn't. A solid afternoon's worth of entertainment, but not if you don't like children.

2601 Las Vegas Blvd. S. (just south of the Sahara Hotel & Casino). ☎ ***702/737-3819.*** **Admission:** *$23.95 adults, $16.95 children under 10, $10.95 seniors over 55, free for children under 3.* **Open:** *April 30–Sept 30 daily 10am–6 or 8pm. Season and hours vary, so call ahead.*

Bet You Didn't Know

Just because everything in Vegas has to break some record, the World of Coca-Cola features a 100-foot glass Coke bottle. Yep, you guessed it—it's the world's largest.

World of Coca-Cola
South Strip

A museum/gift shop devoted to all things Coke. Your visit starts with live-action exhibits detailing the history of the product (from soda fountain to bottling plant). You next move on to the art museum, featuring paintings, murals, and sculptures depicting... you guessed it. Next comes the tasting area, where a wild, musical water fountain will pour you a glass of soda. The grand finale is a two-story gift shop where they've slapped the Coca-Cola logo on just about every possible item.

In the Showcase Mall, 3785 Las Vegas Blvd. S. (just north of Tropicana Ave.). ☎ ***800/720-COKE.*** **Admission:** *$2, free for children under 6.* **Open:** *Sun–Thurs 10am–11pm, Fri–Sat 10am–midnight.*

Attractions Worksheet

Attraction and location	Amount of time you expect to spend there	Best day and time to go
Caesars Magical Empire		
Caesars OMNIMAX Theatre		
Carnaval Fantastique		
Ethel M. Chocolates/M&M World		
Forum Shops at Caesars Palace Fountain Shows		
Fremont Street Experience		
Grand Slam Canyon Theme Park		
Hollywood Movie Museum		
Imperial Palace Auto Collection		
King Tut's Tomb and Museum		
Liberace Museum		
Lied Discovery Children's Museum		
Luxor IMAX Theater/Secrets of the Luxor Pyramid		
Masquerade Village Show in the Sky		
MGM Grand Adventures		
The Mirage Volcano		
New York New York Roller Coaster		
Race for Atlantis IMAX 3D Ride		
The Secret Garden of Siegfried and Roy/ Mirage Dolphin Habitat		
Speedworld		
Star Trek: The Experience		
Stratosphere Tower and Thrill Rides		
Treasure Island Pirate Battle		
Wet 'n' Wild		
World of Coca-Cola		

Chapter 13

More Fun Stuff to Do

10¢ PER RIDE

In This Chapter

➤ More fun things to do, including entertainment for the kids

➤ Where to go get hitched!

➤ Staying active

If you like constant action and variety, Las Vegas is the place for you. There's something going on around the clock (even beyond the gaming tables!). The attractions listed in the preceding chapter are the real biggies, but they're not the whole story by a long shot—there's a lot more sensory overload to be had. Read through the headings below, and see what strikes your fancy.

All the attractions mentioned in this chapter can be found on the maps in chapter 12.

If You Want to Check Out Some Knock-Your-Socks-Off Architecture

Of course, Vegas isn't the place for appreciating great architecture in the classical sense of the term, but there are lots of buildings here that will make your eyes bug out. One of the main activities in town is wandering around and gawking at the gigantic, splashy, gimmick-filled hotels. I've described them in detail in chapter 6, "Hotels A to Z," but for sheer spectacle, these few are my favorites.

Your first stop has to be **New York New York,** 3790 Las Vegas Blvd. S. (☎ 702/740-6969). It's that little place (hah!) on the corner of Tropicana Ave. and the Strip that looks like the New York City skyline, complete with the Empire State Building and the Statue of Liberty. Take time to really appreciate all the silly touches, like the graffiti-covered mailboxes and the change carts dressed up like Checker cabs.

What's that just across the street from New York? A medieval castle? Well, sort of. It's the **Excalibur,** 3850 Las Vegas Blvd. S. (☎ **702/597-7777**), one of the largest hotels in the world. Check out the moat, drawbridge, and fire-breathing dragon.

Next, take the air-conditioned walkway farther south to **Luxor,** 3900 Las Vegas Blvd. S. (☎ **702/262-4000**), where you can experience the Vegas version of ancient Egypt. The Sphinx (don't worry, the real one is still in Egypt) stands guard in front of the 30-story pyramid that's big enough to house nine jumbo jets. Be sure to visit the dizzying interior of the pyramid, especially the second-floor attractions level.

If You've Got the Kids in Tow

Your kids will love a lot of the attractions described in chapter 12 (just look for the kid icon for my suggestions), but if you need even more entertainment for the young ones, the **Scandia Family Fun Center,** 2900 Sirius Ave. (☎ **702/364-0070**), is a good bet. There's miniature golf, bumper boats, miniature-car racing, and a huge video arcade. Take Sahara Avenue west to Rancho Drive (just past I-15), turn left, and go about one-half mile; Scandia will be on your right. Hours vary seasonally, so call ahead.

Bet You Didn't Know

Just when you thought Las Vegas couldn't attain any more obscure world records, try this one on for size: The interior of the Luxor is the biggest indoor atrium in (you guessed it) the world!

Another solid bet is the **Circus Circus Midway,** 2880 Las Vegas Blvd. S. (☎ **702/734-0410**), located inside Circus Circus. Open 24 hours, it has carnival games where the kids can win prizes and arcade games where they can blow up the universe. Ongoing circus acts—trapeze artists, stunt cyclists, jugglers, magicians, and acrobats—perform continuously under the big top every day from 11am to midnight.

GameWerks, 3785 Las Vegas Blvd. S. (☎ **702/432-GAME**), is a 47,000-square-foot facility boasting the latest interactive video games plus a giant rock-climbing wall. It's located in the Showcase Mall just north of the MGM Grand Hotel/Casino. It's open Sunday to Thursday from 10am to 2am and Friday and Saturday from 10am to 4am. Also of note are the video-game arcades in the **New York New York, Excalibur,** and **Luxor** hotels. All are large and feature lots of high- (and low-) tech diversions for the kids.

Tourist Traps

Many of the video- and carnival-game arcades offer winners of certain games tickets that can be redeemed for merchandise. Cynics say this is a way to expose kids to gambling at a young age—I think your kids will learn pretty quick that spending $10 on Skee-Ball just to win a stuffed animal worth a buck doesn't make much sense.

If You Want to Get Hitched

Many of the major hotels have wedding chapels and services, but you'll find the bulk of the independent places between the Strip and downtown on Las Vegas Boulevard.

Your first stop has to be at the courthouse to visit the **Clark County Marriage License Bureau,** 200 S. 3rd St. (☎ 702/455-3156). All they require is for both of you to be there and for one of you to have $35. That's it—not even a blood test. They're open daily from 8am to midnight, except on legal holidays, when they are open 24 hours.

To actually tie the knot, there are a couple of places that I recommend. The first is **Cupid's Wedding Chapel,** 827 Las Vegas Blvd. S. (☎ 800/543-2933), which offers a pretty simple and straightforward setting. It's the staff that sets this place apart; they provide genuine warmth and an infectious sense of romance. Even if you're not getting married, you may be able to watch other couples tie the knot. Just ask. You can decide for yourself whether a $100, 15-minute wedding is as likely to last as a $50,000 ceremony complete with brides-maids.

I also like **A Special Memory Wedding Chapel,** 800 S. Fourth St. at Gass Ave. (☎ 800/9-MARRYU). It's a clean, modern new building complete with a church-like steeple and a demi-shopping arcade for flowers, tuxes, and the like. If you're in a hurry, you can use their drive-up window!

For more information about weddings in Vegas, call **Las Vegas Weddings and Rooms** (☎ 800/488-MATE), or visit the **Wedding Dreams** web site at **www.weddingdreams.com**.

Bet You Didn't Know

More than 100,000 weddings are performed in Las Vegas annually. The two busiest days are Valentine's Day (some chapels perform more than 80 services in one day) and New Year's Eve.

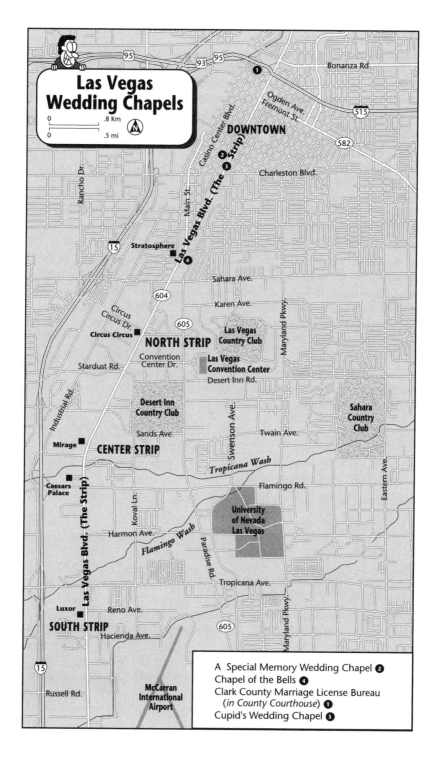

Las Vegas Wedding Chapels

0   .8 Km

0   .5 mi

95

93   95

Bonanza Rd.

①

Ogden Ave.
Fremont St.

515

DOWNTOWN

582

②
③

Charleston Blvd.

Casino Center Blvd.

Las Vegas Blvd. (The Strip)

Main St.

Rancho Dr.

15   **Stratosphere**

④

Sahara Ave.

604

Karen Ave.

Maryland Pkwy.

605

Circus
Circus Dr.

Circus Circus ■

NORTH STRIP

**Las Vegas
Country Club**

Convention
Center Dr.

**Las Vegas
Convention Center**

Stardust Rd.

Desert Inn Rd.

**Desert Inn
Country Club**

**Sahara
Country
Club**

Industrial Rd.

Sands Ave.

Swenson Ave.

Twain Ave.

Eastern Ave.

Mirage ■

CENTER STRIP

Tropicana Wash

Flamingo Rd.

**Caesars
Palace** ■

Las Vegas Blvd. (The Strip)

Koval Ln.

**University
of Nevada
Las Vegas**

Harmon Ave.

Flamingo Wash

Paradise Rd.

Tropicana Ave.

Luxor ■

Reno Ave.

605

SOUTH STRIP

Hacienda Ave.

15

Maryland Pkwy.

Russell Rd.

**McCarran
International
Airport**

A Special Memory Wedding Chapel ②
Chapel of the Bells ④
Clark County Marriage License Bureau
    (in County Courthouse) ①
Cupid's Wedding Chapel ③

If You Like Animals

The first stop for animal lovers has to be the **Mirage Dolphin Habitat,** described in chapter 12, but if that isn't enough for you, try the **Southern Nevada Zoological and Botanical Park,** 1775 N. Rancho Dr. (☎ **702/ 648-5955**). The zoo itself is on the smallish side, but there are more than 250 species from around the world, plus a petting zoo for kids. Admission is $5 for adults and $3 for seniors and kids under 12. Zoo hours are 9am to 5pm daily. To get there, take Charleston west from the Strip to Rancho Drive and turn right. It's up about 2½ miles on your left.

At the **Excalibur,** 3850 Las Vegas Blvd. S. (☎ **702/597-7600**), you can watch an amazing show with the **Royal Lippizaner Stallions**—beautiful horses from Vienna that perform amazing footwork and leaps to classical music. Admission is $7.95 for adults, $5.95 for children under 12 and seniors. Show time is 2pm Saturday through Thursday.

You can also take the **Wildlife Walk** at the **Tropicana Resort & Casino,** 3801 Las Vegas Blvd. S. (☎ **702/739-2222**) and stroll through a natural habitat for exotic wildlife, including cockatoos, toucans, and marmosets. Admission is free, and you can walk through 24 hours a day.

If You Want to Get Away From the Neon

Just about everything has a neon sign in Las Vegas—even the 7-11. In fact, I've often wondered: If I stop long enough, will I myself wind up with a neon sign strapped to my butt?

If it all gets a little much for you, there are places you can go that don't involve bright lights, marble, and concrete. **The University of Nevada Las Vegas (UNLV)** is located between Paradise Road and Maryland Parkway, just east of the Strip and just north of Tropicana Avenue. Yes, there is concrete, but there are also lots of beautifully landscaped paths wandering throughout the campus. It's basically an arboretum with a wide array of plants, trees, and flowers. Overall, a beautiful and relaxing distraction.

Lorenzi Park, the largest in Las Vegas, is located just west of Rancho Drive, northwest of the Strip. There is a lake, a few museums, playgrounds, and jogging paths, plus acres of grassy lawns and lush gardens. To get there, take Charleston Boulevard west from the Strip, turn right on Rancho Drive, and travel about two miles to Washington Street and turn left. You'll see the park on your left in a few short blocks.

If you don't mind a little airport noise, there's also the large, lushly landscaped **Sunset Park** located just south of McCarran International Airport. You'll find jogging paths, a swimming pool, tennis and volleyball courts, playgrounds, a lake, and lots of real plants instead of the fake ones inside most casinos. Head south on the Strip to Sunset Road, turn left, and go a couple of miles to Eastern. The park is on the southeast corner.

If You Really Like the Neon

Barbara Mulasky is heading up a terrific project for the city called **The Neon Museum,** at Fremont Street and Las Vegas Boulevard (☎ **702/229-4872**). The goal is to rescue classic neon signs, restore them, and put them on public display as a means of preserving Las Vegas history. At the end of the Fremont Street Experience (see chapter 12), you'll find the horse and rider from the Hacienda Hotel, the genie's lamp from the Aladdin Hotel, the Anderson Dairy Milkman, and the Chief Motel Motorcourt sign, among others prominently displayed. The future should bring more signs and an indoor facility for smaller exhibits.

The signs that haven't made it to the Neon Museum yet are resting in what is known as the **Neon Graveyard, Young Electric Sign Company,** 5119 Cameron St. (west of the Strip at Tropicana Ave.; ☎ **702/876-8080**). There are no official tours of this place, but the company has made most of the neon signs in Las Vegas for decades. Those that have outlived their usefulness now rest in a dusty lot next to their factory. You can only view them from the fence, but they are a powerful bit of Vegas history.

If You Want a Fun Factory Tour

Henderson is a community just to the southeast of Las Vegas, about a 20- or 25-minute drive from the Strip, where you'll find three functioning factories that offer tours.

Ethel M Chocolates, 2 Cactus Garden Dr. (☎ **702/433-2500**), allows you to see how chocolate (the "M" is for Mars, as in Mars Bars, M&Ms, and more) and other candy is made on a free, self-guided tour. You even get samples in the adjoining gift shop! They're open daily (except Christmas) from 8:30am to 7pm, although it's best to visit on a weekday when the business is up and running. You can catch the free shuttle from M&M World on the Strip (see chapter 12).

Time-Savers

The fastest way to get to Henderson is to take the Strip south to Sunset Road, about a mile past the last of the big hotels. Turn left, and it's a straight shot across to Mountain Vista, where you'll find Ethel M Chocolates. Continue on Sunset Road to Stephanie Avenue (less than a mile) and turn right. Take that a few blocks to American Pacific Road, and you'll see Cranberry World West. Kidd's Marshmallow Factory is right around the corner.

Just down the road is **Cranberry World West,** 1301 American Pacific Dr. (☎ 702/566-7160), an Ocean Spray juice plant. Admission is free here also, and you get to see a short film and play with interactive exhibits; you're also treated to free samples of beverages and baked goods. It's open daily from 9am to 5pm.

Just in case the chocolate and cranberries haven't given you enough of a sugar high, right around the corner is **Kidd's Marshmallow Factory,** 1180 Marshmallow Lane (☎ 800/234-2383). Same concept as the others: a free, self-guided tour with samples and a gift shop. Visit Kidd's Monday to Friday from 9am to 4:30pm or weekends from 9:30am to 4:30pm.

If You Want to Visit a Serious Museum

If the Liberace Museum isn't highbrow enough for you, there are several outstanding museums in town.

The **Clark County Heritage Museum,** 1830 S. Boulder Hwy. (☎ 702/455-7955), takes you through 12,000 years of local history, including exhibits on Native American tribes, pioneer settlements, the gold-rush era, and the dawn of gambling (with old slot machines and a life-size statue of Bugsy Siegel). The 25-acre facility also has an authentic ghost town and several houses from the early to mid-1900s that have been fully restored with period furnishings. Hours are 9am to 4:30pm daily; admission is $1.50 for adults and $1 for seniors and kids 3 to 15. To get there, take Tropicana Avenue east to Boulder Highway and turn right. It's down about eight miles on your left.

Five miles west of the Strip on Sahara Avenue is a big white building that houses the **Las Vegas Art Museum,** 9600 W. Sahara (☎ 702/360-8000). This is a lovely facility that has revolving exhibits of fine art. It's open Tuesday to Saturday from 10am to 5pm and Sunday from 1 to 5pm. Admission is $3 for adults, $2 for seniors, and $1 for students; children under 12 enter free.

Finally, you might want to check out the **Las Vegas Natural History Museum,** 900 Las Vegas Blvd. N. (☎ 702/384-3466), to see exhibits of (stuffed) bears, elk, and the like, plus a few roaring dinosaurs. There's also a hands-on activity room great for kids, and a gift shop for you. It's a couple of miles north of downtown. It's open 7 days a week from 9am to 4pm. Admission is $5 for adults and $2.50 for children 4 to 12.

If You Want to Visit a Not-So-Serious Museum

If the Liberace Museum is *too* highbrow for you, then run over to the **Guinness World of Records Museum,** 2780 Las Vegas Blvd. S. (☎ 702/792-3766), which is on the Strip just north of Circus Circus. It's a hilarious conglomeration of exhibits that celebrate the achievements listed in the Guinness Book of Records (like the collection belonging to Louise, the Magnet Lady). The museum is open daily from 9am to 6pm. Admission is $4.95 for adults, $3.95 for seniors and students, and $2.95 for children 5 to 12.

Inside O'Shea's Casino (between Harrah's and Barbary Coast on the Strip) is the **Magic and Movie Hall of Fame,** 3555 Las Vegas Blvd. S. (☎ **702/737-1343**). The primary focus here is the art of illusion. Your visit starts with a half-hour show and concludes with a visit through a vast museum loaded with interactive exhibits and displays on everyone from Houdini to Siegfried and Roy. You can visit Tuesday through Saturday from 10am to 6pm; there are shows at 11:30am, 1:30, and 4:30pm. Admission is $9.95 for adults and $3 for children under 12.

Dollars & Sense

All over Vegas, you'll have people thrusting flyers and coupons into your hand as you walk around. Many of them are for adult-oriented fare, but some offer discounts to museums, attractions, and restaurants. Many hotels also offer *funbooks* that include coupons and savings on fun stuff all over town.

If You Want to Take a Fun Side Trip from Las Vegas

If you're dizzy from sensory overload, you might want to consider getting out of town for a day, because there's some cool stuff to see nearby. Note: Hotels sometimes run escorted trips out of town, so ask at the front desk for information.

Rent a car and head over to **Hoover Dam**, one of the most magnificent architectural achievements in the world. It took five years to build and stands as high as a 60-story skyscraper. Guided tours are offered by the **Hoover Dam Visitor Center** (☎ 702/294-3522) between 8:30am and 5:30pm; tours vary in price, schedule, and extensiveness. The dam is about 30 miles southeast of Las Vegas and is best reached by taking Tropicana to Boulder Highway and turning right. That road becomes U.S. 93 and will take you all the way to the dam.

Around 20 miles west of Las Vegas is **Red Rock Canyon**, a beautiful and serene natural area highlighted by the natural sandstone sculptures and red rocks that gave it its name. You can either take the 13-mile scenic drive (for a $10.00 per vehicle fee) or spend a few hours hiking and picnicking. Take Charleston Avenue (between the Sahara Hotel & Casino and the Stratosphere Las Vegas) west; it'll become Highway 159. The **Red Rock Canyon Visitor Center** (☎ 702/363-1921) will be on your right, and it's open from 8:30am to 4:30pm.

Even farther afield is **The Extraterrestrial Highway**. This 100-mile stretch of U.S. 375 passes near Nellis Air Force Base, where the infamous **Area 51** is supposedly located and UFOs and aliens are supposedly housed.

Outer-space and flying saucers are the theme at the roadside stands and diners in small towns like Rachel and Warm Springs, where I'm not sure if they think the whole thing is a joke or not. Take I-15 north to U.S. 93, which will connect with U.S. 375. Return via U.S. 6 and U.S. 95, and you're going to go a few hundred miles, but it can easily be done in a day. For more information on services and places to stop, contact the **Nevada Commission on Tourism** (☎ **800/NEVADA-8**) or check the web at **www.ufo-hway.com** or www.ufomind.com.

Also near Las Vegas are Mt. Charleston (a popular ski resort area), Lake Mead (water activities galore for the summer), and Valley of Fire State Park (a natural wonder if there ever was one). For more information on these and other recreation areas, consult the Nevada Commission on Tourism (☎ 800/ NEVADA-8) or check with your hotel tour desk.

If You Want to Work Up a Sweat

For many years, recreation in Las Vegas meant lying by the pool, and exercise came in the form of pulling handles on slot machines. But when The Mirage opened in the late 1980s, it signaled a change in attitude that would revolutionize the way visitors spent their time. This major resort was the first in town to offer such an unprecedented array of sporting and exercise alternatives. Sure, there were other hotels in town that had golf courses and health clubs, but nobody did it quite the way The Mirage did. Virtually every major hotel built since then has tried to imitate the Mirage's success. Odds are that your own hotel will have a huge array of options, and probably even a full-fledged spa.

Biking

Escape the City Streets (☎ **702/596-2953**) is a rental company that offers 21-speed mountain bikes at $26 for the first day, $20 for a half day or whole consecutive days, and $90 for a week (major credit card required). They'll even drop your bike off for you at any downtown or Strip hotel.

Consider taking a trip out to Red Rock Canyon using Charleston Boulevard. There's a nice wide bike lane starting at Rainbow Lane (in the western part of town) that runs all the way to the canyon's visitor center, about 11 challenging but not impossible miles in total. If you're really in good shape, you might consider a bike tour of the canyon itself. Contact the **Red Rock Canyon Visitors Center** (☎ **702/363-1921**) or ask the bike rental agent for other options.

Bowling

Las Vegas hosts major Pro Bowlers' Association tournaments every year, so you know the city has some of the biggest and most modern facilities in the world. One of the best is **The Showboat Hotel Bowling Center,** 2800 E. Fremont St. (☎ **702/385-9153**), which is southeast of downtown. With 106 lanes, it's the largest bowling center in North America. Everything is spotless and high-tech, with a variety of food stands and shops adjacent. They're open 24 hours a day. To get there from the Strip, take Las Vegas Boulevard north to Charleston, and turn right. The hotel is at the intersection of Charleston and Fremont, about three miles away.

The recently completed **Orleans,** 4500 W. Tropicana Ave. (☎ **702/365-7400**), has a great 70-lane facility that's also open 24 hours a day. It's on the second floor of the hotel, which you'll see on your right as you travel west from the Strip on Tropicana Ave.

Extra! Extra!

If you're interested in taking the plunge, literally, I'll bypass my commentary about your mental health and just send you straight to *A.J. Hackett Bungy,* 810 Circus Circus Dr. (☎ **702/385-4321**), which has a 175-foot tower where you can take a flying leap. They offer a variety of price packages, some of which include membership, T-shirts, and videotapes of your bungee jump. They're located next to Circus Circus, just west of the Strip. Their hours vary, so call ahead for more information.

Golf

Las Vegas is a favorite destination for the PGA's annual tour. **The Desert Inn Golf Club,** 3145 Las Vegas Blvd. S. (☎ **800/634-6906** or 702/733-4290), is considered by many golf pros to be one of America's best. It has an 18-hole, par-72 resort course, and everything except for the driving range is open to non-hotel guests. Reservations are required and can be booked up to 90 days in advance for a Sunday-to-Thursday tee time and two days in advance for a Friday or Saturday tee time.

Another exceptional course is located at the **Las Vegas National Golf Club,** 1911 Desert Inn Rd. (☎ **702/796-0016**), which was formerly part of the Las Vegas Hilton Country Club. There's an 18-hole, par-71 public course just past Paradise Road on your left.

Also notable is the **Angel Park Golf Club,** 100 S. Rampart Blvd. (☎ **702/254-4653**), which has a 36-hole, par-70/71 public course that was designed by Arnold Palmer. To get here, take the Strip to Charleston Blvd. and travel west about 10 miles; then turn right on Rampart.

Health Clubs

Just about every hotel in town has a health club/spa, so you'll probably find a place to work out without a problem. I especially like the outstanding facilities at The Mirage, The Desert Inn, the Golden Nugget, the Luxor, and Caesars Palace (which is soon to feature a rock-climbing wall and Zen meditation garden).

Tourist Traps

If you're an avid golfer and intend to play the links in Las Vegas, consider bringing your own clubs. I know of more than one golfer who didn't want to haul his equipment halfway across the country but later found himself horrified at the outrageous rental fees at the local courses.

If your hotel doesn't offer what you want, you can check out the health club at **Harrah's Las Vegas**, 3475 Las Vegas Blvd. S. (☎ 702/369-5000), which is the only hotel facility I know of that's open to the general public. Don't miss the virtual-reality cycles and stair climbers that allow you to steer through various courses (island, snowscape, and more). They even simulate the wind blowing through your hair and have soundtracks accompanying the onscreen action. They're perfect distractions for people who hate to exercise (like me).

You can try the **Las Vegas Sporting House**, 3205 Industrial Rd. (☎ 702/733-8999), which is located right behind the Stardust Resort & Casino. It boasts more than 65,000 square feet of luxurious facilities, including racquetball/handball courts, squash courts, tennis courts, a full gymnasium for basketball and volleyball, indoor and outdoors pools and jogging tracks, and a full range of free weights and Nautilus-type machines. As if that weren't enough, they also offer aerobics and spinning classes. After that hard workout, you can enjoy a sauna, steamroom, Jacuzzi, massage, skin- and hair-care salon, restaurant, bar, and/or lounge (call ahead to book massages and services). Plus, you can leave the kids with the baby-sitter during your entire visit. The facility is open 24 hours a day, in case you have a burning desire to use a Stairmaster at 4am.

Tennis

In addition to the tennis courts at the Las Vegas Sporting House, you'll also find places to play at several hotels. **Bally's Las Vegas,** 3645 Las Vegas Blvd. S. (☎ 702/739-4598), has eight lighted hard courts; the **Desert Inn Country Club Resort & Casino,** 3145 Las Vegas Blvd. S. (☎ 702/733-4557), has five; the **Flamingo Hilton,** 3555 Las Vegas Blvd. S. (☎ 702/733-3444), has four; and you'll find two at the **Riviera Hotel & Casino,** 2901 Las Vegas Blvd. S. (☎ 702/734-5110). All are open to the public, but rates and hours of operation vary, so call ahead to reserve.

If You Want to Catch the Best Spectator Sports

There are no major-league sporting teams in Las Vegas, so most of the local action comes from the **University of Nevada Las Vegas (UNLV).** The main campus is located just off Paradise Road between Tropicana Avenue and Flamingo Road. If you just have to get a football or basketball fix, there may be a game playing at the **Thomas and Mack Center** (☎ **702/895-3900**) on campus. This 18,500-seat facility hosts the college teams and a variety of boxing tournaments, NBA exhibition games, and rodeos.

Caesars Palace (☎ **800/634-6698**) and the **MGM Grand's Garden Events Arena** (☎ **800/929-1111**) host major sporting events year round, including gymnastics, figure skating, and boxing. Remember the bite that Mike Tyson took out of Evander Holyfield's ear in 1997? That happened at the MGM—how proud they must be.

Auto Racing

The **Las Vegas Motor Speedway,** 7000 Las Vegas Blvd. N. (☎ **702/ 644-4443**), is a new 107,000-seat, $100 million–dollar state-of-the-art motor sports entertainment complex. There's a 1.5-mile oval that hosts Indy and NASCAR events, a road course, a drag strip, and a motocross course. Ticket prices vary wildly, so call ahead to find out what's happening and how much it costs. If you're driving, take I-15 north to the Speedway exit (#54) and follow the signs. If you're cabbing it, save your money by catching the shuttle bus that runs regularly from the Imperial Palace.

Bowling

The **PBA Classic** in January and **PBA Invitational** in March are two major stops on the Pro Bowlers Tour. Both are hosted by the **Showboat Hotel,** 2800 Fremont St. (☎ **702/385-9150**).

Golf

The **Las Vegas Invitational,** a major stop on the PGA tour, is held every October on several local courses. For details, call ☎ **702/242-3000.**

Rodeo

Every December, Las Vegas hosts the **National Rodeo Finals,** considered to be the "Super Bowl of rodeos." Nearly 200,000 people attend the two-week event, which is held at the Thomas and Mack Center on the UNLV campus. Everything sells out quickly, so call as far in advance as possible (☎ **702/ 895-3900**).

187

Chapter 14

Charge It! A Shopper's Guide to Las Vegas

In This Chapter

➤ Malls and outlet stores

➤ Standout hotel shopping arcades

➤ Necessities and oddities

Most people don't really think of Las Vegas as a shopper's paradise. But though it's true that there is no Rodeo Drive (otherwise known to people with good credit ratings as the holy land), the city does run the gamut from campy souvenir shops to tony Beverly Hills–style boutiques. Die-hard shoppers will not have a problem finding places where they can part with their money.

This is Las Vegas, and very little comes without some measure of showmanship. It's not enough to be a mall; you've gotta be a "theme" mall, preferably with shows or rides to amuse people as they walk from Banana Republic to The Gap. This chapter will take a look at the basics, the bargains, and the bizarre shopping options.

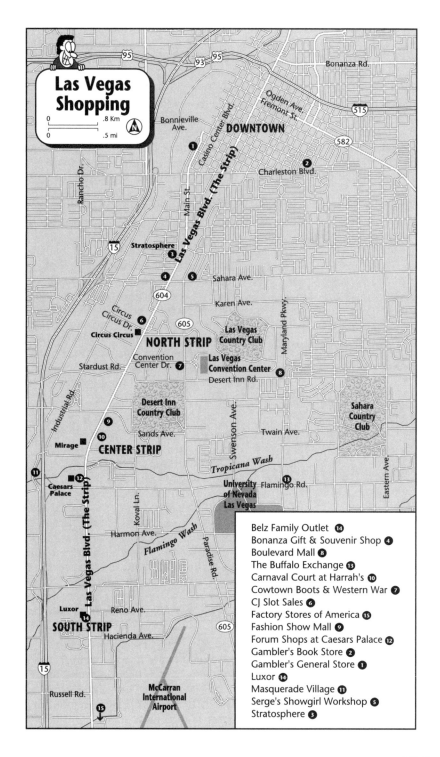

Las Vegas Shopping

0   .8 Km
0   .5 mi

Bonanza Rd.

Ogden Ave.
Fremont St.

Bonnieville Ave.

DOWNTOWN

Charleston Blvd.

Cadino Center Blvd.

Main St.

Rancho Dr.

Las Vegas Blvd. (The Strip)

Stratosphere

Sahara Ave.

Karen Ave.

Maryland Pkwy.

Circus Circus Dr.

Circus Circus

NORTH STRIP

Las Vegas Country Club

Stardust Rd.

Convention Center Dr.

Las Vegas Convention Center

Desert Inn Rd.

Sahara Country Club

Desert Inn Country Club

Sands Ave.

Swenson Ave.

Twain Ave.

Industrial Rd.

CENTER STRIP

Mirage

Eastern Ave.

Caesars Palace

Tropicana Wash

University of Nevada Las Vegas

Flamingo Rd.

Koval Ln.

Harmon Ave.

Flamingo Wash

Paradise Rd.

Luxor

Reno Ave.

SOUTH STRIP

Hacienda Ave.

Russell Rd.

McCarran International Airport

Belz Family Outlet ⑭
Bonanza Gift & Souvenir Shop ④
Boulevard Mall ⑧
The Buffalo Exchange ⑬
Carnaval Court at Harrah's ⑩
Cowtown Boots & Western War ⑦
CJ Slot Sales ⑥
Factory Stores of America ⑮
Fashion Show Mall ⑨
Forum Shops at Caesars Palace ⑫
Gambler's Book Store ②
Gambler's General Store ①
Luxor ⑭
Masquerade Village ⑪
Serge's Showgirl Workshop ⑤
Stratosphere ③

The Malls

Didn't believe me when I said *theme mall*? Your first stop, regardless of your shopping intentions, should be **The Forum Shops at Caesars Palace,** 3570 Las Vegas Blvd. S. (☎ **702/893-4800**). Think of it as Rodeo Drive meets Ancient Rome, with a healthy dash of Disneyland, and you still probably aren't even close to what this place is really like. It's a mall designed to look like a Roman street scene, complete with columns, marble, and animatronic statues under a "sky" that somehow transforms from day to night as time passes. Hardly your typical suburban mall in design or content. You'll find mostly high-rent joints like Louis Vuitton, Christian Dior, Armani, and Versace alongside fancy restaurants like Spago. (Even if they're all beyond your budget, it's a hoot to walk through here and check out the scene.) A new addition has added a three-story FAO Schwarz with a giant moving Trojan horse at the entrance, Fendi, and Polo (among others) plus more talking statues and a giant aquarium. Send the kids (or bored husbands) downstairs to the motion-simulator cinema rides in 3D that simulate space flight, submarine adventures, and roller coasters (the cost is $6 to $8 for a five-minute ride). Then get everybody back together for the every-hour-on-the-hour light-and-laser shows at the Festival Fountain or the Atlantis Fountain. The shops are open Sunday to Thursday from 1am to 11pm, Friday and Saturday from 10am to midnight.

Bet You Didn't Know

Think your utility bill is high? Caesars Palace has an annual electric bill of over $3 million! Apparently, the cost of all that neon adds up—or else the guests keep leaving the lights on when they leave their rooms.

Dollars & Sense

Everything's more expensive on the Strip, and that goes for the merchandise in the stores and malls as well as for hotels and restaurants. If you're more intent on serious bargain hunting than fun browsing, head elsewhere.

Just up the street (across from Treasure Island) is the **Fashion Show Mall,** 3200 Las Vegas Blvd. S. (☎ **702/369-8382**), which is not quite as upscale as The Forum Shops but pretty close. More than 130 shops, restaurants, and services include Nieman-Marcus, Saks Fifth Avenue, Macy's, Louis Vuitton, and the Sharper Image, plus your usual mall denizens, such as The Gap, Bennetton, and Victoria's Secret. No roller coasters here, but you can arrange to have your car washed while you shop. Free self and valet parking is available, and the mall is open Monday to Friday from 10am to 9pm, Saturday from 10am to 7pm, and Sunday from noon to 6pm.

If you're looking for the comforts of home, head over to **Boulevard Mall,** 3528 S. Maryland Pkwy. (☎ **702/732-8949**). This is the largest mall in Las Vegas, and its more than 140 stores are geared to your average traveler. You'll find names such as Sears, J.C. Penney, and Marshalls. All the usual suspects are here, including The Gap, The Limited, Victoria's Secret, and The Disney Store, just to name a few. To get here, take any of the major east-west streets (Flamingo, Tropicana, or Sahara) to Maryland Parkway, which is about two miles east of the Strip. The mall is located just south of Desert Inn Road and north of Flamingo. Hours are Monday to Friday from 10am to 9pm, Saturday from 10am to 8pm, and Sunday from 11am to 6pm.

Where the Bargains Are: The Outlet Malls

Factory-outlet malls are springing up all over the country, and Las Vegas is no exception. For those not familiar with the concept, these outlets are where major chain stores or companies offer big savings on merchandise that wasn't quite good enough to get into the regular stores. In most cases, we're talking about tiny, almost invisible flaws in the material of a shirt or a pattern on a Crockpot that doesn't quite match up. Sometimes it's just where they dump their overstocked merchandise that is completely fine. No matter the reason, you can often get up to 75 percent off what you would pay for the same goods at retail stores.

The biggest and best is the indoor **Belz Factory Outlet World,** 7400 Las Vegas Blvd. S. (☎ **702/896-5599**). There are 145 outlets, including Casual Corner, Levi's, Nike, Esprit, Bugle Boy, Reebok, Oneida, Bose, and Waterford Crystal. As you can see from that partial list, they have a lot more than just clothing and shoes. It's all in a friendly and spacious mall-like setting that has a giant indoor carousel for kids (or bored spouses). Open Monday to Saturday from 10am to 9pm, Sunday from 10am to 6pm.

Dollars & Sense

Before you buy something in a regular mall in Las Vegas, ask the sales staff if the store has a local outlet. You can save big bucks by exploring these alternatives.

Factory Stores of America, 9155 Las Vegas Blvd. S. (☎ **702/897-9090**), is a 30-acre outdoor mall with more than 40 stores, such as Corning/Revere Cookware, Izod, Mikasa Crystal, American Tourister, B.U.M. Equipment, and London Fog. If you find yourself seized with a sudden need to gamble, you can amble over to their on-premises casino/bar/lounge. Hours are Monday to Saturday from 10am to 8pm and Sunday from 10am to 6pm.

You can get to either of these malls by heading south on the Strip. They are both located a few miles past the southernmost major hotel, the Luxor.

Hotel Shopping Arcades

Just about all the big hotels have some sort of shopping arcade where you can find fancy clothing emporiums, sundry stores, and logo shops (that's the

1990s term for gift shop). I recommend avoiding these places like the plague if at all possible, since you'll pay a lot more for whatever you buy than you will elsewhere. They get away with charging $1.50 for a pack of gum or $8 for shampoo because they assume hotel guests or fervent gamblers won't want to leave the property for these kinds of items.

A few places, however, have taken the shopping arcade to a new level. **Masquerade Village,** 3700 W. Flamingo Rd. (☎ **702/252-7777**), is a new 60,000-square-foot addition to the Rio Hotel & Casino that includes two levels of shopping and dining surrounding a casino. It's done as a European village and sports mostly upscale clothing boutiques and small curio or jewelry shops (only a few national chains like Nicole Miller and Speedo). Be sure to stop by the **'Nawlins** store, which sells voodoo items, Mardi Gras masks, and the like. I question the authenticity of any of it, but it's fun to look around.

There's also a large shopping arcade at the **Stratosphere Las Vegas,** 2000 Las Vegas Blvd. S. (☎ **702/380-7777**), which you have to pass through to get to the tower itself. It has more than 40 stores set in different international streetscapes that attempt to evoke Paris, Hong Kong, and New York City. One notable gift shop sells functioning and decorative slot machines.

Tourist Traps

Most of the hotel shopping arcades are adjacent to or in the middle of casinos. Perhaps they hope you'll use your shopping money on a slot machine instead? Avoid these machines if at all possible, since they are rumored to offer lower winnings than machines in other areas of the casinos.

Harrah's Las Vegas, 3475 Las Vegas Blvd. S. (☎ **702/369-5000**), has recently remodeled from top to bottom, and that includes their outdoor shopping arcade, the **Carnaval Court**. The party, logo, and magic stores are accompanied by a Ghirardelli Chocolate shop. It all surrounds a covered courtyard where lights, lasers, fireworks, and acrobats provide entertainment after dark.

The **Luxor,** 3900 Las Vegas Blvd. S. (☎ **702/262-4000**), has a new arcade with eight stores ranging from men's and women's fashions to toys and upscale gifts. There's also a Cairo Bazaar section with street vendors selling a variety of trinkets and doodads from carts.

Where to Pick Up Necessities

You never know what's going to come up while you're on vacation (or what you'll forget to pack), so it's always good to know where those dependable, low-cost chain stores are located.

You can find everything from clothes to aspirin and hair spray at **Target,** 4001 S. Maryland Pkwy. (at Flamingo; ☎ **702/732-2218**), or **K-Mart,** 2975 E. Sahara (about three miles east of the Strip; ☎ **702/457-1037**). The K-Mart also has a pharmacy.

You can also fill medical prescriptions at **Sav-On,** 1360 E. Flamingo Rd. (at Maryland Parkway; ☎ **702/731-5373**), which is a large national pharmacy chain. Another, closer option is **White Cross Drugs,** 1700 Las Vegas Blvd. S. (just north of the Stratosphere Tower; ☎ **702/382-1733**). If you go there, you can have a great hamburger at the Liberty Cafe (see chapter 10, "Making Your Restaurant Choice") while you're waiting.

If you're traveling with a child (or someone who is acting like a child) toys and stuffed animals are cheaper at **Toys 'R Us,** 4000 S. Maryland Pkwy. (at Flamingo; ☎ **702/732-3733**) than at your hotel gift shop.

For those who took a road trip, you may want to know about **Pep Boys,** 637 E. Sahara (just east of Paradise; ☎ **702/796-0600**), a major auto parts and service chain that can be helpful if you're concerned about making it home.

I've Just Gotta Have a Campy Souvenir

Desperate for a pair of dice earrings or a snowglobe of Las Vegas? Well, look no further than **Bonanza Gift and Souvenir Shop,** 2460 S. Las Vegas Blvd. (at the northwest corner of Sahara; ☎ **702/384-0005**). They bill themselves as the "largest souvenir shop in the world," although I'm not really sure what particular organization certifies such things. I can tell you that it is very large and filled with a wide array of souvenirs—from the ultra-tacky to the expensive.

Dollars & Sense

Most of the hotels have small gift shops (A.K.A. *logo shops*) that offer a variety of trinkets for you to bring home to friends and family. If you can, try to get out to one of the independent souvenir shops. You'll usually find better deals and more interesting stuff.

If all those designer clothing stores are making you nervous, take a drive over to **The Buffalo Exchange,** 4110 S. Maryland Parkway (☎ **702/791-3960**). It's one of a chain of used-clothing stores filled with hip, alternative, and plain old weird outfits. Hours are Monday to Saturday from 11am to 8pm, Sunday from noon to 6pm. It's in a small shopping strip at the southeast corner of Maryland Parkway and Flamingo Road (next to Tower Records).

If you have a sudden hankerin' to do some serious two-stepping but don't have the right apparel for the task, mosey on over to **Cowtown Boots and Western Wear,** 2989 Paradise Rd. (across from the Las Vegas Hilton;

☎ **702/737-8469**). You'll find a big barn full of boots, jeans, hats, and assorted cowboy paraphernalia. You can yee-haw it there Monday to Saturday from 9am to 6pm, Sunday from 10am to 5pm.

Time-Savers

If you're into the alternative music scene, check out the local newspapers and flyers at The Buffalo Exchange. You can also ask the staff what's happening in town. They are knowledgeable and informed about local bands and clubs. Consider it a one-stop-shopping resource for the alterna-set.

If you're not content blowing your money at the blackjack table, you can blow it on gambling-related stuff downtown at the **Gambler's General Store,** 800 S. Main St. (eight blocks south of Fremont; ☎ **800/322-CHIP**). Another "World's largest" (who decides these things?), the store has actual gaming equipment (dice, craps tables, old slot machines, and more) and a virtual library of gambling books. The store is open daily from 9am to 5pm.

You can also find a wide array of used slot machines, video poker, keno, and even blackjack tables at **CJ Slot Sales,** 2770 Las Vegas Blvd. S. (just north of Circus Circus; ☎ **702/893-0660**). They have everything from antiques to the latest gadgets, but it ain't cheap! Hours are Monday to Saturday from 9am to 5:30pm.

If you want to read up on strategy, try the **Gambler's Book Shop,** 630 S. 11th St. (☎ **800/522-1777**), near Charleston Road. There are more than 4,000 gambling-related titles here designed to help you beat the odds.

For another only-in-Vegas experience, stop in at **Serge's Showgirl Wigshop,** 953 E. Sahara #A-2 (in the Sahara Commercial Center just east of Paradise; ☎ **702/732-1015**). This place has been around for more than 20 years and has some 2,000 wigs costing from $130 to $1,500. They have wigs by Dolly Parton and Revlon, men's and women's hairpieces, or they can customize your own special creation. If the prices are a little steep, there's an outlet store just across the shopping center for discontinued wigs that run around $50–$60. They are open Monday to Saturday from 10am to 5:30pm.

If you're an antique hound, you'll want to poke around East Charleston Road, where more than 20 small antique stores of very good quality are located within a few blocks of each other. Go north on the Strip to Charleston Road and turn right—the stores begin about the 1600 block. You can also stop at **Silver Horse Antiques,** 1651 E. Charleston (☎ **702/385-2700**), to pick up a map that highlights all the individual shops, complete with phone numbers and business hours.

Part 6

On the Town: Nightlife & Entertainment

Las Vegas is a 24-hour town, and come nightfall, the city really lights up. (With so much neon, what else would you expect?) Vegas nightlife has something for everyone, so try to pull yourself away from the slot machines to sample it. And plan on becoming a night owl; many bars and other hotspots don't really start to swing until midnight.

Although Vegas has a sophisticated side, it's not exactly known for symphony or theater. Nobody ever came to Vegas looking for a dose of Beethoven or Shakespeare. Nightlife in Las Vegas means dropping some of your gambling dough on big, splashy production shows and checking out the hippest clubs and bars. This section of the book will help you plan your Vegas nights.

Chapter 15

The Shows A to Z

Though long famous for its slick, larger-than-life production shows, Vegas has a lot more to offer these days than just magic acts and bare-breasted showgirls with Cadillac-size headdresses. The Mirage Corporation shattered the conventional model a few years ago, bringing the avant-garde Canadian circus troupe Cirque du Soleil to town. That resounding success has spawned a slew of big-budget imitators. These days, the trend in major production shows is toward bigger, louder, brighter, and more expensive creations—perfect for Vegas.

But never fear, this is still the town of Sigfried & Roy and showgirls. If you want to see big-time magic acts or topless dancer revues, you won't go home disappointed. This chapter will walk you through your options.

Given the spectrum of nightlife in Las Vegas, ranging all the way from glitz to sleaze, choosing what to do at night is a highly personal matter. While I'm a huge fan of Cirque du Soleil's Mystère and Lance Burton's magic show, I've tried to give equal treatment to other popular shows. Some may not win any critical acclaim, but are certified mass-audience pleasers. These shows, as well as outings for more adventurous travelers, can be found here. There are other big shows in the major hotels, but I've seen them all, and if I didn't think they measured up, I didn't include them. Why waste your time?

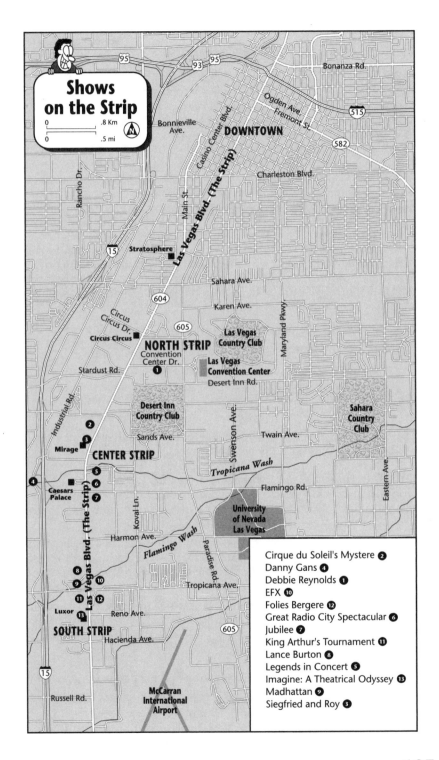

Shows on the Strip

0   .8 Km
0   .5 mi

DOWNTOWN

Bonnieville Ave.

Stratosphere

Sahara Ave.

Karen Ave.

Circus Circus Dr.

Circus Circus

NORTH STRIP

Las Vegas Country Club

Convention Center Dr. ❶

Las Vegas Convention Center

Stardust Rd.

Desert Inn Rd.

Desert Inn Country Club

Sahara Country Club

Sands Ave.

❷

❸

Mirage

CENTER STRIP

Twain Ave.

Tropicana Wash

❹

❺

Caesars Palace

❻

❼

Flamingo Rd.

University of Nevada Las Vegas

Harmon Ave.

Flamingo Wash

❽

❾ ❿

⓫ ⓬

Luxor ⓭

Tropicana Ave.

Reno Ave.

SOUTH STRIP

Hacienda Ave.

McCarran International Airport

Russell Rd.

Cirque du Soleil's Mystere ❷
Danny Gans ❹
Debbie Reynolds ❶
EFX ❿
Folies Bergere ⓬
Great Radio City Spectacular ❻
Jubilee ❼
King Arthur's Tournament ⓫
Lance Burton ❽
Legends in Concert ❺
Imagine: A Theatrical Odyssey ⓭
Madhattan ❾
Siegfried and Roy ❸

197

Price Categories

Categories for shows are based on a single adult ticket that may or may not include taxes, gratuities, drinks, or dinner (see each description for details).

$$$$$	Very Expensive	$75 and up
$$$$	Expensive	$60–$74
$$$	Moderate	$45–$59
$$	Inexpensive	$30–$44
$	Very Inexpensive	$30 or less

A Few Words About Logistics

You Be the Judge

Just as in chapter 12, "The Top Attractions A to Z," I encourage you to take a pen and scribble down your own informal rating next to each listing to indicate your level of interest. That'll make it easier to put your itinerary together later on. Use the same 1 to 5 scale to keep track of which shows you definitely want to see and those you don't:

1 I absolutely cannot miss this show!

2 I'm very interested in this show.

3 This is something that I'd like to do if there's time.

4 Only if I'm really bored.

5 You couldn't drag me.

A little later in this chapter, you'll find one of those handy worksheets that you can use to keep track of these extravaganzas.

What's This Gonna Cost & How Do I Get In?

I've included admission prices on every listing that follows. But use these only as guidelines. Recent show changes or special promotions may result in slightly different prices than those listed here.

If you don't see a separate price for children's admission, it's a fair bet that this show is geared toward adults. It doesn't necessarily mean that the show is obscene, but it may contain racy material or skimpy costumes that some parents don't want their kids to see.

Reservations are required everywhere, but you can often get a last-minute ticket at the box office for many shows. I'll tell you how far in advance you can make reservations.

Showroom Policies

Most showrooms these days are non-smoking and have preassigned seating.

Old Vegas rules are still in effect in some places with maitre d' seating; these are the places where you may want to haul out some extra cash to tip for a better seat. For such an upgrade, you'll probably need to part with $5 to $20 per couple, depending on the original price of your ticket. The higher figure applies to the larger showrooms. If you wish, you might tip the captain who shows you to your seat rather than the maitre d'. If he or she leads you to a satisfactory seat, you won't have to give him anything. If you want something better, discreetly show the captain what you are prepared to tip.

Most shows are found in the large hotels, so you'll find free self or valet parking unless otherwise noted.

Nightlife A to Z

Cirque du Soleil's Mystère
$$$$. Center Strip.

This is an unforgettable and innovative spectacle, unlike any other Las Vegas show. Cirque du Soleil is a Canadian circus troupe from Montreal that performs highly choreographed, imaginative acrobatics and hypnotic feats of human strength. This is not your standard old-fashioned three-ring circus (in fact, there are no animals at all). Expect suspense, laughs, and eroticism in this beautiful spectacle. It is true performance art: surreal, engaging, whimsical, dreamlike, and occasionally, bewildering. However, it may be a bit too sophisticated and arty for some kids' tastes. The show is presented in a customized showroom with state-of-the-art hydraulics; it has the huge dimensions required of a showstopper.

Dollars & Sense

Be sure to check with your hotel to find out if it offers discounts on shows, especially shows staged on its premises. If you're gambling, ask about discounted admission or even free passes to shows and nightspots.

In the Treasure Island, 3300 Las Vegas Blvd. S. (☎ 800/392-1999). Reservations accepted up to 90 days in advance (the word's out about this show, so do reserve as early as possible). **Admission:** *$69.85 adults, $34.84 children under 12 (drinks and tax extra).* **Show times:** *Wed–Sun 7:30 and 10:30pm.* **Showroom policies:** *No smoking, preassigned seating.*

Danny Gans: The Man of Many Voices
$$$. Center Strip.

Impressionist extraordinaire Danny Gans consistently rates as the "best in Las Vegas," according to local polls. Gans, a former Broadway theater star, does uncanny and hilarious impressions of Frank Sinatra, Dr. Ruth, Clint Eastwood, Paul Lynde, Bruce Springsteen, Katherine Hepburn, Stevie Wonder, and of course, Elvis. In the course of the show, Gans dazzles his audience with more than 100 personas. He performs a mind-boggling rendition of "The Twelve Days of Christmas" in 12 different voices. Even the performers he is imitating call him the best. Not only are his impressions dead-on, but Gans's comedy is sophisticated and sharp.

In the Rio Hotel & Casino, 3700 W. Flamingo Rd. (☎ 800/PLAY-RIO). Reservations accepted up to 30 days in advance. **Admission:** *$60.00, including two drinks, tax, and gratuities.* **Show times:** *Wed–Sun at 8pm.* **Showroom policies:** *No smoking; maitre d' seating.*

Tourist Traps

Shows that charge extra for drinks usually charge exhorbitant prices for even the most modest cocktails. Don't plan on doing a lot of drinking during the show unless you won big that day; have a nightcap later at a more reasonably priced bar.

Debbie Reynolds Show
$$. Paradise Road.

Reynolds, a living legend of screen and stage, has a song, dance, and impression show that's a lot of fun. Her voice is still crystal clear on songs from her famous movies, like *Singin' in the Rain.* Her anecdotes and wicked impressions (of fellow stars such as Barbra Streisand and Dolly Parton and TV characters such as Edith Bunker) are hysterical. With her recent film success (*Mother, In and Out*), Reynolds is more in demand in Hollywood, and this show goes on hiatus when she is working. Call ahead to find out if she'll be in town. If you catch the show, hang out afterward in the showroom for the chance at an autograph or photo with Debbie.

In the Debbie Reynolds Hotel & Casino, 305 Convention Center Dr. (☎ 800/ 633-1777). Reservations accepted up to three days in advance. ***Admission:*** *$39.95, including two drinks, tax, and gratuities $55 for dinner and the show.* ***Show times:*** *Mon–Fri at 7:30pm.* ***Showroom policies:*** *No smoking, maitre d' seating.*

EFX
$$$. South Strip.

This $40 million extravaganza stars (as of this writing) former Partridge Family member and one-time teen heartthrob David Cassidy. The skimpy plot involves Cassidy as a man who has lost his imagination and first love. His mission is to travel through time to locate both; along the way, there is singing, dancing, magic, acrobatics, and a slew of remarkable special effects. The sets and effects (*EFX*, in Hollywood terminology) are quite incredible, Cassidy is charming, and the show's choreography is entertaining. You can get away with sitting in the cheap seats; the view is just as good far back as it is up close (and that way, you won't get enveloped in fake fog).

In the MGM Grand Hotel/Casino, 3799 Las Vegas Blvd. S. (☎ 800/929-1111). Reservations accepted any time in advance. ***Admission:*** *$51–$72.* ***Show times:*** *Tues–Sat 7:30 and 10:30pm.* ***Showroom policies:*** *No smoking, preassigned seating.*

Folies Bergère
$$$. South Strip.

This topless revue is a veritable Vegas institution and one of the few remaining dinner shows in town. Beautiful showgirls dance and sing in lavish costumes (the headdresses are only the size of a two-seater). Scenes feature music from a variety of eras and styles (Parisian, American oldies) and are punctuated by acrobatic and comedy acts. *Showgirls* fans rejoice: you've found nirvana!

In the Tropicana Resort & Casino, 3801 Las Vegas Blvd. S. (☎ 800/468-9494).
Reservations accepted up to seven days in advance. **Admission:** *$45–$55, includ-*
ing dinner and drinks. Taxes and gratuities extra. **Show times:** *Fri–Wed at 8 and*
10:30pm. **Showroom policies:** *No smoking, preassigned seating.*

Bet You Didn't Know

The old Dunes Hotel was destroyed by a spectacular explosion staged by the
people who bought it, The Mirage. The explosion was timed to appear as if it
were triggered by cannon fire from the Treasure Island pirate battle nearly one-
fourth mile away.

The Great Radio City Spectacular
$$$. Center Strip.
The world-famous Rockettes deliver this wholesome version of a showgirl
revue. There's always a headliner (Susan Anton, Paige O'Hara from *Beauty and
The Beast*, and others) leading the proceedings, but leggy chorus-line kicks are
the true stars. The musical numbers and the variety acts sandwiched between
them change from time to time, and while there are few surprises, expect to
see lots of dancing, comedians, jugglers, and (if you're lucky) a charming
trained-dog act. It's a smooth, entertaining show.

In the Flamingo Hilton, 3555 Las Vegas Blvd. S. (☎ 702/733-3333). Reservations
accepted up to 14 days in advance. **Admission:** *$54–$65 dinner show includes*
full meal, tax, and gratuities. $46 cocktail show includes two drinks, tax, and gra-
tuity. **Show times:** *Nightly 7:45 dinner show and 10:30pm cocktail show.*
Showroom policies: *No smoking, maitre d' seating.*

Imagine: A Theatrical Odyssey
$$. South Strip.
Dancers, magicians, and acrobats fill the stage for this hour-and-15-minute
show, a combination of Cirque du Soleil feats and Vegas extravaganza. The
magic and dancing segments are merely so-so, but the aerialists, twirling and
bungee jumping 30 feet above the audience, are spectacular. Also of note is a
three-person human-sculpture team. A troupe of astounding Chinese acrobats closes the show. The unique Egyptian-theme showroom and compara-
tively low ticket price make this a fun night out.

In the Luxor, 3900 Las Vegas Blvd. S. (☎ 702/262-4000). Reservations required
up to seven days in advance. **Admission:** *$39.95, including tax.* **Show times:**
Wed–Mon at 7:30 and 10:30pm. **Showroom policies:** *No smoking, preassigned*
seating.

Jubilee!
$$$. Center Strip.

This is another quintessential Las Vegas extravaganza, complete with singing, dancing, fantastic costumes, elaborate sets, and variety acts. And, oh yeah, bare breasts. Lot's of 'em. It's a huge show, with more than 100 dancers and over-the-top sets. Wild production numbers abound, including Samson and Delilah and a musical re-creation of the *Titanic* sinking (with all the silicone on stage, you'd think it would float!). It's probably the only show of its type in town (and you can interpret that statement any way you want).

*In Bally's Las Vegas, 3645 Las Vegas Blvd. S. (☎ **800/237-7469**). Reservations accepted up to six weeks in advance. **Admission:** Starts at $49.50, including tax. Drinks and gratuities extra. **Show times:** Sun–Wed at 8pm, Thurs and Sat at 8 and 11pm. **Showroom policies:** No smoking, preassigned seating.*

Bet You Didn't Know

The movie *Showgirls*, a "tribute" to Vegas showgirl productions, wasn't exactly a documentary. After it bombed in theaters and received a merciless drubbing from critics, it was re-released and marketed as high camp, drawing late-night revelers who hooted it up with (and even dressed up as) the onscreen characters. It even became a gay cult favorite.

The Kenny Kerr Show
$. Paradise Road.

Kerr leads his absolutely fabulous female-impersonator troupe through this revue, sending up Dolly Parton, Liza Minnelli, and Marilyn Monroe—even Pocahontas. The show, previously called *Boylesque,* is the longest-running female impersonator production in town: Since 1976, Kerr has sung, danced, and rapped with his devoted audience. His crew of guys/gals, in brilliant costumes (and often lace panties and bras), looks great.

*In the Debbie Reynolds Hotel & Casino, 305 Convention Center Dr. (☎ **800/ 633-1777**). Reservations accepted up to three days in advance. **Admission:** $21.95, including tax. **Show times:** Tues–Sat at 10:00pm. **Showroom policies:** No smoking, maitre d' seating.*

King Arthur's Tournament
$. South Strip.

Knights in shining armor battle for the hand of a fair maiden in highly choreographed jousts—and all the while, you eat dinner with your hands.

King Arthur's is full-blown medieval tournament fare with audience partici-
pation encouraged to the point of overkill. There's a whole lot of hooting
and hollering going on. Think of it as dinner theater mixed with professional
wrestling. If you're into the WWF, Renaissance fairs, or are just a child at
heart (underneath your armor), you might find it entertaining. But actual
children are the ones who most enjoy this show; their parents usually look
like they'd prefer to be at "Jubilee!"

*In Excalibur, 3850 Las Vegas Blvd. S. (☎ 702/597-7600). Reservations accepted
up to six days in advance.* **Admission:** *$29.95, including dinner, beverage, tax,
and gratuities.* **Show times:** *"Knightly" (their word, not mine) at 6 and 8:30pm.*
Showroom policies: *No smoking, preassigned seating.*

Lance Burton: Master Magician
$. South Strip.
There are a number of big magic shows in town, but this one is by far the
best. A lush, Victorian-style theater is home to the down-home charm of
Burton's magic. The folksy Kentuckian favors up-close-and-personal illusions
over big-budget special effects. There are a few big-set pieces, but Burton's
laid-back personality makes even these routines seem less silly and overpro-
duced than those of his competitors. Although some find the show a bit
modest given the grand surroundings, I'd highly recommend Lance Burton
even if the ticket price weren't so agreeable.

*In the Monte Carlo Resort & Casino, 3770 Las Vegas Blvd. S. (☎ 800/311-8999).
Reservations accepted up to 60 days in advance.* **Admission:** *$34.95, including
tax. Drinks are extra.* **Show times:** *Tues–Sat at 7:30 and 10:30pm.* **Showroom
policies:** *No smoking, preassigned seating.*

Extra! Extra!

When making show reservations, be sure to coordinate them with your dinner
plans so you're not stuck racing through your meal or destined to arrive late for
the curtain. Allow more time than you think to get from place to place on the
Strip; this is when traffic can really stress you out—and you're supposed to be
having *fun.*

Legends in Concert
$. Center Strip.
Another ongoing Vegas tradition is the impersonator show; this one is probably the best. There's no lip-synching here; it's all live performances by impersonators of Neil Diamond, Elton John, Diana Ross, The Four Tops, and Elvis

(performers rotate, so don't count on seeing these every night). The quality of individual acts varies—some performers look like the celebrities but don't really sound quite right or vice versa—but overall, it's a lot of cheesy fun. The show is fast-moving and up-to-date, a real crowd-pleaser—which is why it's been running continuously since 1983.

In the Imperial Palace, 3535 Las Vegas Blvd. S. (☎ 702/794-3261). Reservations accepted up to 14 days in advance. **Admission:** *$29.50, including two drinks. Tax and gratuity extra.* **Show times:** *Mon–Sat at 7:30 and 10:30pm.* **Showroom policies:** *No smoking, maitre d' seating.*

Tourist Traps

Celebrity impersonator shows have sprouted up all over town. Many of them, however, are pretty awful rip-offs featuring look-alikes lip-synching to prerecorded music. Be sure that any impersonator show you are going to features actual singing and live bands.

Madhattan
$$. South Strip.
The theater is decorated to evoke New York (a bus, subway, stoplights, graffiti), and the show itself aims to put you in a New York state of mind. Songs (mostly blues and doo-wop) and dance (tap and street) hark back to Gotham, including selections from recent Broadway hits like *Bring in Da Noise, Bring in Da Funk; Stomp;* and even *Rent.* The cast (all former New York–street performers) is quite talented. The show will probably appeal mostly to young, urban types who like their entertainment loud. Ear-splittingly loud.

In New York New York, 3790 Las Vegas Blvd. S. (☎ 702/740-6815). Reservations required up to seven days in advance. **Admission:** *$40. Tax and gratuity extra.* **Show times:** *Tues–Sat at 7:30 and 10:00pm.* **Showroom policies:** *No smoking, preassigned seating.*

Siegfried & Roy
$$$$$. Center Strip.
These two gents are probably the most famous illusionists in the world, and their $30 million show is a nonstop pageant of magic, dancing, explosions, special effects, white tigers, lions, and elephants. It's all high-drama and very stylized; S&R didn't get rich pulling rabbits out of a hat. Their show is staggering, even overwhelming, and elaborately staged. Many call this magic-act-turned-spectacle a must for every Vegas visitor; if tickets cost about half of

what they do, I'd probably agree, but those are pretty shocking prices for a couple of hours of entertainment.

In The Mirage, 3400 Las Vegas Blvd. S. (☎ **800/627-6667** *or 702/791-7111).* *Reservations accepted up to three days in advance (and this is one of the hottest tickets in town, so act fast).* **Admission:** *$89.35, including two drinks, tax, and gratuity.* **Show times:** *Fri–Tues at 7:30 and 11pm.* **Showroom policies:** *No smoking, preassigned seating.*

Bet You Didn't Know

Siegfried and Roy have performed for approximately 4 million people in Las Vegas. At last check, they were the highest paid performers in the history of Vegas entertainment.

Rating the Nightlife	
Nightlife Entertainment	**Your Rating (1–5)**
Cirque du Soleil's Mystère	
Danny Gans: The Man of Many Voices	
Debbie Reynolds Show	
EFX	
Folies Bergère	
The Great Radio City Spectacular	
Imagine: A Theatrical Odyssey	
Jubilee!	
The Kenny Kerr Show	
King Arthur's Tournament	
Lance Burton: Master Magician	
Legends in Concert	
Madhattan	
Siegfried & Roy	

Headliner Showrooms

Many of the major hotels have showrooms that book big-name singers, bands, and comedians. You can find listings of who is in town by consulting the local free alternative papers *Scope* and *City Life*. You can also call the **Las Vegas Convention and Visitors Authority** (☎ 702/892-0711) and request a free copy of *Showguide* and *What's On in Las Vegas*. For the most up-to-date information and prices, you might also call the showrooms direct.

I'm not going to waste your time describing the venues below, because you're not going for the decor. It would also be pointless to list policies, prices, or show times, since they vary for each performer. What you'll find below is a list of the major showrooms with addresses, phone numbers, and a few examples of the performers who have played in each. I'm including the latter not because it means they'll ever play there again, but to give you a sense of the type and caliber of performers the management tends to book.

Bally's Celebrity Room, in Bally's Las Vegas, 3645 Las Vegas Blvd. S. (☎ 800/237-7469), offers 1,400 seats, and is where everyone from superstars to still-popular has-beens play: Hall and Oates, Barbara Mandrell, Liza Minnelli, Andrew Dice Clay, and George Carlin, among others.

Bet You Didn't Know

Marlene Dietrich and Louis Armstrong shared the Riviera stage in 1962 and showed the audience how to do the twist, the dance craze of the decade.

Caesars Circus Maximus Showroom, in Caesars Palace, 3570 Las Vegas Blvd. S. (☎ 800/445-4544), is a 1,200-seat venue that has featured big-name headliners since 1966, including David Copperfield, Jerry Seinfeld, Julio Iglesias, Natalie Cole, and Rosie O'Donnell.

With only 650 seats, the **Desert Inn Crystal Room,** in The Desert Inn Country Club Resort & Casino, 3145 Las Vegas Blvd. S. (☎ 800/634-6906), is a great place to catch a star. Frank Sinatra made his Vegas debut in the Desert Inn's Painted Room in 1951 (one night, the whole Rat Pack stormed the stage while Eddie Fisher was performing.) Smokey Robinson, The Temptations, Dennis Miller, Neil Sedaka, and Rita Rudner are among those who have performed here since.

The **Hard Rock Hotel's The Joint,** in The Hard Rock Hotel & Casino, 4455 Paradise Rd. (☎ 800/693-7625), opened in 1995 with 1,400 seats. This is the place for current rock headliners, including Melissa Etheridge, Marilyn Manson, Hootie and the Blowfish, Lyle Lovett, and even Bob Dylan.

At the **Las Vegas Hilton,** 3000 Paradise Rd. (☎ 800/222-5361), headliners are once again dominating the showroom that Elvis used to perform in now that *Starlight Express* has closed permanently. Acts like Bill Maher, Johnny Cash, The Monkees, and Al Jarreau join the ghost of Elvis to fill the 1,500 seats.

Bet You Didn't Know

The Las Vegas Hilton, once known as The International, was where The King played when he was in town. Elvis played a record–setting 837 shows here and sold out every one of 'em. (Those were the fat years, indeed.) Today, the Hilton has a large statue of Elvis (okay, it's a shrine) adjacent to the lobby.

Follow the crowds to the 15,225-seat **MGM Grand Garden,** in the MGM Grand Hotel/Casino, 3799 Las Vegas Blvd. S. (☎ **800/929-1111**), for sporting events and the biggest pop concerts: Bette Midler, The Rolling Stones, Janet Jackson, and Elton John. Tickets are available through Ticketmaster (☎ **702/474-4000** or through your hometown number). In the same hotel is the 650-seat **MGM Grand Hollywood Theatre,** where smaller shows can be seen in a more intimate setting. It's hosted Wayne Newton, Dennis Miller, Randy Travis, and Las Vegas tapings of *The Tonight Show with Jay Leno.*

The 450-seat **Orleans Showroom,** in the Orleans, 4500 W. Tropicana Ave. (☎ **800/ORLEANS**), hosts acts like Chuck Berry, The Pointer Sisters, and The Oak Ridge Boys.

Recently renovated, the 750-seat **Sahara Hotel Showroom,** in the Sahara Hotel & Casino, 2535 Las Vegas Blvd. S. (☎ **702/737-2878**), schedules musical acts and comedians such as Rita Rudner and Elayne Boozler.

Hitting the
Bars & Clubs

This chapter will explore some of your nightlife alternatives. There's a bit of everything for just about every taste. Many of you will remain glued to the slot machines or entranced by the roulette wheel, but if you can pry yourself away, there's a lot of fun to be had just by wandering around, checking out the neon spectacle and bar-hopping from hotel to hotel.

By now, you've probably figured out that much of Las Vegas is open around the clock, and that definitely applies to bars and nightclubs as well. If you're still up at 4am and suddenly feel like having a cold beer or going dancing, you're in luck—you're in Las Vegas. Liquor can be sold legally 24 hours a day, and a lot of joints take advantage of that fact by never closing. Most bars and nightclubs don't really start jumping until late. Since lots of folks don't want to give up that slot machine and many locals work in the casinos or shows, it's not unusual for a spot to begin to pick up past midnight.

A word to the wise: You should know that Nevada has extremely tough laws regarding drinking and driving, public intoxication, and disorderly conduct, so go out and have a good time, but don't think that *anything* goes—there are boundaries, despite the hedonistic, party-zone atmosphere.

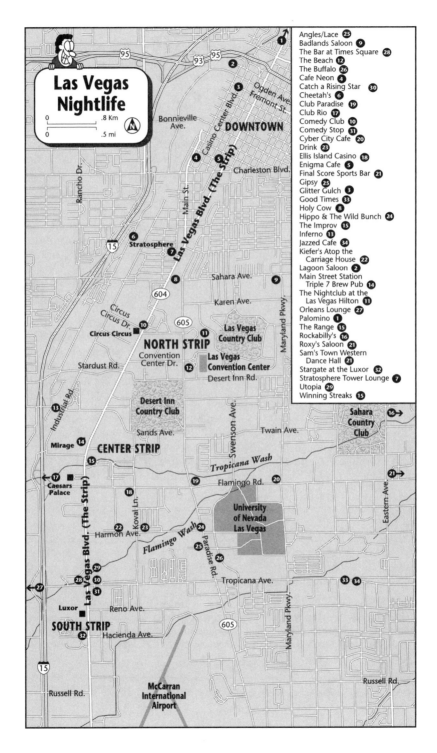

Las Vegas Nightlife

0 ——— .8 Km
0 ——— .5 mi

Angles/Lace **25**
Badlands Saloon **9**
The Bar at Times Square **28**
The Beach **12**
The Buffalo **26**
Cafe Neon **4**
Catch a Rising Star **30**
Cheetah's **6**
Club Paradise **19**
Club Rio **17**
Comedy Club **10**
Comedy Stop **31**
Cyber City Cafe **20**
Drink **23**
Ellis Island Casino **18**
Enigma Cafe **5**
Final Score Sports Bar **21**
Gipsy **25**
Glitter Gulch **3**
Good Times **33**
Holy Cow **8**
Hippo & The Wild Bunch **24**
The Improv **15**
Inferno **13**
Jazzed Cafe **34**
Kiefer's Atop the
  Carriage House **22**
Lagoon Saloon **2**
Main Street Station
  Triple 7 Brew Pub **14**
The Nightclub at the
  Las Vegas Hilton **11**
Orleans Lounge **27**
Palomino **1**
The Range **15**
Rockabilly's **16**
Roxy's Saloon **21**
Sam's Town Western
  Dance Hall **21**
Stargate at the Luxor **32**
Stratosphere Tower Lounge **7**
Utopia **29**
Winning Streaks **15**

If You're Looking for a Good Laugh

Stand-up comedy is a Vegas institution; there are several hotel-based comedy clubs in town, and many prominent comics have made a name for themselves in Vegas. While the clubs may not currently feature acts you've heard of, they do book the up-and-coming comics that may soon appear on a national sitcom. Show times and prices vary, but I've listed what was quoted at press time.

Catch a Rising Star, in the MGM Grand Hotel/Casino, 3799 Las Vegas Blvd. S. (☎ **800/929-1111** or 702/891-7777), books pretty big acts for shows nightly at 7:30 and 10:00pm. Cover is $15.40 (tax and drinks are extra). You can call the box office and charge tickets up to 30 days in advance, and there's maitre d' seating.

The **Comedy Club,** in the Riviera Hotel & Casino, 2901 Las Vegas Blvd. S. (☎ **800/634-3420** or 702/734-9301), features comics, hypnotists, and occasional theme shows (shock comics, X-rated, all gay, and so on) at 8 and 10pm nightly, with a bonus 11:45pm show on Friday and Saturday. Prices range from $19 to $25 and include two drinks and tax. Tickets must be purchased at the box office (you can't call ahead and charge over the phone), and there's maitre d' seating.

The **Comedy Stop,** in the Tropicana Resort & Casino, 3801 Las Vegas Blvd. S. (☎ **800/468-9494** or 702/739-2411), has 8 and 10:30pm shows nightly. The $16 cover includes two drinks, tax, and gratuities; tickets can be charged in advance, and there's maitre d' seating. It's also the only comedy club that permits smoking.

Finally, **The Improv,** in Harrah's Las Vegas, 3475 Las Vegas Blvd. S. (☎ **800/392-9002** or 702/369-5111), has a 400-seat showroom that often books the top comics on the comedy-club circuit. You can catch shows every day but Monday at 8 and 10:30pm for $16.45 (tax and drinks extra). Call ahead to charge tickets; there's preassigned seating.

Bet You Didn't Know

Some big-name comedians will put in special, unannounced appearances at Las Vegas comedy clubs to test out new material. In fact, many of the jokes you hear from Jay Leno on *The Tonight Show* were told to Vegas audiences beforehand. The clubs won't tell you in advance, so there's no way to know ahead of time, but you may be in for a good surprise.

If You Want to See a Lounge Act

Just about every hotel has a lounge with some sort of live, nightly entertainment. Once you could find a flood of top-drawer acts in hotel lounges, but Sinatra's long gone, unfortunately. These days, you can expect stand-up comedy and impersonator shows (played straight or for laughs, featuring imitators of Cher, the Blues Brothers, and, of course, Elvis and Liberace). Quality and camp factors vary tremendously. Still, some solid musical entertainment can be had; here are a few places to check out.

For the dance/pop scene, I highly recommend **The Nightclub at the Las Vegas Hilton,** 3000 Paradise Rd. (☎ **702/732-7111**). Recording artists like Kristine W. and Louie Louie (both dance-club divas) entertain twice nightly in this 350-seat hotspot with a large dance floor. Cover and schedule vary; call ahead for details.

Fans of salsa and reggae should head to the **Lagoon Saloon,** in The Mirage, 3400 Las Vegas Blvd. S. (☎ **702/791-7111**), where live lounge acts perform in a tropical rain forest atrium nightly.

At **Orleans,** 4500 W. Tropicana Ave. (☎ **702/365-7111**), you'll hear *zydeco* bands (Southern Louisiana music combining French dance melodies, Caribbean music, and the blues) and other New Orleans sounds in the lounge adjacent to the front doors.

If You've Got Boogie Fever

There's no shortage of places to put on your dancing shoes. Prepare yourself, though, for dress codes (some much more strict and formal than you'd expect in an otherwise casual town), steep cover charges, and a little attitude.

And women beware! These places are meat markets, so if you're not obviously with a date, you may be hit on endlessly. (If you want to avoid that, and you're just into dancing, you might check out **Inferno** or **Gipsy,** two predominantly gay nightspots listed later in this chapter.)

The ultimate party bar in Las Vegas is **The Beach,** 365 S. Convention Center Dr. (☎ **702/731-9298**), located at the corner of Paradise Road across from the Las Vegas Convention Center. It's a huge two-story building with eight separate bars surrounding a giant dance floor, all done in a PG-13 *Gilligan's Island* theme. (Think of it as a giant frat party; witness "Bikini Boxing Night.") Women in bikinis and shot belts filter through the crowds dispensing liquid merriment. A recent Friday night had a $10 cover charge, and the place was packed to the rafters.

A little more high class (and sporting a little more attitude and a pricier cover charge) is **Club Rio,** in the Rio Hotel & Casino, 3700 W. Flamingo Rd. (☎ **702/252-7777**). I'll be honest, I hated this place for its almost draconian dress code, $20 cover charge, and snooty staff, but the young, trendy, party types in town don't seem to mind. This place is always crowded, and locals insist this is the place to be.

Dollars & Sense

If you want to avoid paying high cover charges at nightclubs, go earlier in the evening before they go into effect. The club may not be going full tilt, but the lack of huge crowds on the dance floor might be a plus, and some of us just can't keep our eyes open 'til 4am anyway.

If you're looking for a slice of New York's underground, head straight to **Utopia,** 3765 Las Vegas Blvd. S. (☎ **702/740-4646**). On Saturday nights only, the young and hip take over the Epicenter nightclub for an evening of techno-tribal-rave partying.

My favorite dance club is simply called **Drink,** 200 E. Harmon Ave. (☎ **702/ 796-5519**). No beating around the bush with the name, huh? It's got a terrific layout with several different rooms featuring their own drinks and music. Check out the Drink Vodka room with its mind-boggling array of vodka choices and alternative and retro music. Maybe you'd prefer the Drink Beer room, which seems to have almost every brew known to mankind. There are seven or eight rooms in all, in a meandering layout surrounding a three-story, cave-like dance floor. The crowd and staff are friendly and the prices affordable; I've even spotted a celebrity or two shaking their booties here. To find it, take Harmon Avenue east from the Strip (near the MGM Grand) to the next major street, Koval Lane. Drink is on the corner.

Finally, **Stargate at the Luxor,** 3900 Las Vegas Blvd. S. (☎ **702/262-4000**), is scheduled to open shortly after this guide goes to press, and while I can't give you specifics, the plan sounds auspicious. They've gotten actual props from the movie *Stargate* (Kurt Russell and Jaye Davidson in Egyptian outer space) and are building a 600-person, high-tech dance club in the Luxor pyramid. The Stargate promises to be a major nightspot.

If You Want to Two-Step to Country & Western Tunes

Just can't get enough of two-stepping or line dancing? No problem.

Sam's Town Hotel & Casino, 5111 Boulder Hwy. (☎ **702/456-7777**), has two separate places for you to boot-scoot-boogie. **Roxy's Saloon** features live country bands and dancing (on a very small dance floor) daily from noon until 6am. **Sam's Town Western Dance Hall** has a huge dance floor and a DJ spinning the best country music from 9pm to 3am Monday through Saturday. Get here early to take the line-dancing lessons from 7:30

to 9pm every night. Sam's Town is in the eastern part of Las Vegas and is best reached by taking Flamingo Road east from the Strip about eight miles to Boulder Highway. Make a right, and you can't miss it on your left.

If you follow the directions above for Sam's but turn left on Boulder Highway and head north, you'll see **Rockabillys,** 3785 Boulder Hwy. (☎ **702/ 641-5800**), a country-and-western nightclub featuring a 2,000-square-foot dance floor and free lessons Monday to Saturday at 7:30pm.

If You Want a Bar with Personality

After a while, many bars start to look alike. But not in Vegas, which offers some pretty memorable places to have a beer.

Holy Cow, 2432 Las Vegas Blvd. S. (☎ **702/732-COWS**), is located on the north end of the Strip, across the street from the Sahara Hotel & Casino. It's all about cows. Sounds silly? Sure, but silly in a giggle-inducing way. Outside is a giant heifer on the roof and hoof prints sunk into the concrete, à la Mann's Chinese Theater. Inside, cow puns abound alongside the bar, cafe, gift shop, and microbrewery. Plenty of gambling machines compete with the cows for your attention.

But why limit yourself to a bovine theme? **Hippo & the Wild Bunch,** 4503 Paradise Rd. (☎ **702/731-5446**), provides all sorts of wild animals to party with. The interior is a cartoon version of a tropical forest, and the bar area has an upbeat feel. You can grab a bite at the restaurant (see the review in chapter 10, "Making Your Restaurant Choice"), and there's dancing every night from 8pm to 3am except on Mondays. It's located directly across the street from the Hard Rock Cafe at the corner of Harmon Avenue.

Bet You Didn't Know

Although New York City is known as the city that never sleeps, Vegas is really the place where things never shut down, and the time of day is inconsequential. Casinos have no clocks. You can scamper out to pick up your dry cleaning at 3am.

Animals aren't your thing? Check out the **Main Street Station Triple 7 Brew Pub,** 100 Main St. (☎ **702/387-1896**), inside the Main Street Station, located downtown. In addition to the microbrewery, which has a good selection of ales, there's a sushi bar, an oyster bar, a grill, and two grand pianos, where someone tinkles the ivories nightly. It's all done in an attractive, postmodern warehouse style.

Extra! Extra!

There's no more memorable view in town than the nighttime vista from the cocktail lounge on the 107th floor of **Stratosphere Tower,** 2000 Las Vegas Blvd. S. (☎ **702/380-7777**). It costs $6 to get up there and, while drinks are pricey, it's very cool to sip a martini while gazing down at the sea of neon displayed at your feet. The lounge, like the restaurant directly below, revolves slowly, so give yourself an hour to make a 360-degree trip around the city.

If You Want a Piano Bar

Quiet, intimate settings, although not what many visitors come to Vegas for, are the draw at most piano bars. **Kiefer's,** atop The Carriage House, 105 E. Harmon (just east of the Strip; ☎ 702/739-8000), is one of the most romantic spots in town. Its floor-to-ceiling windows offer stunning views of the Strip from the rooftop lounge, and the bar offers piano entertainment Thursday through Saturday nights from 9pm until they feel like stopping.

Another great view can be had from the lounge at **The Range Steakhouse,** in Harrah's Las Vegas, 3475 Las Vegas Blvd. S., just north of Flamingo (☎ 702/369-5000). Its intimate lounge, featuring nightly piano music, sits right above the Strip.

On the other hand, if a quiet piano bar is not your style, try the more boisterous party that's always in swing at **The Bar At Times Square,** in New York New York, 3790 Las Vegas Blvd. S. (☎ 702/740-6969). Here, you'll find nightly entertainment for the young and trendy, cigar-smoking crowd, including sing-alongs and lots of good-natured swayfests.

If You Want to Catch the Big Game

Some of the best places to watch sports (lap dancing is not considered a sport) in Vegas are the Sports Books at the major hotel casinos.

One terrific game-watching spot is **Final Score Sports Bar,** located adjacent to Sam's Town Hotel & Casino, 5111 Boulder Hwy., East Las Vegas (☎ 702/456-7777). It's a unique environment featuring interactive sports, video games, a basketball court, pinball, pool, an outside volleyball court, and dozens of televisions on which you can catch just about any major game from across the country. It's open daily from 10am to 4am.

Another good spot is **Winning Streaks,** in Harrah's Las Vegas, 3475 Las Vegas Blvd. S. (☎ 702/369-5000). Although more restaurant than bar, it's open to the casino and has a parade of televisions, terrific hamburgers, and some cool specialty drinks.

If You Want a Karaoke Bar

"Feelings... whoa, whoa, whoa, feelings..."
Isn't it everyone's dream to embarrass your
friends by singing that song in public?

The **Ellis Island Casino,** 4178 Koval
Lane (☎ 702/733-8901), will give you
the chance; it has karaoke nightly from
9pm to 3am. Koval Lane is just east of the
Strip, and Ellis Island is right behind
Bally's Las Vegas.

On the one night of the week (Sunday)
that it isn't doing the country thing,
Sam's Town Western Dance Hall,
5111 Boulder Hwy. (☎ 702/456-7777),
also has karaoke, starting at 9pm.

Bet You Didn't Know

According to karaoke hostess-
with-the-mostest Jackie Enx,
the all-time most-requested
karaoke songs are Frank
Sinatra's "My Way" and
"New York, New York."

If You Need a Caffeine Jolt

Yes, there are Starbucks here, too, but you can get that at home. For a
true local coffeehouse environment, try **Cafe Neon,** 1018 S. Main St.
(☎ 702/388-4088), a funky space above a vintage clothing shop. It's located
near Charleston Ave., five blocks west of the Strip, and is open Monday to
Friday from 10am to 6pm, and Saturday and Sunday from 10am to 7pm.

A few blocks closer to the Strip is the **Enigma Cafe,** 918½ S. Fourth St.
(☎ 702/386-0999), featuring a huge menu of coffees and smoothies, plus
an art gallery, live acoustic and folk music, and poetry readings. It's open
Monday from 7am to 3pm, Tuesday to Friday from 7am to midnight, and
Saturday and Sunday from 9am to midnight.

The **Jazzed Cafe,** 2055 E. Tropicana (☎ 702/798-5995), is a European-style
cafe—small but cozy, candlelit, and featuring nonstop jazz music. It's about
three miles east of the Strip at Eastern Avenue and is open Tuesday to Sunday
from 6pm to 3am.

Cyber City Cafe, 3945 S. Maryland Pkwy. (☎ 702/732-2001), is sort
of a techno-geek version of a coffeehouse (but I mean that in a good way).
Computer terminals dominate the space (Internet access is available for a
small fee), but there are also intimate non-cyber chatting areas and a large
alternative newsstand. Although not strictly gay, it is very gay friendly—and
is open 24 hours. You can find Maryland Parkway about two miles east of the
Strip; Cyber City is near Flamingo.

If You Want to Check Out the Gay & Lesbian Scene

Probably the hottest gay club in town is a relative newcomer called **Inferno,** 3340 S. Highland Ave. (☎ 702/734-7336). It's close to the Strip (take Spring Mountain west less than one-half mile to Highland and turn right) and features a dance floor, games, and a professional staff. It's almost always packed with a solid mix of locals and tourists but has surprisingly affordable drinks and cover charges. The bar features shows, dancers, beer busts, and theme nights and is open 24 hours.

A longtime favorite, **Gipsy,** 4605 Paradise Rd. (☎ 702/731-1919), has a new look, but everything that made it popular for so long has been maintained, including dancing, go-go boys, and shows. The recent $750,000 remodeling, part of an upscale trend, created an odd Indiana Jones look on the dance floor. There's a nightly cover of $5 or $6. You'll find it just south of Harmon Road; it usually opens around 10pm and closes whenever they feel like it—usually after the sun comes up.

Right next door is **Angles/Lace,** 4633 Paradise Rd. (☎ 702/791-0100), a 24-hour video bar divided into two parts: the predominantly male Angles and the predominantly female Lace. The club sports video poker and billiards.

The leather-and-Levis crowd can go right across the street to **The Buffalo,** 4640 Paradise Rd. (☎ 702/733-8355), which often has beer busts and is open 24 hours. Drinks are cheap, and you can try your hand at billiards, darts, and the ever-present video poker.

If you're looking for something a little quieter, try **Good Times,** 1775 E. Tropicana Ave. (☎ 702/736-9494), a cozy neighborhood bar with a small dance floor. You'll find it right next to the Liberace Museum, a most auspicious location, you might agree.

Finally, country and western fans should check out **Badlands Saloon,** 953 E. Sahara (☎ 702/792-9262). It's a friendly place with lots of good ol' boy fun on tap nightly. Head east on Sahara from the Strip about a mile (between Paradise and Maryland Parkway), and you'll see the Sahara Commercial Center. Turn right into the parking area; Badlands is in the northeast corner.

Time-Savers

Other gay and lesbian bars in town can be found by picking up a copy of the *Las Vegas Bugle* or *Las Vegas Nightlife,* two free publications available at any of the bars listed in this book. They will give you all the information on all the bars, parties, and special events.

If You Want to Go to a Strip Club

If topless dancers are even remotely on your mind, you've come to the right place. Welcome to Decadence Central. Some are actually clean, respectable establishments (relatively speaking). I'll stick to these; they're generally the safest and nicest of the bunch. There are down-and-dirty, much raunchier places in this town—but you're on your own.

FYI: In Las Vegas proper, topless bars can serve alcohol, but all-nude clubs cannot. Only the Palomino, an all-nude joint in North Las Vegas, is allowed to serve stiff drinks (the exception due to a grandfather clause in the Clark County ban). And touching the dancers in a strip club is usually forbidden. Some clubs, however, allow a restrained bit of physical interaction between clients and dancers. Be sure to check at the door for the rules and regulations so you don't get yourself into trouble.

Cheetah's, 2112 Western Ave. (☎ **702/384-0074**), was the club featured in the movie *Showgirls*; you may vaguely recognize the main stage. It's a clean, friendly place that actively courts a young party crowd. It has a bit of a frat-house atmosphere, but you'll also find couples here. Table and couch dances are available. Cover charge varies, and the club is open 24 hours. (Western Avenue is just east of I-15, and the club is between Sahara and Charleston Avenues.)

Club Paradise, 4416 Paradise Rd., just north of Flamingo (☎ **702/734-7990**), targets an upscale market, with brighter lighting, glittering marble, champagne, and cigars. Oh yeah, and topless dancers. Can't forget that. The place is glitzy and attracts a white-collar crowd. The dancers, called "actual centerfolds," have had the requisite boob jobs. The bar is open daily 6pm to 6am, and cover varies (usually includes a drink minimum).

Glitter Gulch, 20 Fremont St. (☎ **702/385-4774**), is a downtown landmark of sorts, right in the heart of the Fremont Street Experience. You'll find the usual topless dancers, table dancing, and lap dancing, plus a gift shop (you read that right) and limo service to and from your hotel. Cover charge varies, and hours are Sunday to Thursday from noon to 4am, Friday and Saturday from noon to 6am.

If topless isn't enough for you, then you'll have to travel a bit of a distance to **Palomino,** 1848 Las Vegas Blvd. N. (☎ **702/642-2984**). This large, two-level facility boasts a bunch of stages, semi-private rooms, and total nudity. Once one of the nicer strip clubs in Vegas, it's now on a descent into seedier goings-on. But if you're looking for a private, totally nude lap dance, you can get it here. It's a straight shot up Las Vegas Blvd. (the Strip) past downtown, but it'll take 15 to 25 minutes, depending on traffic. It's open daily from 1:30pm to 4am.

Until recently, male strippers were nowhere to be found. But ladies (and men escorted by women) can check out **Olympic Garden,** 1531 Las Vegas Blvd. S. (☎ **702/385-8987**), where there's a male strip show most nights upstairs in a second room.

217

Designing Your Itinerary

I can give you recommendations and suggestions until I'm blue in the face, but ultimately it's up to you to decide what you want to do, where you want to eat, and how much time you're going to spend at each stop. Below are some worksheets designed to help you come up with an itinerary of your own. (Pretend you're in school and use a pencil in case you need to erase.)

Immediately following the itinerary pages is a reference worksheet where you can jot down all your important phone numbers, reservation or confirmation numbers, and travel arrangements.

When planning your time, don't forget to block out approximately two hours just after your arrival. This is the time it will take to get your bags, get a rental car, perhaps, check into the hotel, and so on. Set aside another two hours prior to your departure.

I suggest that you don't try to make a super-detailed plan for your stay in Las Vegas—something that I might recommend if I were talking about London or New York. Las Vegas is about going with the flow, wandering around and gawking, popping into a casino and gambling when the mood strikes you, lounging by the pool, and having fun.

You won't want to schedule every minute, since a lot of the experience is about spontaneity. However, you may want to indicate a time frame for seeing the attractions that interest you the most, and there may be restaurants and shows you definitely want to experience (some of which you should select ahead of time, since they require reservations).

With these caveats in mind, it may be helpful for you to fill in this very general itinerary planner. Since shows are the least flexible as far as times and dates, start with those. I'd put in restaurant choices next, followed by any attractions you really don't want to miss. You'll also need to block a substantial amount of time (at least half a day) if you want to take a side trip out of town, say to the Hoover Dam.

DAY 1

Morning:

Lunch:

Afternoon:

Dinner:

Evening:

DAY 2

Morning:

Lunch:

Afternoon:

Dinner:

Evening:

DAY 3

Morning:

Lunch:

Afternoon:

Dinner:

Evening:

DAY 4

Morning:

Lunch:

Afternoon:

Dinner:

Evening:

Some Helpful Hints

Some more pointers about budgeting your time:

➤ Remember to allow sufficient time to get from place to place. Traffic on the Strip is always congested, especially at night, and it often takes more than an hour to get from one end to the other.

➤ The heat in Las Vegas takes a greater toll than you'd expect. It's not humid, so the heat sneaks up on you. If you can reserve two or three midday hours for a nap or swim, your energy wattage will get a boost.

➤ This is your vacation, for heaven's sake! You don't have to keep a schedule, put on a tie, or check your voice mail. Don't try to overload your schedule or do too much. Too many people ruin their trips by trying to cram in too much. You don't want to return from your vacation feeling like you need a vacation.

Las Vegas A to Z: Facts at Your Fingertips

AAA The nearest regional office for the nationwide auto club is located in Carson City (☎ **702/883-2470**).

American Express If you lose your American Express Travelers Cheques, dial ☎ **800/221-7282** 24 hours a day. There's an American Express Travel Services office in Caesars Palace (☎ **702/731-7705**).

Baby-sitting Both **Around the Clock Childcare** (☎ **800/798-6768** or 702/365-1040) and **Children's Babysitting Service** (☎ **702/255-5955**) have experienced and licensed childcare available 24 hours a day. Their workers are screened by the health department, sheriff, and FBI and will provide extensive references upon request.

Camera repair Most major hotels offer photo and camera service in their primary gift shops. Check with your concierge or guest services desk.

Doctors & dentists Most major hotels have physician-referral services, but you can also call the free service at **Desert Springs Hospital** (☎ **800/ 842-5439** or 702/733-6875) Mon–Fri 8am–5pm. For a dental referral, call **Clark County Dentist Society** (☎ **702/255-7873**) weekdays 9am–noon and 1–5pm.

Dry cleaners Most major hotels offer laundry and dry-cleaning services, but you might want to try **Steiner Cleaners,** 1131 E. Tropicana (at Maryland Parkway near Vons; ☎ **702/736-7474**). Why? They were Liberace's personal cleaners what else do you need to know? They're open Mon–Fri 7am–6:30pm, and Sat 8am–6pm; closed Sun.

Emergencies Dial 911 to contact the police or paramedics. Round-the-clock emergency service is available at **Sunrise Hospital and Medical Center,** 3186 Maryland Parkway (between Desert Inn Road and Sahara Avenue; ☎ **702/731-8080**). For less-critical emergencies, there's a 24-hour urgent care facility on the eighth floor of the **Imperial Palace,** 3535 Las Vegas Blvd. S. (just north of Flamingo; ☎ **702/731-3311**). It's independently run, retains a full staff of doctors, and has all the latest medical equipment. No appointment is necessary.

Gambling laws You must be 21 years old to enter a casino area.

Highway conditions For recorded local information, call ☎ 702/ 486-3116.

Hotlines In a crisis, you can contact the Rape Crisis Center (☎ 702/ 366-1640), the Suicide Prevention Hotline (☎ 702/731-2990), or Poison Emergencies (☎ 800/446-6179).

Information All the major hotels have tour and show desks, but you can get additional information from the **Las Vegas Convention and Visitors Bureau,** 3150 Paradise Rd. (☎ 702/892-0711) or the **Las Vegas Chamber of Commerce,** 3720 Howard Hughes Pkwy. (☎ 702/735-1616). The LVCVB is open Mon–Fri 8am–6pm, Sat–Sun 8am–5pm; the LVCC is open Mon–Fri 8am–5pm.

Liquor laws You must be 21 to buy booze or get served. Liquor is sold at bars and stores 24 hours a day, including Sunday. You can drink from open containers on city streets—a practice banned in most other cities.

Maps All major hotels have basic city maps available to hotel guests. You can buy more detailed maps at any hotel gift shop.

Newspapers/Magazines There are two major newspapers in the city: *The Las Vegas Review-Journal* and *The Las Vegas Sun.* Both are available at almost every hotel gift shop. In addition, there is a variety of free local magazine publications that have information on local happenings. The best of the lot are *What's On Las Vegas* and *Showbiz Weekly,* available in hotels and restaurants throughout the city. There's a major newsstand near the Strip: **The International Newsstand,** 3900 Maryland Pkwy (in the Citibank Plaza; ☎ 702/796-9901), is open daily 8:30am–9pm and has a vast selection of newspapers from around the country and virtually every magazine you can think of.

Pharmacies Sav-On, 1360 E. Flamingo Rd. (at Maryland Parkway; ☎ 702/ 731-5373), is part of a large national pharmacy chain and is open 24 hours. Another option closer to the heart of town is **White Cross Drugs,** 1700 Las Vegas Blvd. S. (just north of the Stratosphere Tower; ☎ 702/382-1733). The latter will make deliveries to your hotel.

Police For emergencies, dial 911; for non-emergencies, dial ☎ 702/ 795-3111.

Rest rooms All the major hotels have public rest room facilities. They are, for the most part, clean and safe.

Safety As long as you stick to well-lit tourist areas, crime is usually not a major concern. However, there is a problem with pickpockets who target people coming out of casinos (or people in the casinos who are entranced by gambling). Men should keep wallets well-concealed, and women should keep pocketbooks in sight and secure at all times. Be warned—these thieves tend to be particularly bold during outdoor shows like the Volcano at The Mirage or the Pirate Battle at Treasure Island. Many hotel rooms have safes for cash or valuables. If yours does not, the front desk can offer you a safety deposit box.

Taxes Clark County hotel room tax is 9 percent, and sales tax is 7 percent.

Taxis Basic fare is $2.20 for the first mile, $1.50 for each additional mile, with time penalties for standing still. Major operators include **ABC** (☎ 702/736-8444), **Ace** (☎ 702/736-8383), **Checker** (☎ 702/873-2000), **Desert** (☎ 702/386-9102), **Henderson** (☎ 702/384-2322), **Star** (☎ 702/873-2000), **Western** (☎ 702/736-8000), **Whittlesea** (☎ 702/384-6111), and **Yellow** (☎ 702/873-2000).

Time zone Las Vegas is in the Pacific time zone, three hours earlier than the East Coast (New York, Florida), two hours earlier than the Midwest (Iowa, Texas), and one hour earlier than the Mountain states (Colorado, Wyoming).

Transit information Call **Citizen's Area Transit (CAT)** at ☎ 702/CAT-RIDE.

Weather and time Call ☎ 702/248-4800 for an update.

Weddings Neither a blood test nor a waiting period is required to marry in the state of Nevada. Licenses can be obtained at **Clark County Marriage License Bureau,** 200 S. 3rd St. (at Bridger Ave., downtown; ☎ 702/455-3156), for $35.00. They are open 8am–midnight Mon–Thurs, and 24 hours a day on weekends and holidays. For more information, see "If You Want To Get Hitched" in chapter 13, "More Fun Stuff to Do."

Handy Toll-Free Numbers and Internet Addresses

Airlines

Air Canada
☎ 800/776-3000
www.aircanada.ca

Alaska Airlines
☎ 800/426-0333
www.alaskaair.com

America West Airlines
☎ 800/235-9292
www.americawest.com

American Airlines
☎ 800/433-7300
www.americanair.com

British Airways
☎ 800/247-9297
☎ 0345/222-111 in Britain
www.british-airways.com

Canadian Airlines International
☎ 800/426-7000
www.cdair.ca

Continental Airlines
☎ 800/525-0280
www.flycontinental.com

Delta Air Lines
☎ 800/221-1212
www.delta-air.com

Frontier
☎ 800/432-1359

Hawaiian Airlines
☎ 800/367-5320

Kiwi International Air Lines
☎ 800/538-5494
www.jetkiwi.com

Midway
☎ 888/226-4392

Midwest Express
☎ 800/452-2022

Northwest Airlines
☎ 800/225-2525
www.nwa.com

Reno Air
☎ 800/736-6247

Southwest Airlines
☎ 800/435-9792
iflyswa.com

Sun Country
☎ 800/359-6786

Tower Air
☎ 800/34-TOWER (800/348-6937)
www.towerair.com

Trans World Airlines (TWA)
☎ 800/221-2000
www2.twa.com

United Airlines
☎ 800/241-6522
www.ual.com

USAirways
☎ 800/428-4322
www.usair.com

Virgin Atlantic Airways
☎ 800/862-8621 in Continental U.S.
☎ 0293/747-747 in Britain
www.fly.virgin.com

Western Pacific
☎ 930-3030

Car-Rental Agencies
Advantage
☎ 800/777-5500
www.arac.com

Alamo
☎ 800/327-9633
www.goalamo.com

Allstate
☎ 800/634-6186
www.bnm.com/as.htm

Avis
☎ 800/331-1212 in the
Continental U.S.
☎ 800/TRY-AVIS in Canada
www.avis.com

Budget
☎ 800/527-0700
www.budgetrentacar.com

Dollar
☎ 800/800-4000
www.dollarcar.com

Enterprise
☎ 800/325-8007
www.pickenterprise.com

Hertz
☎ 800/654-3131
www.hertz.com

National
☎ 800/CAR-RENT
www.nationalcar.com

Payless
☎ 800/PAYLESS
www.paylesscar.com

Rent-A-Wreck
☎ 800/535-1391
rent-a-wreck.com

Thrifty
☎ 800/367-2277
www.thrifty.com

Value
☎ 800/327-2501
www.go-value.com

Major Hotel & Motel Chains
Best Western International
☎ 800/528-1234
www.bestwestern.com

Clarion Hotels
☎ 800/CLARION
www.hotelchoice.com/cgi-
bin/res/webres?clarion.html

Comfort Inns
☎ 800/228-5150
www.hotelchoice.com/cgi-
bin/res/webres?comfort.html

Courtyard by Marriott
☎ 800/321-2211
www.courtyard.com

229

Days Inn
☎ 800/325-2525
www.daysinn.com

Doubletree Hotels
☎ 800/222-TREE
www.doubletreehotels.com

Econo Lodges
☎ 800/55-ECONO
www.hotelchoice.com/cgi-bin/res/webres?econo.html

Fairfield Inn by Marriott
☎ 800/228-2800
www.fairfieldinn.com

Hampton Inn
☎ 800/HAMPTON
www.hampton-inn.com

Hilton Hotels
☎ 800/HILTONS
www.hilton.com

Holiday Inn
☎ 800/HOLIDAY
www.holiday-inn.com

Howard Johnson
☎ 800/654-2000
www.hojo.com/hojo.html

Hyatt Hotels & Resorts
☎ 800/228-9000
www.hyatt.com

ITT Sheraton
☎ 800/325-3535
www.sheraton.com

La Quinta Motor Inns
☎ 800/531-5900
www.laquinta.com

Marriott Hotels
☎ 800/228-9290
www.marriott.com

Motel 6
☎ 800/4-MOTEL6 (800/466-8536)

Quality Inns
☎ 800/228-5151
www.hotelchoice.com/cgi-bin/res/webres?quality.html

Radisson Hotels International
☎ 800/333-3333
www.radisson.com

Ramada Inns
☎ 800/2-RAMADA
www.ramada.com

Red Roof Inns
☎ 800/843-7663
www.redroof.com

Residence Inn by Marriott
☎ 800/331-3131
www.residenceinn.com

Rodeway Inns
☎ 800/228-2000
www.hotelchoice.com/cgi-bin/res/webres?rodeway.html

Super 8 Motels
☎ 800/800-8000
www.super8motels.com

Travelodge
☎ 800/255-3050

Index

235

X-Y-Z